SELECTIVE
MEMORY

SELECTIVE MEMORY

KATHARINE WHITEHORN

virago

VIRAGO

First published in Great Britain in 2007 by Virago Press
Reprinted 2007 (four times)

A CIP catalogue record for this book
is available from the British Library.

The author gratefully acknowledges permission to quote extracts
from the following:
'A Map of Verona' from A Map of Verona by Henry Reed (Jonathan Cape,
1946, and OUP). 'I Yield to My Brother' or 'Is There a Candlestick Maker
in the House?' from Candy is Dandy: The Best of Ogden Nash by Ogden
Nash with an Introduction by Anthony Burgess (André Deutsch, 1994).

ISBN 978-1-84408-240-7

Typeset in Goudy by M Rules
Printed and bound in Great Britain by
Clays Ltd, St Ives plc

Virago Press
An imprint of
Little, Brown Book Group
100 Victoria Embankment
London EC4Y 0DY

An Hachette Livre UK Company

www.virago.co.uk

'If you can look back on your life with contentment, you have one of man's most precious gifts – a selective memory'

JIM FIEBIG

This life was made by
my parents Alan and Edith Whitehorn,
Jack Gallagher, George Seddon
and
Gavin Lyall

CONTENTS

PROLOGUE

Have you ever taken anything back out of the dirty-clothes basket because it had become, relatively, the cleaner thing? How many things are there, at this moment, in the wrong room – cups in the study, boots in the kitchen – and how many on the floor of the wrong room?

Thus ran the most remembered thing I have ever written: an article on sluts, in the *Observer*, in 1963. I discussed how we sluts could outwit our doomed condition, using Indian ink instead of darning-wool when our black stockings had holes, giving up any idea of little white collars, bulk-buying since we would never remember to replace stuff in time. It had an amazing response: readers wrote in to say, 'Yes! Yes! That's exactly how I am!' One said hers was the only baby in Ruislip with blue nappies; another had found she was wiping the kitchen table with the kitten; another rejected the notion of resorting to aspirin tablets when the button was off one's suspenders, as sluts never have any, using gin for headaches instead – she said she had used the buttons off her husband's pyjamas until he sewed them on again.

Why should that article have had such an impact?

This was a turning-point. We were poised at the moment when writing for women ceased to be a matter of exhorting them to be perfect – at the stove, round the cradle, head down in the broom cupboard if necessary – and started telling it how it really was: a confusion of purposes, a mess, against which we all struggle. It was ceasing, too, to be a separate ghetto occupied only by women. George Seddon, when he was made the women's editor of the *Observer*, was required by the editor David Astor to create some serious women's pages. Before that, they'd had just the fashion, expertly done by Alison Settle, and a recipe column by a bloke who wrote as Syllabub, and that was all. George had taken the pioneering ideas of Mary Stott of the *Guardian* and moved them on: he thought such pages should cover anything and everything that wasn't work. Food, yes, clothes certainly – but also human relationships, visits to the dentist, holidays good and frightful, struggles with babies and children, gearboxes and hairdressers, bosses and fathers, bed and board.

I had the great good luck to be part of all this, as George commissioned me to write one of the first such personal columns; but it took me a while to get there – and I wasn't a 'child of the sixties'. My path led from a childhood in Mill Hill in north London to six schools here and there, two universities and about a dozen jobs; from two families similar in some ways, very different in others; a journey in which I was set on the road by some men, nearly derailed by others. It led from far further back, and was to lead far further forward than that explosive sixties moment; and even if, at the time, it seemed the exact opposite, I now realise I have had good luck almost all the way.

SELECTING MEMORIES

When you walk along a street and pass hoardings that hide building work, you discount it in your mind; then suddenly the hoardings are down – and how on earth did that eight-storey building spring up overnight? In the same way, boring bits of the past simply fail to register. I know I went to Finland, I know why I went, and I have a vague memory of a British Council advertisement. But how did I apply, who interviewed me, how did I get a Finnish work permit? No idea. I found a mention of writing something for the *Mirror*, and doing a column for the *Sunday Dispatch* which I could have sworn I never did. There's a letter I came across regretfully resigning from something I apparently helped found with Cyril Ray and fellow journalist Jean Robinson, the Women's Wine Club – I had no memory of any such thing.

Sherlock Holmes refused to remember things he thought of no importance, of no use to him; but not many of us can order our minds so neatly. The memory makes its own selections, its own decisions about what is fun, interesting, moving or even excruciating to remember, and what is simply too boring to store. What's more, you can remember things that didn't happen – and you aren't lying, either. The brain apparently sees thing A and thing C, and if it is puzzled by the gap, officiously fills in what it thinks should be there, thing B; then you remember that, and when you've recalled it two or three times it's a genuine memory – but of the last time you ran this construct past your consciousness.

Digging around among old papers and letters, as I have been, I was occasionally staggered to find just how wrong my memory of something could be. I would have said I never consulted my father about personal things – yet here was a letter asking whether, having dropped a brick with a lecturer whom I admired to the point of adoration, I should apologise or hope he hadn't noticed. Again, I was dumbfounded by a tender if lousy poem, written to someone I knew I'd been involved with – but *like that*?

Confronting or trying to call up memories has been one of the most daunting tasks of writing the book you're now holding. As the poet Henry Reed wrote:

> It is strange to remember those thoughts and to try to
>   catch
> The underground whispers of music beneath the years,
> The forgotten conjectures, the clouded, forgotten
>   vision,
> Which only in vanishing phrases reappears.

Strange to remember, indeed; but not futile – at least not to me.

PART 1

WHERE I CAME FROM

EARLY DAYS

My parents, who already had a boy, both very much wanted their second child to be a girl. So I was born luckier in one respect than about half the world's female babies, who are greeted as an unfortunate second-best. This birth took place in a small house in Mill Hill, and I can't go and visit my birth-place because it was knocked over by one of Hitler's flying bombs. I do know, though, the large white Collinson House, to which my father Alan Whitehorn, who taught classics and cricket at Mill Hill School, was appointed housemaster about a year later. He was young for a housemaster, but the previous housemaster's wife had apparently gone off her head, so the husband had to be replaced. That wasn't necessarily preju-dice; a housemaster's wife in those days was expected to run a staff of ten servants and cater for sixty people. This job my mother Edith assumed, without any training at all, at the age of twenty-six.

I and my elder brother John had a nanny; apparently there was one called Nurse Firth who was credited with ruining my character, but she was succeeded by Molly Leefe, who became an integral part of the family. She was pretty and fun and a bit like my mother to look at, and she owned the only pet we ever had: a daft dog called Micky. He was a black and white wire-haired terrier who, shrewdly realising that his only asset was a talent to amuse, decided not to give up clowning even when he was quite old enough to know better. I have a vivid memory of him when he happened to be suffering from eczema: he had a mackintosh bonnet and mackintosh bootees on his paws, eliciting undeserved cries of 'Oh, the poor little doggy!' as he hammed it up for all he was worth. My mother got a bit fed up because my father preferred playing with this idiot dog to playing with us.

Growing up in a school was, I suppose, rather strange. Our part of the house was separate from the boys' part, at which I would sneak fascinated glimpses during the holidays. The house tutor and the matron would have their evening dinner with my parents; we children ate in the nursery during term time, and had to eat up everything — Molly once gloomed that she doubted if my parents would have insisted on this if they'd had to force the stuff into us themselves. I do remember one triumph when, made to eat my revolting mutton fat in the dining-room during the holidays, I contrived to be sick of it with maximum drama; one up for Kath, one down for the carpet. I also remember sneaking back into the dining-room to eat potatoes out of the serving dish after lunch; no wonder my father's nickname for me was 'Pudding' ('more pudding, Pudding?'), and till the end of his life I signed letters and cards to him with a drawing of a Christmas pudding – even if I sometimes felt, I suppose, like the pudding in the Goons' *Great Christmas Pudding Hunt*, found in the bushes angrily lashing its holly.

For he was a pretty strict father, as schoolmasters so often are. I never really felt close to him or friendly until the end of my teens, but I was always close to my endlessly patient and loving mother. She had had spinal meningitis when she was sixteen, narrowly escaped dying and had tinnitus all her life, ultimately growing completely deaf; but she was, none the less, an extremely happy woman. She was an excellent housewife, but scarcely valued her skills: coming from a large poor family that valued plain living and high thinking, not gracious living and certainly not money, she always regretted what she saw as her own lack of intellectualism – she had won a place at Cambridge but wasn't allowed to take it up; they thought the meningitis had made her too frail.

You don't realise, until later, the assumptions, the culture in which you have grown up. Both my parents were left-wing, horrified by the conditions of the two million unemployed, the slums, the means test that meant you hid your last remaining treasures in the coal bin lest your dole be cut until you sold them. And like so many of their generation, the horrors of the First World War – during which my father had been a conscientious objector – had made them passionately pacifist. They saw a clear distinction between the conservative, class-conscious assumptions of Church and state (my father used to denounce with impartial scorn the pronouncements of the weather forecast, the Archbishop of Canterbury and the then head of the London County Council) and left-wing idealism. This largely came from my mother's Christian socialist family, the Grays, for whom the belief that all men were equal in the sight of God exactly matched their conviction that all men had an equal right to a decent life. It still enrages me when Christian fundamentalists talk as if *they* were the only idealists.

My parents were determined to bring us up in a free and modern way: we wore 'sensible' clothes – Clarks sandals, hand-kitted jerseys – neither the doll-like frills of the nineteenth century nor the round-the-clock fancy dress they wear today – though I remember with horror my first struggles with a Liberty bodice, from which my first long stockings were to be suspended. I was supposed to have a cold bath every morning; in practice, I swished the water noisily with my hand and stayed dry; my parents weren't deceived for long and finally gave up on the idea. We had sex instruction from a book called *Peter and Veronica*, greatly concerned with the reproductive life of squirrels. We were encouraged to say what we thought, though apparently when I once said, 'Here comes the old grump' at the approach of my father, my mother didn't know whether to be more horrified that I should want to say it or pleased that I thought I could. And I was sent to a progressive school, The Mount, halfway down the hill from where we lived; sometimes I walked and braved the terrifying dogs along the way, sometimes my mother drove me at breakneck speed in our old Morris; I can't, at this distance, say which was the more alarming.

The school did not have prep as such, but set 'assessments' which you were supposed to complete in your own time, which I didn't. My main trouble there, though, was that I never had any friends. I couldn't take teasing, which naturally made the other girls tease me more and more; I tended to be the last picked for any team, and if ever I drew a popular girl when paired off for something, a certain amount of scuffling would always ensure that she was exchanged for someone as unpopular as me. Once someone – the headmistress? – urged them to include me more in their games; so they did. They invented a splendid game in which I was a princess and they were evil spirits, circling me and making horrible faces at me – not much of a fun experience.

I knew all this made me unhappy, but I suppose I never grasped just why until I saw how much my own grandchildren, both girls, value their friends above absolutely everything else; and read Deborah Tannen's books, explaining how differently males and females use talk – males, even little boys, trying to establish status or discussing action, while females, even little girls, endlessly try to make connections with other little girls, which I never quite seemed to do. Why? No one ever decided. Probably bumping me up a class because I was supposed to be bright took me away from my first natural group; and growing up in a boys' school was odd, and different from the others' experience – I apparently once wailed that I wished I could be an 'ordinary child on an ordinary pavement'.

No wonder I longed for the holidays, and especially the summer holidays, which we always spent in Scotland. Sometimes we were packed into the back of one of our awful old cars – the journey took three days then; sometimes, if our father went on a cricketing week, my brother John and I shared a four-berth sleeper with our mother who, terrifying in her hairnet, would scold us every three minutes until anyone who'd been assigned to the fourth bunk would beg the guard to be moved. My mother's family, Scottish to the core, always went there, and my father, also half Scottish, had met my mother at the little house they owned at Lochearnhead; they were both great hill walkers, and scaled all the hills of the Spey Valley – Braeriarch, Ben Macdui, Cairn Gorm – no lift up it in those days. As a child I wasn't too keen on the walks, but I hated to be left out of anything, which explains how, apparently cursing and spluttering every step of the way, I was up

Ben Nevis, highest mountain in the British Isles, at the age of eight.

Of course, what I remember about my childhood isn't necessarily how other people saw it. My mother kept a book, which like all baby books started with when I slept and fed and so on, but went on to quote my infant remarks, some of which seemed fairly prescient of what was to follow.

'Says *far* too often "Kaffrin can do it a self."' 'She often gets quite angry and jealous of John' – well, yes, I was jealous of him all the time I was growing up: the foundation for my deeply jealous personality, no doubt. He was older, he was a boy, so he was allowed to do more things; and when he went away to boarding-school he naturally attracted more attention in the holidays.

When they tried to stop me spending all my pocket money at once, because there'd be none left, I said: 'But I don't want any left, I just want lots and lots of toys' – not an attitude to endear one eventually to a cautious spouse. Then: 'No one could possibly call me naughty now cos I'm very kind and good doing all this weeding.' Oh, God, yes, the avoidance of blame and finally: 'Bother! There's my tongue speaking before I'm ready for it – it's always doing that.' I can add that I also could blow a trumpet at fifteen months – I can't think why they let me.

I think they found me fairly tiresome, even in Scotland. I've been told (often) of one time when I'd been larking with my young aunt Margaret, my mother's much younger sister, on a moor; I inadvertently got scratched, was furious and stomped off into the heather. It was a wonderful light evening, and after a while my mother said: 'Oh Katharine, how can you be cross on this glorious evening?' to which I apparently replied: 'It's not *my* fault it's sunny; *I* can't help the weather; if it was up to me it would be *pouring with rain*.' It usually was, of course, up there; but having a whole month to stay there gave one a quite different view: if you've only got a week and it rains every day, you hate the place; if you're there for a month and can wait for the good weather there's a surprising amount of it.

I loved the picnics we would have by a loch or a river. I remember my grandmother at Feshie bridge in the Cairngorms, where there are wonderful tea-coloured pools and white water-falls and huge rocks, cooking potatoes over a fire; you'd dip the scalding potato in the river just enough to get it cool enough to eat. It is only now that I wonder about the ease and frequency with which they built fires in among the pines: pyromaniacs, the lot of them, the Grays. Years later I remember waking from a snooze to find my mother, then in her seventies, making a roaring fire in a high wind on the shores of Loch Morlich; if I hadn't happened to wake up in time to make her put it out I reckon she'd have burned down the whole of Rothiemurchus forest.

MY FATHER'S FAMILY, THE WHITEHORNS

The Whitehorns were solid respectable bourgeois people, entirely English, though I can claim studious Scottish divines there as well, through my grandmother Lizzie Drummond. The Whitehorns were blacksmiths in Berkshire at the end of the eighteenth century, in the jewellery business in London throughout the nineteenth; eventually my grandfather Joseph Whitehorn was High Warden of the Goldsmiths' Company and ran Collingwood's in Conduit Street for many years. When he retired, he turned the firm over – as it transpired – to a crook; Joseph went back into the firm, put in his own money and managed to pay off almost all the debts. So while the firm still remembered him (it's been taken over now), we enjoyed a privileged relationship. My husband Gavin, when he had become a crime writer, once wanted to know if pearls would be harmed by being soaked in petrol. 'I don't know,' said Mr Morrell, who ran it in the sixties; he simply took a pearl out of a drawer – 'Put that in lighter fluid and we'll see.' The pearl was OK – so in his novel *The Wrong Side of the Sky* the stolen jewels were hidden in the petrol tank of an aeroplane. And once when I had to give a speech at the Lord Mayor's summer banquet, he lent me thousands and thousands of pounds' worth of diamonds: a diamond tiara on my head, I had, though Marks & Spencer shoes as usual.

Mrs Whitehorn was not liked by her daughter-in-law, my mother Edith. On one occasion when Edith, Alan and small John were staying with his parents, someone, to their delight, asked them out to a rather festive dinner – as a hard-up schoolteacher's family they had very little money and few treats.

'And who,' said Mrs Whitehorn, 'will look after John?'

My mother thought perhaps the maids . . .

'The maids have their own work.' She then invented some reason why a sister who was also staying there couldn't do it, and she herself never offered.

'So with five women in the house I had to hire someone to babysit,' Edith remembered.

No wonder she didn't want my children to call her Granny, since that was what we'd called *her*. So what did they call Edith? I'd once read that question in the advice column of Marcelle Ségal in *Elle* magazine, and her answer was: '*Laisse*

bébé le faire.' (Leave it to the baby). So we waited till our first
son Bernard attempted his version of the word, and called my
mother Danny from then on. She liked that.

At what point the Whitehorns, English, from Wantage,
switched to being Baptists I don't know, but they later switched
again to the Presbyterian church in Marlborough Place in
north London, which was where my grandfather Joseph met
Lizzie Drummond, his future wife. Joseph, the grandfather
whom I barely remember, was apparently a bit of a joker,
though looking unbelievably saintly behind his abundant
white moustache by the time I knew him. My father said
Joseph would occasionally take a spoon hot from his soup and
lay it on the bare arm of the lady next to him at dinner: they
would be bewildered because surely *he* couldn't have done that?
Two of his daughters – he had three – married men who had
gone abroad – Robin Sawers was in the Argentine, Reg Fenn
in Hong Kong. Before their weddings he escorted both overseas, so that if they took one look at their intendeds and
thought better of it, they could come right back with him.
The detail that fascinated me was that they went, of course,
accompanied by a lavish and brand-new trousseau, but wearing
the last of their ordinary underwear – each piece of which they
would simply drop out of a porthole when it got dirty.

Roy, my father's eldest brother, was a warm and jovial
Presbyterian minister, eventually Principal of Westminster
College in Cambridge, which taught Presbyterian ministers.
That sounds highly serious, but his approach wasn't. One of his
exam questions was: 'What is your favourite heresy, and why?'
I was always fond of him; he gave the address at our wedding;
and I remember him every time I put a towel through a rail
because he taught me to pull it up from the back instead of
trying to stuff it down from the front – which is actually the

kind of reason you do remember someone, all the time. Both his sons became ministers, and his daughter Hilary married a Methodist minister from Jamaica. 'I think it's so splendid of Hilary,' said my mother. 'We all *talk* about racial equality but she's actually *done* something.' Gently we suggested that Hilary probably hadn't married George solely in the interests of good race relations. Roy's son John had, on the face of it, the most interesting career: as a missionary in the hills of what was then Formosa. He found that his potential flock had no written language, so he made them one. Then he translated the New Testament into it, though even so, I fear, he didn't make any mass conversions.

My cousin Michael Whitehorn, alas dead now, wrote a little book, or perhaps I should say pamphlet, called *The Whitehorns in Five Centuries*. The first few centuries contain some pretty speculative connections: a possible early Scottish link, a just believable line to a madrigalist, and one hard-and-fast one to an ancestor who was child number twenty-four of his parents: he was called Gad, which apparently means 'Behold a troop cometh.' Or so we were brought up to believe. And it turns out that I'm not the first to fall for (as well as into) the Thames. When I was on the *Observer* someone wrote and said they'd read in some heritage magazine of a booklet called *The Whitehorns on the River* – did I want it? Yes indeed – though it was sent without return address or invoice, alas. It was written by my great-uncle Percy and describes the way they would go up to Oxford by steamer, and then row back down; one of the great-uncles was so keen he had his own rowing boat made especially. It pleased me to think that I had roots in the Thames valley as well as all those links north of the border.

MY MOTHER'S SIDE, THE GRAYS

My father used to say that while he, a Whitehorn, would go the sensible way up a mountain, zigzagging to take the ascent steadily, a Gray would say: 'There it is – what are we waiting for?' – and swarm straight up the side. Maybe not exactly true; but the approaches of the two families were certainly very different.

The Grays, I have come to realise, were in many ways ahead of their times. My aunt Margaret, ten years younger than my mother, went to Cambridge in the thirties and didn't think it odd, because her own aunts had gone before the First World War. (Once on a Highland walk my father came across a body lying in the heather, but it was only Aunt Hester, happily reading Homer in the original Greek.) It never occurred to my parents – and I know much of this was my mother's doing – to give me a worse education than my brother.

Much of the spirited rashness actually came from my maternal grandmother's side, the Dodses. My great-grandfather, Marcus Dods, was the last man to be tried for heresy by the Church of Scotland: he was acquitted, but what had alarmed them was his interest in textual criticism of the Bible, how and when it had been written, translated, evolved – heresy indeed to fundamentalists. My great-aunt Ursula was not a Dods by birth but might as well have been – she married the next-generation Marcus Dods, a judge, who collected antique furniture and used to knit on the train going 'through to Edinburgh' during the First World War. Before she married, Ursula had to be sent to Australia to curb her suffragette sympathies (it didn't). She and her husband had a lovely house called Easter Laggan near Dulnain Bridge where we spent our summer holidays during the war. I have vivid memories of her seen through the haze of a picnic fire smoking a pipe. (Their son was the Marcus Dods who conducted film music in the fifties – one of the many pacifists who, faced with the actuality of Hitler, finally changed their minds and joined up.)

Mamie Dods, Marcus's sister, married my grandfather, the poor clergyman Herbert Gray – rather to the consternation of her family, for the Grays were 'in trade'. They had an iron-monger's store in George Street, Edinburgh. But weren't the Dodses in trade too? Ah, yes, but they were wholesale, which apparently made it better. Herbert Gray, who went to Glasgow University on a scholarship earmarked for the best scholar of the year named Gray, was a remarkable man. I never knew him very well, but he is something of a legend in the family – and elsewhere. He was a Presbyterian minister, and before the First World War had a church in an up-scale parish; terribly aware of the other side of Glasgow life, though, he put up a trestle table outside his church showing the shirts sewn by sweated labour in the slums, to make his posh parishioners aware of what went on, and of just how little the poor who had sewn them had been paid. During the war he was a padre in France, and was most deeply influenced by the horror he saw; he came back a passionate pacifist and was among the founders of the Peace Pledge Union.

But what he is most remembered for is his work with family and sexual troubles. He wrote a book in the 1920s called *Men, Women and God* which was the first to tackle the down-to-earth messy problems of sex and marriage from a Christian viewpoint. It sold many editions in the twenties and thirties, was reprinted, remarkably, in the eighties, long after his death, and overall sold more than a million copies. He was a friend of Dr Helena Wright, one of the first pioneering doctors in the twenties to help women with sexual problems – my mother went to her to sort out some technical difficulty in the early days of her marriage, which she plainly did, since my mother never gave me any impression of sex but that it was absolutely gorgeous.

There is a contradiction here, though. My grandfather Herbert Gray wrote books about married love, insisting that it was not sordid or sinful but God-given and splendid, and contributed prefaces to the kind of discreet sexual manuals they had before the war. But what Mamie his wife told her own daughter – my mother – was 'You won't enjoy it but you must never say no.' Yet my grandmother was a profoundly happy woman, and assumed her daughters would have the same sort of life, with marriage and children. When her youngest daughter Margaret had to have a hysterectomy in her thirties, her view was that this was the worst news she had ever heard – which somewhat annoyed her other daughters. 'What about Kitty's diabetes?' said my mother, 'and my deafness?'

Herbert Gray's books, predictably, led to a large number of people with marriage difficulties seeking his advice; and in 1938 he, with others, founded the Marriage Guidance Council. At the headquarters in Rugby of what is now Relate is Herbert Gray Hall, and on their fiftieth anniversary a rose was named after him to celebrate his achievement. He also wrote a book called *God in the Slums* which caused his irreverent children to discuss the dread dental disease 'slod in the gums'.

They were an interesting lot, the Gray children. The eldest boy was Arthur, who was going to be a factor on a Scottish estate, arranged by his uncle Henry Dods, who worked for Lord Novar. But that never happened, because Henry's entire family, who had been kind to the officers from HMS *Natal*, a battleship anchored in the Cromarty Firth, were invited on board for Christmas dinner in 1916 and the battleship was blown to bits that day by enemy action (I suppose a proper socialist would say, serve them right for having their attendants wait in the carriage on shore all the time they were enjoying their Christmas dinner). Arthur finally went into industry instead.

Kitty, my mother's elder sister, was extremely pretty when she was young, and was courted unsuccessfully by John Reith, later to be the founder of the BBC. She married James Macgregor, who also worked for the BBC – until he took his typist away for the weekend and got sacked. Kitty had to go to her old beau and ask him to reinstate her husband, which he did, and James wound up as Head of News at the BBC during the war – but was never, according to my mother, nearly so much fun ever again. They had four daughters, the middle pair being twins. This meant a lot of cast-offs – one for their younger sister, one for me, it usually went.

The true eccentric, however, was my uncle Marcus. His first words in this world, addressed to his mother, were 'Come here, silly woman'; he had a very tender conscience, so much so that his parents knew when he had been naughty because he would put a bowl by his bedside to be sick into if need be. At the end of his teens he resolved to be a missionary and set off for India, having first had all his teeth out, fearing the attentions of funny foreign dentists. He married Beatrice, nine years older than him and something of a puritan – she had had relatives *who drank*. For years they were ardent followers of the Oxford Group, or Moral Re-Armament. After they returned from India Marcus became a teacher, but eventually went to his headmaster and said: 'I can't go on any longer, I hate them [the pupils] too much.'

'But what are you going to do instead?' he was asked.

'I have a job with the local joiner, for whom I've been working on Saturdays for some time.'

The story ought to end there, of course, but it doesn't: they lived in Marlborough, where his son, young Marcus, was teaching at the public school, and got him a job teaching carpentry to these far more disciplined and civil boys. When Beatrice died, my uncle Marcus married her best friend Pat, and while they were engaged they went to stay with Margaret.

'One bed or two?' she asked.

'Oh, one – we're very much in love,' said eighty-something Marcus. 'Only we can't get married before Pat's sixtieth birthday or she'd lose her widow's pension.'

I knew my Gray cousins much better than I knew the Whitehorn ones. But I had plenty to choose from – eighteen; my mother had a dozen. My sons have only three, Gavin's sister Barbara's boys, whom they hardly ever see. Sad, really.

EDITH, MY MOTHER

After my mother died, I found among her things a piece of paper in which, when the war ended in 1945, she had written the pros and cons of having another baby. She used to say she was overmaternal the way some people were oversexed – they had had just the two of us because that was all they could afford to educate properly. So now she had another chance. But she was deaf by then; one con was doubt about having a baby with a deaf mother. The pros included 'Another chance to bring up a girl'; the con '*But it might turn out no better this time.*' Just as well I knew by then how proud of me she became – and that she'd actually brought me up wonderfully.

Edith grew up in Glasgow, was very happy at school, did well, and insisted on taking part in the hurdling race of a class higher than her own and won it. Then at sixteen disaster struck: she got spinal meningitis. In those days you mostly died of it, but a doctor uncle was working on this in London, and sent up a new horse serum – which saved her life, but left her with permanent tinnitus. She went to Glasgow University for a year but married Alan before she was twenty-one (having commented when she first met him: 'Well, if that's your charming young Englishman give me a dour old Scot any day'), and never had a paid job, though she was an excellent housemaster's wife.

She wanted to write and certainly wrote at least one novel, but nobody wanted to publish it and I think, with two small children and Collinson House to cope with, she didn't keep it up. But it meant that when I made writing my trade, I was fulfilling, for her, lost ambitions of her own. And, maternal as she was, she never *once* said, 'When are you going to get married?'; she never once said, when I was married, 'When are you going to have a baby?' She did once say she thought I'd be happiest living in the country, and when I said I'd be bored stiff, she said: 'No, you wouldn't; any daughter of mine can adapt to anything.' My husband disagreed: 'You don't adapt to things – you change them,' Gavin said.

When the war came, Mill Hill School evacuated to St Bees on the coast of Cumberland, and my mother had to cope with the evacuation, catering with all the wrong supplies, organising the masters' evening meal and rescuing stuff from London, where Collinson House was commandeered to be a mental hospital for the shell-shocked. Compared to many people's war, what they put up with was minor; but St Bees was bleak. When John went into the RAF she was, of course, worried stiff about him; and usually, I'm afraid, she was worried about me and my various school troubles. And just before John went abroad, she went to spend a week with him in Liverpool and caught scarlet fever – which put paid to the rest of her hearing.

Eventually she learned to lip-read and we all grew used to checking automatically, when we spoke, that Edie was looking at us, that there was enough light; but some of her friends were absolutely asinine about it. They'd expect her to lip-read in a rotten light, they'd talk with a cigarette in their mouths, they'd turn away in mid-sentence. Edith was pretty brave about her condition, and amazingly cheerful and relaxed. She adored Alan, she adored us; she kept up correspondence with several of her best friends from school, and made new ones in Marlborough. And in one respect she was more fortunate than some deaf people: her voice remained absolutely normal. She used to sing, because she'd been told that was one way to keep it from changing; it was a heartbreaking sound because it sounded all wrong, but it plainly did the trick.

It was when she became completely deaf that she realised she must learn to lip-read, but no one seemed to know how you did it; she had to write to a friend's husband, a doctor in Inverness, to find out about lip-reading classes. Compared to the wealth of help there is now – ways of turning sound into light, the use of signers at lectures, the hear-see TV pro-grammes and far better hearing aids (though those wouldn't have helped Edith), the deaf were appallingly served. Edith thought the provision of hearing aids to ordinary poor people – 'bringing the deaf out of their holes and corners' – in itself jus-tified the NHS.

One trouble with being deaf, she said, was that it didn't show – people just thought you were stupid: 'It would be easier if our ears turned purple or something.' There's another snag, too. If you put your hands over your eyes, or turn out all the lights in an enclosed room, you can easily imagine some of the horror of being blind. But if you put your hands over your ears, it may even seem quite a relief not to be bothered with the noise of other people's telephones and car alarms. So you don't have any immediate experience of the real disadvantages of being deaf – of the dreadful isolation. Of course, a lot of things like booking tickets or asking prices or striking up a conversation with someone new are dauntingly difficult for the deaf; but the real misery is that deafness cuts you off from people. It's an effort for hearing people to make themselves understood; so most of us simply make three minutes' conversation and then talk to someone else, as polite foreigners do when you're in a country where you hardly know the language. When it comes to communication the deaf are strangers in their own country, for ever.

For deaf people, technology is a real help – and I don't just mean hearing aids, which don't work for everybody (even if, says she sourly, the hard-of-hearing can be persuaded to wear them). For my mother, when she came to look after my first baby, the National Institute for the Deaf provided a device which turned his cries into flashing light, and later she had a doorbell that did the same. It is heartbreaking to think how much she'd have relished fax and especially email – she'd have chattered away all day.

PART 2

WHERE DO I BELONG?

BOARDING-SCHOOLS

It was at the beginning of 1940 that I achieved my ambition to be sent to a boarding-school – too many girls' school stories, hatred of the school I was at – it seems amazing now that this was what I passionately wanted. And I think I would ulti-mately have liked Downe House, in Berkshire, where I was sent first. But when the invasion scare came, they sent back all the girls whose families were in the north lest they get sepa-rated, and after much agonising about finding a good academic school my parents sent me to Roedean, which had also been evacuated to Cumberland.

The school was housed in the grand Keswick Hotel, on Bassenthwaite Lake under Skiddaw; we trooped for morning assembly to a neighbouring Methodist chapel, where Miss Tanner, the headmistress, a large woman with wobbly chins, presided grandly from the central pulpit. On wet days we wore huge woollen cloaks with hoods big enough to go over our hats (I only discovered later that they were the same as the Kerry cloak used in Ireland for pregnant brides). I don't remember much about the classrooms, or the bedrooms, except that in winter we sometimes found icicles inside the windows, and in those pre-duvet days often stuffed the eiderdown under the sheet; we also perfected the art of getting dressed or undressed under the bedclothes. There was a tendency to keep up pre-war traditions: the uniform was a strange navy garment called a djibbah, a loose tunic with a V-shaped insert at the neck; under it you wore a top – not a blouse – that had an elastic under the bosom, if you had one (if you were lucky, that is; if you weren't, it cut across). In the evening you changed into another one made of velvet or silk with embroidery in the V. Everyone did change for the evening, including the mistresses.

For me, things went wrong at Roedean from the start. A mix-up about train times meant I arrived from St Bees twenty-four hours later than the other new girls, so I didn't belong even to that small start-up group; and the one girl who lived near us and had been told to keep an eye on me was, I discovered, unpopular herself, so that didn't help. I was hopelessly bad at games and I was in the wrong uniform – Downe House's green and purple (the colours, I discovered decades later, of the suffragettes). But I was in the wrong mental uniform too: my background was non-conformist, professional, left-wing, pacifist; theirs, I suppose, fully Church and state and certainly money-conscious; we were issued with little yellow cheque books, no cash, to prepare us – at twelve! – for what they no doubt thought was the real world. The ethos was certainly Spartan, very much that of a boys' public school – we even sang the Harrow school song, which featured 'the tramp of the twenty-two men'. If anyone *had* become the tramp of twenty-two men she'd have been expelled.

My personal miseries there were compounded of being teased, being useless at games and being the fat girl who gets stuck trying to vault the horse; the gym mistress would look on with the half-concerned, half-exasperated expression of a circus trainer trying to back the elephant into a truck; Girls, this is Not Funny. And maybe, even more – what it took me years to work out – the captivity. At boarding-school you're never free: of the school, the rules, the other girls' opinions and the stiff-upper-lip expectation that stopped some girls, who were just as unhappy as I was, ever saying so in their letters home.

But even years later, when I'd got over all that, I rejected – and still do – the whole ethos of toughening up girls in the way that, I suppose, made some sort of sense when you were building boys to go out and run the empire. The attitude to illness is a good enough example. One of our matrons was tough: no good going to her just because you felt too awful for cricket; the other showed signs of humanity – and was regarded as soft. Yet which are women supposed to be – good at comforting the suffering or good at spotting malingerers? I probably did malinger, if I could get away with it: though it was actually at Downe House that I contrived to have German measles, in the peace and safety of the sanatorium, twice running. (My father maintained that no one could prove, at any one time, that he *hadn't* got German measles, since you could have them without spots, without a temperature or a sore throat, without feeling bad.)

My father got on well with the mistresses, at least with my house mistress, Miss Patterson. In the hall of the hotel there was a larger-than-lifesize lamp-holding statue of a naked black woman. 'Distinguished old girl?' suggested my father; Miss Patterson laughed, but I was mortified. For I did try to fit in: I tried clowning it a bit which sometimes worked; I did get up for fielding practice before breakfast, though I don't know whether I had a choice; as far as lacrosse was concerned, they finally gave up and simply had me practise 'cradling' on the sidelines most of the time.

Were there no bright spots? There must have been: I remember rejoicing when I was put in the choir, and I was some sort of animal in a masque of Milton's *Comus* they put on. I played one of the schoolchildren in a production of J. M. Barrie's *Quality Street*, in which Jill Balcon played the lead – she who married Cecil Day-Lewis, the divorced husband of my mother's cousin Mary, and would star as Mrs Jackaman in the TV version of my husband Gavin's *The Secret Servant*. I did occasionally have the odd friend and was, though seldom, on the teasing side rather than being teased, which I was not proud to remember later.

But I lost a stone every term from sheer misery, my parents later told me. And at the end of the second year I got on my bicycle and rode home to St Bees, having plotted my course over weeks from the hotel's huge relief map of the area. (The bike had two flat tyres, but a pair of kindly strangers mended them for me.) When I got back, there had to be a session with my father. He said he thought I ought to go back; he also said he couldn't make me – 'It would ill beseem me to be seen brawling with my daughter on St Bees station platform' – and I agreed. The school said never mind, it's almost the end of term, and we understand you're taking her to a child psychologist, so let's see what she says.

The amiable psychologist was called Dr Blau. She lived in Edinburgh; my mother and I visited her and what she said in essence was 'She's been at that school for two years and she's miserable; why don't you send her to a different school?' It sounds obvious, but to be fair to my parents, it wasn't: I'd been homesick at Downe House, a misfit at The Mount; they must have thought, with some justice, that the trouble was me, not the schools. But Dr Blau's words were the order of release; I remember that day well. We bought my first 'high' heels (about an inch at most) and my first cherry-coloured suit; my mother and I, who enjoyed doing things together, had a joyful, joky day in town before going back to the Highlands for the summer.

Then they set about finding somewhere else. What they found was the Glasgow High School for Girls, in the town where my mother had been blissfully happy at school; and so, from then on, was I. When I arrived in the new school, on a Wednesday, I joined my class; on the Friday a girl called Sheila Haydock said: 'We all know each other, but you don't know us; so would you like to come to tea tomorrow?' I couldn't believe my ears: at Roedean a new girl spent at least a term having it drummed into her what an insignificant little squit she was; and here were these girls being welcoming!

The difference from Roedean was the difference, for me, between a wet November evening and a sunlit June morning. For years I could cheer myself up just by remembering I wasn't at Roedean any more; my worst nightmare was dreaming I was back; and for the rest of my life I have always known I was happy *when* I was happy, and not just later. We all try passionately to give our children an unclouded youth; but, if it doesn't warp you entirely, there is this upside to having once had a rotten time.

AT SCHOOL IN GLASGOW

Of course the girls weren't all wonderful, but one of them was a sweet-natured girl called Isabelle Baxter, the daughter of a Church of Scotland minister who lived in Dowanhill. And when the couple who had first given me a billet said they couldn't do it any longer (Mrs Mackenzie was going to have another baby – but another explanation was that the help had said either I left or she did), my parents asked the Baxters to take me in. It was wartime; they were incredibly good-hearted; so in spite of not really having room, they did. For the first term or two I even had to share a big double bed with Isabelle. She had a very pretty elder sister, Agnes, and two brothers, Wallace and Richard, with whom I was able to fall quietly and gently in love; first with Wallace, who was devastatingly handsome, and later with Richard, who was nearer my age, more accessible and more fun. On one occasion, for a bet, he undertook to go to school wearing a different pair of trousers (or kilt) every day for two weeks; not to be outdone, I undertook to wear a different hairstyle every school day for a fortnight. I enjoyed watching the stunned glances of my teachers as, towards the end of the second week, my hair resembled various forms of birds' nest, cat's cradle or lampshade. Not a touch was ever exchanged between the Baxter boys and me, but I was able safely to adore them: honest, clever, good-looking middle-class boys. Maybe it's not a coincidence that the only two people I ever seriously wanted to marry were cast in the same mould.

My form mistress, like me, was English, not Scots, and occasionally that made a comfortable bond. Ethel Barlow was a woman of elegance and a fantastic teacher; she taught English, which I was good at, and history, which I wasn't. For history we also had Miss Robertson, a formidable lady with a grey bun; she was ambidextrous and used to amaze her class by starting a sentence on the blackboard with her left hand and continuing the other half with her right. She also spelled out words in such a way that you remembered the spelling: 'In-de-pen-dent' still remains at least one word I never get wrong. In those days, in Scotland, there was an item in the History Highers – the Scottish equivalent of the School Certificate – called Significances. The pupils were given the name of an event, a date, a person, and told to say in a couple of lines when or what they were and what was their significance – so 'Salamis – 5th century BC – a sea battle fought between Athens and Sparta which established Athens's supremacy over the Aegean'; or 'Marie Curie – nineteenth-century Frenchwoman who discovered radium which is used to treat cancer'; or '1066' or 'Abraham Lincoln' or 'Rembrandt', and you had to say what each of those was. The teachers understandably loathed teaching these snippets, but they had an immense usefulness for us, and at least they stopped whole generations of schoolchildren from thinking that Nelson protected us from Hitler or that Botticelli was a cheese.

There was a loopy eccentric called Miss Meldrum who taught us art, and, meeting a couple of us in the street one weekend, swept us into a marvellous exhibition of Chinese art and porcelain; there was appalling Miss Morrison, large and ugly, who taught maths and spat, and called me Kathleen Whitthorn till the end. I sat and actually passed in maths under her tuition, which included calculus; but I never at any point understood what calculus *was* – as far as I was concerned it could have been a philosophy or a food or a piano (years later someone explained it to me in two sentences).

I was inclined, as a fellow Sassenach, to stick up for Miss Barlow if the class disapproved of anything she said; and I remember one occasion when she had defended the Church's tendency in the Middle Ages to swing incense: 'If you have four hundred unwashed people gathered in a cramped space it's quite a practicable idea to provide an alternative smell.' To the little Presbyterians, *any* approval of *anything* Catholic was a no-no: 'How can she say they're practical when they believe the bread and wine actually change . . .!' I said she only said it was practicable, not that their ideas were practical; as the next class began Isabelle in the seat behind leaned forward and hissed the ultimate insult: 'You're a wee nun!'

Living in a minister's household, I went to church a lot, and I also for a while had to bang out the Sunday School hymns on an old piano, which I almost never did without a mistake. I can't now remember how much of that religion I actually believed. School religion has its drawbacks, of course, but at least you do end up knowing the words to a lot of hymns (it was a test of being a bit gone on somebody when you started substituting their name for a holy one – 'How sweet the name of Wallace sounds/In a believer's ear'). Miss Barlow wrote in one of my reports: 'I doubt if any organised religion will ever hold her.' I and my brother had our reports read to us. We weren't shown them, on the very sound theory that if there was something our parents didn't want us to see, we'd smell a rat at once if they suddenly withheld the report. Only, of course, that didn't stop us – didn't stop me, at least– getting hold of them anyway.

Interestingly, my father, who had once thought he might become a missionary and had belonged to the Student Christian Movement, tried very hard to get John to consent to being confirmed at Rugby. John put a up strenuous resistance – he didn't hold, he said, with an institution that preached the Sermon on the Mount and then blessed bombers; they had a vigorous correspondence about it all. Once John sent a postcard to our father which ran: 'If religion only moral imperative what about God?' As it was marked 'Urgent', Alan replied by telegram: 'GOD ONLY MORAL

IMPERATIVE DRESSED UP IN TROUSERS AND LONG
WHITE BEARD.'

My father had not urged confirmation on John because he
favoured the Church of England, but because he thought
John's path would be smoother if he was C of E like his peers.
Alan had undoubtedly suffered as a schoolmaster from not
being C of E; he had several times applied to become a headmaster and been turned down because he was a nonconformist.
Just as well, actually: he was a brilliant classroom teacher, but
I don't think he would have been a particularly good headmaster. He wasn't good at imaginative change (he never, for
example, understood what rebellious sixties students were on
about, and thought they should simply be grateful to get a university education). Safe with the Baxters, I was unaware of
any of this, and just thought all grown-ups were church-going
one way or another.

The Baxters used to invite lone servicemen to tea, if they
showed up in church; and one of these, a sailor from
Kentucky, took a fancy to me and we began to exchange letters. It was always terribly exciting when an airmail letter
arrived in that universal looped American handwriting, and
after a bit the question of marriage came up. I said no, of
course, having only met the guy a couple of times, though we
kept on writing; I suppose I can say I got my first proposal
before I got my first kiss – which was *disgusting*. It was at a
school dance where there were kissing games, during which a
lanky stranger put his revolting tongue halfway down my
throat.

After the Baxters, I boarded with a doctor's family, the
Campbells; they too had a couple of sons, though the eldest,
John, was away in the Navy. When he was home on leave he
was great fun. Once he complained he'd left without his

pyjama cord; his mother asked why on earth he hadn't written for it: 'But it would have made such a silly parcel' – and we immediately imagined it, one inch wide and a yard and a half long – as pyjama cords were in those days. (My mother used to say she thought my father had only got married to have someone there to do something when the cord got stuck halfway round the back.)

David was my sort of age, and he and I did have certain snogging sessions in the back of a car; though I can't remember whose car it was or how on earth, in 1944, we got hold of it. He was a friend – I never had a crush on him; and by this time I had friends at school, too; you could say I was approaching normality at last. My best friend was Marion Gibb, also a fan of Miss Barlow (we took her to the theatre once), also a contender for the English prize – thank goodness they had the wit to split it between us. We both idolised Rupert Brooke, and I didn't know whether to be more horrified or envious when she cut his photograph out of the library copy of his poems. She didn't share, though, my obsession with G. K. Chesterton, many of whose poems I still know by heart, some of whose paradoxes I would tediously quote and whose amazing gusto and appetite for life had me enthralled. I imagine that for most adolescents there is one writer, or teacher, or leader more than another, through whom one first learns about what are in fact quite commonplace or universal truths; you think that author or person alone has thought of them, and idolisation follows.(This, I suppose, may also explain why, during my time at Cambridge, so many otherwise sensible people thought D. H. Lawrence had invented sex.)

Marion was brilliant at school, in spite of having an enormous amount to battle with at home. Her mother was dead, she had an insensitive and demanding father and a younger sister that she had to look after, as well as doing all the cooking and housework. When, later on, the question of university came up, her father was predictably against it.

'But what about my career?'

'*This* is your career,' said he, waving his hand round the kitchen.

But she did get to university in spite of him. She and I kept up off and on for years.

I was back at St Bees for the holidays, of course. The adults had a pretty thin time of it there, though they were certainly out of the way of bombs and danger. The younger men were all away at the war and of course my parents were worried all the time about my brother John, in the RAF. St Bees had a horizontal wind that pierced the staunchest topcoats. But for me, it was fine in lots of ways: I could stride across endless sand when the tide was out, or brood my way among lorry-sized sandstone rocks under St Bees Head to sit for hours gazing at the sea. In those days, the only thing my parents would worry about in my case was maybe my breaking an ankle with an incoming tide, not serial rapists lurking among the boulders. They even let me go youth-hostelling by myself with my bicycle in 1945 – in time to celebrate VE day in Winchester, picking up a soldier and clambering over the rings of fences that circled the Mound where the bonfire blazed. He, the soldier, presented no risk: he was absolutely winded by the climb and said between gasps: 'My God you're fit.' Well, that was then.

But Glasgow had to come to an end, there had to be a future; and I didn't seem to be all that good at academic things (I got – just – Higher English and Art, Lower Maths and French and History, though I apparently only passed when they'd taken my chequered wartime career into account). So it seemed a good notion to go for something artistic, and I enrolled at the Architectural Association School in London. But not before I'd had a splendid farewell dance in Glasgow; it was my seventeenth birthday, but Richard Baxter told them it was my twenty-first, so I got a cake and a silver cardboard Key of the Door and a good clap all round. A happy end to three super years.

LONDON, AND ANOTHER SCHOOL

The winter of 1945–6, though, was pretty bleak. I was slowly learning – the school learned a lot quicker – that I would never even begin to make an architect. And my mother was living with her parents in Hampstead Garden Suburb while she learned to lip-read. My father had just got the best job of his life as senior classics master at Marlborough, and they decided, probably wisely, that it would make sense for him to start off there on his own, while my mother stayed in London and only went down at weekends. A sound idea, but hardly fun for her: she and I would meet gloomily for lunch in a Lyons tea-shop where, as I remember, the meat patty cost fivepence (not to be confused with a Lyons Corner House where, in my mother's words, you could eat yourself blind for two and ninepence).

Come Christmas, and I informed them I wished to go back to school and try to get to university. It never occurred to me that they might say no if I could just convince them that this was the best thing for me. All the time I was growing up, the way they ran things was that if I *should* have something – a certain school, for example – the money would be found. At the beginning of the war, my father's salary was £500 and our school fees were £450; the difference had been made up by an overdraft. If I *shouldn't* have it – well, if it was *Mickey Mouse Weekly*, of which they disapproved – I could pay for it out of my pocket money. Years later my aunt Margaret told me that Alan had despaired of yet another stab at my education, but Edie persuaded him to let me try.

They found a sort of sixth-form school or boarding crammer to get girls into university, and in 1946 I went there. By train, where there was, I suppose, a reserved carriage; the others didn't speak to me at first because, as I later learned, they had thought I couldn't be a new girl like them – I'd arrived thirty seconds before the train left, wearing a red suit and carrying a gramophone.

Blunt House was in Oxted, in Surrey; it had about thirty girls. Here we had long philosophical conversations lasting for days; here we read intensively on a few limited subjects; here I made several friends with whom I'm still in touch. June Stonestreet, who married George Grun, my great Cambridge buddy – George is long dead, but I still see June most weeks. Caroline Naylor, who in many ways seemed a bit older than us and no wonder: she'd been caught in France by the German invasion and somehow made her own way home. Another, with whom I have lost touch, was Jeanie Campbell, the granddaughter of Lord Beaverbrook. She was great fun, and took first Caroline and then me over to Cherkley where Beaverbrook lived. It was an unnerving experience. For some reason we approached the house up a series of grassy terraces; as we puffed our way to the top we were confronted by Prince This and Sir That; Beaverbrook greeted Jeanie, then: 'And where's the *pretty* girl you brought last week?'

But worse was to follow a few months later. And I practically gave up social life for good – almost decided to go away and live in a cave – after my first cringe-inducing attempt at smart London, when Jeanie asked me to a party in a restaurant. Big thrill.

Trying to make conversation, I asked a beautiful young man wearing a tie that looked like my brother's: 'Ah, you're an Old Rugbeian?'

'Old Etonian, ectually,' said the demigod.

Abashed, I turned to another who had a stripe down his trousers, like someone I knew in the Marines: 'Royal Marines?'

'Brigade of Guards, ectually'.

So, realising that the high life was not for me, I groped my way to the wrong one of two identical cloakroom stairways, and ended up in the Gents.

In November 1946 I sat the Cambridge entrance exam, and I got an interview. It seemed to go well enough at Newnham, but the Girton one lasted hardly any time at all. I was convinced I'd failed; I remember crying in the rain on Andover platform on the way home: I knew there were other places, but – boo-hoo – my father had been to Cambridge. So had Roy and Margaret and my cousin Michael, and my brother John was there; and Reading had a *milkchurn* on the cover of its prospectus (sniff). But some days later I got the telegram: 'PLACE OFFERED NEWNHAM'. Thereupon was total joy. Edie, who had been unable to take up the place she was offered at Cambridge in the 1920s, rejoiced that I could now do what she had wanted to do – as she did in so much else. And even John's horrible schoolfriend John Longrigg, who routinely sneered at John's kid sister as a matter of principle, treated me with respect for a day or two.

CAMBRIDGE, GATEWAY TO HEAVEN

'Do you suppose we will ever meet any men?' asked a fellow Newnhamite a few weeks after we went up. A pretty odd worry, given that in those days there were thousands of men for every one girl in Cambridge – and I haven't used those words incorrectly: the likes of me came straight from school, but all the men had done National Service and a good many had fought in the war as well. So we didn't have callow boys to relate to, but Real Men.

My entry into mixed company was my brother. John had come out of the RAF and gone back to Trinity, the college that had educated my father and uncle, my great friend George Grun, and later on my ill-starred fiancé Jimmy Wickenden and my great guru Jack Gallagher. John was about to leave for a job with what was then the Federation of British Industries, and I still remember with horror that his leaving party, at Churchill's, a nightclub in London, was attended by me in total contravention of all the college rules. John didn't invite me but one of his friends did; I remember reciting large chunks of Milton's *Lycidas* at three in the morning on the club steps to prove I hadn't had too much to drink – which it plainly didn't. It seems incredible, after all the efforts to get me to Cambridge, that I should have risked it all like this; thank goodness my luck held.

We were young; we were optimistic, and we thought we were very grown-up, now that we were proper undergraduates. And grown-up was what, in those days, we aspired to be: we had never been teenagers with their own youth culture – they hadn't yet been invented. We'd been adolescents aching to be adults. We aspired to the manners of the grand, with proper ball gowns and black ties – indeed, for my first ball my partner had a white tie and tails. I borrowed my aunt Margaret's best evening gown for one May Ball – who would borrow an aunt's garment now?

It was soon enough after the war for all of us to be scraping together what we could – we looked decidedly dreary most of the time, and we used to dye our clothes when we couldn't bear them any longer – I did once try to dye a faded evening dress, mucked it up, and found myself on the morning of the Downing Ball with no dress to wear. But we had a sewing-machine in Newnham, and we all knew how to use it (though only a few could change the thread, so you mostly sewed with what was there already). At ten a.m. I hadn't even bought the material, by seven I was wearing the dress – the only time I followed a Vogue pattern exactly, because I didn't have time to rectify any mistakes.

However bad we were at sewing, we aspired to the same clothes as adults. I remember going up to London once wearing a hat – not a fun hat, a real one such as mothers wore – and being highly delighted that someone saw me and reported I looked very elegant, in my New Look dress, gloves, proper handbag . . . it seems another world. We aspired to permanent waves – I went on having them for decades – and our mothers had a shampoo and set every few weeks – a far cry from today's girls who wash their hair three or four times a week. (Mind you, I've never been very up-to-date about hair – through the seventies I was perming my straight hair curly at the same time as our secretary was *ironing* hers straight.) These were the days when trousers for women were sporty or associated with air-raid warnings, and it was said that one woman of great distinction had been refused a seat on the board of the Bank of England because she had, once, during the war *worn trousers in the City of London.*

Our social lives were fine, but oddly the intellectual side was initially rather disappointing. At Blunt House we had actually had the heady experience of starting an intellectual argument over breakfast and carrying it on for about three days; in Cambridge it didn't seem to be happening, and at one point I and some other Newnhamites started a club rather self-consciously called the Blue Nylons. We invited people like Noel Annan to speak to us and our guests (one of whom, to his discomfiture, had heard him give exactly the same speech the night before to an august male club).

I was reading English, and at that time Cambridge English was dominated by F. R. Leavis, against whom I was unalterably inoculated by the fact that he didn't hold with Milton, whom I revered. What he and his school *said* they did was the exact opposite of what they actually did. The theory was that you didn't just take Great Men for granted; you scrutinised their work to see what it was really like, line by line. But what happened in practice was that Leavis lectured to his acolytes, had only to mention names like A. E. Housman or Shelley to get an appreciative laugh; and they all just knew that D. H. Lawrence was the greatest writer in the world, though George Eliot was also granted his approval. None of his students, I suspect, had actually read a word of the poets he sneered at, let alone scrutinised them – though it was rumoured that occasionally English undergrads of his college, Downing, would creep away to secret meetings where they would read Shelley.

Under the Cambridge system you were usually supervised by dons in your own college, writing about one essay a week, and went to lectures anywhere in the university. I don't recall learning much the first year or so, though I suppose I must have done because I did have to read my essay on Euripides'

The Bacchae aloud to the lecture audience. I have no idea whether a word of it was audible: probably not, since when I auditioned for a part with the Marlowe Society I came on stage and was halfway through my piece before a voice from the audience said: 'You can begin now.' But I did play a heroine in a Queens' College production of a J. B. Priestley 'Time' play, and went out for a while with one of the cast. What I chiefly remember about that was borrowing a very expensive ring as part of my costume, and losing it, and contemplating suicide/going on the streets/stealing the college silver, before it was discovered between the floorboards of the stage.

The ring belonged to Leonie, who played a very important part in our lives. Her parents, or one of them anyway, came from Brazil, and were not married – on principle – though they'd been together half their lives. Leonie was very advanced, she was The One Who Knew About Birth Control – in detail, not just as a concept. There was no Pill then but there were condoms, of course; we may not have actually acquired our Dutch caps until much later on, presenting ourselves at the Marie Stopes clinic in Whitfield Street in London, pretending to be married; but at least, thanks to her, we knew something of the possibilities.

Sometime in my second term I became the girlfriend of Jimmy Wickenden. He was one of the war returnees, extremely handsome to my way of thinking and sophisticated about things like restaurants; I hadn't had a serious boyfriend before and I fell for him in a big way. But he was extremely possessive and a past master, as I later came to realise, in the art of emotional blackmail. He would go into a martyred huff any time I wanted to do anything with anyone else – even a girlfriend, let alone another man. But to begin with I didn't care, I was seriously in love for the first time.

In those days there was nothing automatic about having an affair à *l'outrance*; you discussed it endlessly with your female friends – should we or shouldn't we? – and sometimes had to keep the doubting conversation going long after the matter had been deliciously resolved, lest anyone realise you'd finally given in. But we did eventually become lovers; I remember that on that first evening he said: 'You're not a virgin any more, darling', and I liked the sound of it so much I made him say it again.

We went to the Trinity May Ball; we went away to Cornwall on holiday – he had to pay; my parents weren't prepared to stump up. They had regarded this growing attachment with utter dismay. Having got me to Cambridge, they thought at last that I was behaving myself, working hard, going to get a good degree and make my way in the world; and here I was, apparently, being completely blown off course by a man they actively disliked. And if they suspected, as they probably did, that he had seduced me, or planned to, they would have been furious; this was 1948 and nice girls were still supposed to resist.

As the months went on the pressure to get engaged grew stronger. I finally gave in and said yes, and it went into *The Times*. My father's reaction I only knew about later: 'My daughter, engaged to that little bastard!'

Jimmy was going down from Cambridge that summer, and he wanted me to quit Cambridge and get married. I was shocked: in some deep way, till then, Cambridge and work were to me serious, and love almost an optional extra.

'What about my career?' I pleaded.

'Well, lots of jobs don't need a degree anyway.'

'Like what?' I said sceptically.

'Receptionist,' he suggested.

I should have finished it there and then but I didn't. However, by the autumn I realised I really couldn't go on; and with floods of tears and misery and returning of the ring I broke it off. That should have been the end of the relationship, of course; but it wasn't: it was on again, off again, throughout the Michaelmas term, and finally came to an end only after Christmas of my second year.

By my twenty-first birthday that March I was a free woman, and I only needed a tall, dashing man to make life perfect. Enter Bob Gatehouse of Trinity Hall; he must have been overjoyed at my ponderous explanations of why I *absolutely did not want to get married yet*. He was a glamorous ex-officer; he even had that rarity, a car. But at Trinity Hall they chucked the women out at ten p.m., as opposed to Trinity itself, where it was midnight. ('What is it that a Trinity Hall man will think of at ten past ten that a Trinity man won't think of till after midnight?' Ha ha.) Which was how I came to be lowered over the wall of Trinity Hall wearing a man's Homburg hat and mackintosh – heaven knows why that was supposed to make it better. Newnham, of course, didn't have late-evening men at all in those days and you were supposed to be in at a given time; but they were building a new wing that year and I remember once coming down the scaffolding carrying a rug and a bottle of milk. (Why *milk*?)

There was some suggestion, come the summer, that I might go on holiday with Bob and his friends, but I'd done so little work it was decreed that I should stay and catch up. So without telling me he took his other girlfriend, whom I thought he'd given up. Much later, after we'd split up, I was talking to one of his friends, who casually mentioned that this girl had been in France with them; and I realised that I had, at some level, known all along.

This question of how consciously you know what you know intrigues me, and it comes into the sort of work I do nowadays as agony aunt for *Saga* magazine. One of the earliest queries I had to answer was from a woman who, after endless affairs with men, had at last found happiness with another woman: did she have to tell her aged parents? After much thought I said no, I thought not. Her father, by her account, was fairly set in his ways and conventional, and if he reacted badly, he was so old it might be hard to get their relationship back together again before he died. And as for her mother, I thought it likely that, at some level, she *did* know. But if she were to be told, she'd have to confront it; to decide how to behave towards her daughter's lover, the 'friend' whom she already knew well, she'd have to decide who to tell; to examine whether she was pleased or sorry about it. Better to leave it lie. Which is also, to my mind, why those who tell a wife 'for her own good' that her husband is cheating on her should probably be boiled in oil.

It was my last year at Cambridge which actually did something for my brain – to the extent that it got to my emotions as well – or, just possibly, vice versa. The first discovery was purely intellectual. Third-year English offered a choice of optional papers, which changed from time to time; on offer were the English moralists – Hobbes, Locke and Adam Smith and so on. Enid Welsford, our excellent wren-sized tutor, rightly supposed we wouldn't have the faintest idea what they were on about unless we had a bit of background; so for the first term at least we had what amounted to a potted Moral Sciences tripos – Plato and Aristotle and St Augustine and such. And that *was* of some use.

The other great revelation came from T. R. Henn, head of St Catherine's, who gave totally inspiring lectures on W. B. Yeats. If lecturers hope to light a fire in the hearts of their students, he certainly did: so much so that I determined, somehow, to be taught by him. I wrote to Francis Cammaerts, an ex-pupil and friend of my father's who was also a terrific admirer of Henn and had been at St Catherine's, saying, 'You've got to fix it that I am taught by this man, he's the most inspiring thing that's happened to me at Cambridge.' I expected him to write a carefully worded diplomatic request; what he did was simply to forward my letter to Henn, who added me to the Monday evening seminars otherwise confined to his St Catherine's pupils (all male).

My feelings for him, which were strong and totally one-sided, were Platonic in the real, accurate sense: in his *Symposium* Plato writes of people adoring a person because that person stands as their gateway to The Good. I showed him some of my poetry, which he accurately described as being written 'from the teeth out', and once he returned an essay with a totally illegible remark in red ink at the bottom. I took it up to him after the lecture and said, 'What does this say?'

'It says "You must improve your handwriting,"' he replied.

There was a huge photograph of him in the window of a photographer's in King's Parade; an icon. A week or two before my final exam he suggested that I might possibly get a First. I was appalled; I'd thought he didn't think I had a hope, would have done *far* more work if, if, if . . . He implied he'd not said I might be up to it so as to egg me on: which showed that whatever skills he had with his men – he always required himself to be called the Brigadier – he'd got it quite wrong about me: it's people who believe I *can* do it who get me to work. Anyway, it was too late, I hadn't done nearly enough; anyway, it wouldn't have done me any good in Fleet Street; anyway, I got a respectable 2.1 without anyone having required me to read *Ulysses*, or *Pamela*, or any Scott or Proust or Henry James or

Trollope. I don't know why I'm owning up to this. I got a vast amount out of Cambridge, and the place was never supposed to be all about books.

COMING DOWN

So in 1950 I came down from Cambridge, and my father gave me £70 with stern instructions not to spend all of it. I spent the best part of two months hitch-hiking round Europe by myself; I'd been going with a friend, but she got a plum job with J. Walter Thompson so I went alone. Apparently my parents, understandably worried, asked John, as a contemporary young man, if he thought this was all right. And he said he thought the trouble I might get into with lorry drivers was as nothing to the trouble they'd be in if they tried to stop me. So on condition I sent a postcard every other day, I went, calling on Francis Cammaerts's Resistance contacts en route – he had been a king pin in SOE during the war.

I started in Paris, where I met Richard Mayne and Edward Behr from Cambridge; they were very knowledgeable about the place, very intellectual; they sat in bars and talked about Sartre and *nouvelle vague* cinema and I thought them incredibly sophisticated.

After a couple of months roaming around France, mostly on my own, having stayed with those various Resistance friends – some of whom were very various indeed – resisted sundry lorry drivers, slept under a funeral cover in a youth hostel because that was all there was left; having been bitten by four million mosquitoes, run out of money at the beginning of a three-day bank holiday in Marseilles and had the top of my home-made seersucker swimsuit float away from my chest in shallow water (the only time I ever heard a Frenchman actually say 'Ooh la la!') – when, as I say, I got back to Paris I found them still sitting round in cafés being intellectual. and was rather less impressed. But smitten with Paris I have never stopped being.

Before that, though, I'd spent a few damp days in the Auvergne with Jack Gallagher, who became, apart from Gavin, about the most important person in my life. We had got to know each other during my last term at Cambridge and had arranged to meet in France, making contact via adverts in the newspaper *France-Soir* (I sent one enthusiastic message to a completely baffled tailor whose firm was named Jack et Jack – I thought it was just Gallagher playing around).

Jack was a Trinity fellow and a remarkable man. His father was a railway checker in Birkenhead; when he was only four he would read the papers to his illiterate Irish aunts and uncles; he made his way to Cambridge via the Birkenhead Institute, with one of the very few state scholarships available in 1936 plus a scholarship from Trinity College. When he first had to go to formal college dinners as an undergraduate, his tutor Kitson Clark asked him why he hadn't worn – as protocol demanded – a dinner jacket. Jack hadn't got one, or the money to pay for one. There are various ways of dealing with that. You can abolish dinner jackets because some can't afford them. You can shrug and let the lad simply stay away from occasions where one must be worn, or tell him that he, personally, needn't wear one – and he'll stand out like a sore thumb. What Kitson did was to send Jack to his own tailor to make him one – a very Cambridge solution.

Jack Gallagher was, by any measure, an extremely good historian and astoundingly bright: at the end of the war he came out of the Army – he'd been in tanks – in March and got a

First in May, which was given with an apology that it wasn't – quite – a starred First. He specialised in the British Empire and related it, as most historians apparently did not, to everything else in the world, neither saying what a Jolly Good Thing it was nor blaming it for everything that's ever gone wrong with any nation it touched. But what made him exceptional was that he was so intensely interested in everything else as well. He hung out with scientists such as Fred Hoyle and Tommy Gold and Hermann Bondi, not just with other historians; he was always coming across a new book or idea and had an extremely funny way of describing them to his students – he was a marvellous teacher. And he had a world view leavened with unexpected streaks of compassion: 'We are all poor bastards,' he would say.

Coming from such a tough working-class background, Jack had a particularly beady eye for any sort of pomposity or pretence – he was an expert on the slave trade, for example, but one often got the impression he hated those he thought hypocritical (Wilberforce, for one) far more even than the slave traders. He could be uncouth, usually on purpose, and he lived in a perpetual mess: once, when he'd been in a particular set of rooms in Trinity for several years, someone he hadn't seen for a long time visited him, took one look at the piles of books all over the floor and said, 'Ah! just moving in, I see.' Long years later, after researching in Africa and India, catching amoebic dysentery in the latter and lying for two months in a hotel room, and after passing some terms at Oxford, he came back to Cambridge, ending up as Vice Master of Trinity when Rab Butler was Master. He and Molly Butler it was said, 'pretty well ran the college' till he became ill – with diabetes, among other things – and died in 1980. We got to know each other in 1950, and never lost touch again.

TAKING ON LONDON

The London I came to in 1950 would seem like another planet, I suppose, to anyone arriving today. It was still shabby after the war; there were still paralysing fogs that left yellow greasiness over everything; a lot of food was still rationed. But it wasn't depressing. There's been a tendency to look on the fifties as simply a damp patch of ground between the battleground of the forties and the fairground of the sixties; yet it was anything but. It's true there were still austerities, but we were used to them, and as they gradually ebbed away, we had the heady sense that everything was getting better. In 1951 we had the Festival of Britain, a huge exhibition on the South Bank with installations like the Skylon – a pointless and wonderful structure – and a glorious metal sculpture that scooped water from one plane to another with hypnotic repetition. The Festival staged exhibitions and displays of new materials and had all the exuberance that we were supposed to get with the ill-fated Millennium Dome fifty years later. It worked, it let off steam, it was full of optimism.

When it came to the coronation of a new young queen, people started talking about a New Elizabethan Age. There were the joyous explosions of the American musicals; the Ealing Studios were going great guns; John Osborne's *Look Back in Anger* carved the Angry Young Man out of the bedrock of British conformity; in 1954 a single review in the *Daily Telegraph* covered Kingsley Amis's *Lucky Jim*, Iris Murdoch's *Under the Net* and William Golding's *Lord of the Flies*. We revelled in the gradual easing of restrictions, being able to travel to Europe; with the ending of clothing coupons we swished our full-skirted dresses, preened in our upstanding collars. We still aspired to look like ladies, though: we squeezed ourselves into roll-ons, had permanent waves; we never wore trousers, and none of us middle-class girls had pierced ears – it simply wasn't done.

It's the details you half forget that are so different: the prevalence of uniforms on the streets while there was still National Service; the emergence of coffee bars as something new, and the fact, for example, that no one drank wine except with a meal – girls were supposed to drink sherry or occasionally gin. I remember a traditional family being quite thrown even years later to be asked for wine *before* the meal and having to make a lengthy visit to the cellar.

Old grumps who could remember the pre-war years moaned about the absence of deference and parlour maids, thought it dreadful that a working-class woman could say, as one did to a certain middle-class woman, 'We is what you was'; but we on the Left welcomed the welfare state, thought it would solve everything, with its free healthcare and free secondary education. Attractive council houses were being built, and they were much sought after, too, and only given to the clean and worthy – there are tales of a carpet being passed along the road as the inspectors called on first one then another. Even when the postwar Labour government gave way to Conservatives, they were very pink Conservatives indeed compared to the current crop, let alone the old guard of the thirties.

We were, some of the time, seriously worried about the atom bomb; but it sometimes had the opposite effect of making us feel that it was eat, drink and be merry for there may not be a tomorrow. I remember Jack Gallagher ticking me off for asking whether there was any point in going for a serious career when there might be no future, and his disapproval of the antiheroes of the time who seemed only 'to want to get by till a week on Tuesday'. But except for a few serious protesters against nuclear arms, the misgivings of the fifties seem much more like the mock despair of the privileged student than the gritty dismal nihilism, the listless despair of, say, the late seventies.

The thirties may have had Gertrude Lawrence and Noël Coward and Cole Porter and Mies van der Rohe's Barcelona chair, but it also had massive unemployment and means tests. People forget how the shadow of unemployment hung over the interwar years; and those of us who were young and hopeful thought it was gone for ever, that we would always be able to get jobs whenever we wanted them.

I found a bedsitter, as we all did: it was a single room in Streatham with a gas ring, use of a bathroom and washing up at the end of the corridor. The landlady, though herself quite young and sparky, had no intention of letting anyone else be so, and no males were allowed in; if Jack came to pick me up he had to wait in the road. I wasn't there long, finding a better place in Notting Hill Gate, anything but smart in those days. It was in a grand house that had been carved up and I had a tiny room with a high ceiling, but the gas fire was in my bit and I could turn it on from the bed. The kitchen was down steep dark stairs, down which I occasionally crashed with my tray; whereat the Polish landlady would emerge sourly to remark that if I washed up oftener, I wouldn't break so much at once. From these grotty surroundings we would all occasionally try to copy people with proper kitchens and give proper dinner parties: it was all part of trying to be 'in adult mode' – like Julian Barnes's schoolboys in *Flaubert's Parrot* trying to be called 'Sir'.

I got my first job when I wasn't in London looking for it, which I should have been, but home with a cold in Marlborough. Dr E. V. Rieu, the distinguished translator of Homer, was staying with my father to talk to his sixth form. The Doctor (as he was always known, like Dr Johnson) said there was a job going at Methuen, where he was a director; I applied and got it, I think, largely because I could quote G. K. Chesterton's entertaining description of his own work at a publisher's. I was to be the junior publisher's reader, the one who reads all the stuff that comes in unsolicited, either from authors or from agents; anything that looked at all hopeful was then passed on to more senior people.

Given that I was and am the slowest reader in Europe, it was an odd job for me to have, but I learned to skip effectively. I worked for John Cullen, an uninspiring general editor, who would regularly ask me, 'Where are the young authors?' as if there was a corral of them somewhere. Every week there was a conference, attended by us all, as well as the Doctor and the managing director of Chapman & Hall, Methuen's sister firm, who was a suave master of tact. I remember one occasion when there was a book to be discussed. 'This book,' said the Doctor, ' – is the author a *woman*, Thornhill?'

'Well, not as far as I know,' said Patrick Thornhill of the academic side; 'I wrote it myself.'

Ugly pause, relieved by the MD: 'Surely authors, like cats, are always supposed to be female unless there's some sensible reason for supposing the contrary?'

I was at Methuen for three years, and I can't say I made my mark in any way. One or two good things we did, though. I nudged them into printing the first British Dorothy Parker selection for ten years – we'd all read it at Cambridge; they let me edit a small collection of G. K. Chesterton's essays; and I persuaded them to publish a little book for the deaf, to which I thought up the title *The Listening Eye*. It was the first book on lip-reading written for the ordinary deaf person, not for teachers of lip-reading or other professionals. There'd been nothing like that at all when my mother finally became completely deaf. And I had the idea that we should publish an anthology of advertisement verse, of which there was quite a lot of amusing stuff at that time, and that John Betjeman should edit it. He visited me in my office, left a gold-tipped cigarette in my ashtray which I protected from the cleaners for three days; decades later someone from the British Library sent me a letter from him to someone who might have been interested, saying that 'An extraordinarily beautiful girl called Katharine Whitehorn' had suggested this. Sometimes I wish I'd known I looked that good when I did – but perhaps it was lucky that I didn't. If I had thought to make my fortunes depend on my looks, I'd have been in a right mess when they wore out.

I had a decent job, some friends, but not enough; life was pretty flat after the glittering heights of Cambridge. I came down to earth with a bump, realising I wasn't half as sophisticated as I'd thought, and did several perfectly stupid things, like buying a hat for the office outing and then taking it off in the Ladies so no one saw it; and winning the office Derby sweep, putting some of the money away in a drawer, going down to Cambridge to celebrate – and having to borrow money to get home.

You think if you've had a love affair or two that you're sophisticated and know it all: not so. I was befriended by the author G. B. Stern, to whom my mother had sent some of my writing. On one occasion she undressed in front of me; she was so totally hideous that it never even occurred to my simple mind that she might have been trying to seduce me. And L. A. G. Strong, who was connected to Methuen, got me some reviewing on *John O'London's Weekly*, which I enjoyed; it was only later, because he'd grumbled to a friend, that it occurred to me that a quid pro quo had been expected. He took me out to lunch somewhere rather grand, I remember, and I put ginger on my melon and choked; I was almost as embarrassed as the first time I went to a posh hairdresser, and didn't know the form, and tried to kneel at the backwash.

To make ends meet I taught English to foreigners in the evenings without ever really discovering how to do it; I went on holiday with Jack, and once to France to stay with Sylviane Rey, whom I had met on my hitch-hiking tour. I arrived there with a galloping appendix which had to be removed in a clinic in Crest, near Valence. Whether I can really claim to have been sick over a nun I don't remember, but it was certainly a shock to get nothing to eat for days and then be presented with a three-course meal plus wine.

The bonus of that break, though, was that they hired Anna Bostock to do my job at Methuen while I was ill, and she became a great friend. Years later it was she who rented Gavin and me our first flat; in all the eight years we stayed there she, as a Communist, never put the rent up, since her own lease stayed the same. She belonged to a set of extreme left-wingers, mostly of foreign origin – I think they were called the Geneva Club. They used to have weird parties where they played games, but with a highly intellectual slant – I vividly remember doing charades where someone was, preposterously, trying to mime *Nibelungenlied*.

My main companion through these years was Jack, who was always my guru and blessed friend. But he wasn't attractive. He wasn't Prince Charming or Mr Right or every maiden's prayer, and my efforts to make him become so do me no credit at all. He propped me up emotionally, he educated me far beyond anything schools and Cambridge had done, gently demolishing all the neat platitudes with which students kid themselves they've solved the mysteries of the universe; he was a rock and a comfort and the best companion in the world – but I couldn't fall in love with him. Eventually, of course, I went to bed with him, but that didn't change anything, and he was bitterly aware of it, describing himself once as 'every woman's favourite husband for her later middle age'. On one occasion we were going to see *Kiss Me, Kate*, then on its first time round in London. I wanted the bright lights, I wanted to be taken to a nightclub; Jack prevaricated, produced various reasons why not, said it was too expensive. I tried to solve that by equipping myself with a bottle, but when it became clear, after the theatre, that we simply weren't going on anywhere, I angrily smashed it across the railings outside the National Gallery.

We spent time together, we had holidays together – in Ireland, in Brittany, where I knew, enviously, that my brother John and his first wife Jo had had a good time. I went down to Cambridge to visit him, and in June 1953 it was with Jack that I spent an uncomfortable night on the pavement in Oxford Street to watch the coronation and learn about the thrilling first ascent of Everest. (The man who thought up the wonderful headline 'All This And Everest Too!' apparently never got the credit for it: his superior suggested it to *his* superior as his own inspiration, who then did the same thing when talking to the editor. (And perhaps the editor to Lord Beaverbrook? I don't know.)

There were good bits and bad bits during those London years, but I was getting nowhere, either personally or professionally. I didn't think I had a particularly rewarding job; I wasn't finding the right man; surely life had to hold more than this? I badly wanted a change, and in those days it didn't seem rash to throw up a safe and bearable job; it always seemed easy – or at least possible – to get another one.

One day I answered a British Council advertisement for jobs abroad; and in 1953 I left Methuen and set off for Finland.

TAKING ON THE WORLD: FINLAND

Finland was to make me feel I had come alive again; but not at the beginning. When I arrived in Mikkeli, a quiet town in the middle of Finland, there was no one to meet me; I didn't speak any Finnish and the station people didn't speak any English. Nobody, it seemed, was expecting me. A few frantic phone calls by the stationmaster eventually raised a nice woman who rushed round and collected me, though it was clear that no one had made any plans about where I was to go. Finally they put me in with a couple of pleasant retired schoolteachers and I began what I was there to do: teach English to small classes of adults and run various social events for the newly founded anglophile club.

Somehow during that summer someone must have taught me a bit about teaching English to foreigners – I can't remember when or how, but I do know I realised that while I'd been doing it in London I hadn't had a clue. The first few weeks were pretty bleak: Finns are kindly but amazingly reserved. I was moved from the two old ladies to a saintly family who put me in their drawing-room; but they didn't speak any English at all, which had its drawbacks. I remember one time when the mother was telling me I could have a bath; I was trying to tell *her* I'd just had the bath; eventually, after any amount of miming water and washing, she rang someone up who did speak English and I was allowed to remain dry.

Before the snow came I was taken to my first sauna. I went with some sixteen or seventeen schoolmistresses: '*Now* ve shall see each other in *Eve's* clothing,' said one. I hadn't been naked in front of anybody but a lover or two since I was a child, but here we went: seventeen bodies of assorted shapes and sizes into that amazing heat that made you feel you could hardly breathe, and then out with hefty splashes into the lake. Of course, once you got used to it, it was marvellous. It was also, which I hadn't realised, distinctly social; you sat there steaming away and chatting. In fact it was a terrible tongue-loosener and if you weren't careful you'd confess all your secrets; you worried when you came out for a long coffee what you'd actually said. In those days – I've no idea if it's the same now – the Finns were very formal: you had your coffee filled up in rounds, like a round of pub drinks; when visiting you never turned up without a flower – though one, precious, expensive rose was the norm; and they called each other by their work titles, as the Germans do. After a time it ceased to strike me as incongruous that large women would sit starkers on the pine-smelling benches in the sauna, still addressing each other as Rouva Insinööri (Mrs Engineer) Kekkonen.

It was only later on, when I was spending a couple of days with the Harma family outside Mikkeli, that the question of rolling naked in the snow came up. I said to Liisi, the substantially built mother of five and by then my great friend: 'I will if you will.' I was certain she never would, but alas, she somehow felt the honour of Finland was at stake so out we went. You rolled from side to side before rushing back to the heat; your imprint in the snow was therefore twice as wide as your actual body – and there it stayed, dammit, till spring.

But the snow was wonderful. I got skis, overland ones, the kind they use for cross-country skiing – it was like going for a walk in the woods, not alarming, not fast. At one point Lilja Reunanen, who became a friend I am still in touch with, took me for a week up into Lapland to ski. This was before they had any lifts there, so you walked half crab-like up everything you were going to slide *down*; it was the only time in my life I have eaten everything I could lay hands on, even reindeer meat, and still lost weight.

Skating, to my surprise, was something only children did – children and speed racers or ice hockey men. I didn't learn to skate very well there, but on one occasion I was taken on a picnic: Alte Harma, Liisi's husband, and a friend crossed my arms in front of me, held me then raced me a breathtaking mile across a frozen lake. Then we made a fire and cooked sausages on sticks, with the sausage sizzling at one end while our gloves froze to the other.

I loved it. After the first couple of months the Finns unbent, and I got the hang of the job; and got them to play games to improve their English. And I fell for an army officer named Martti who was a dead ringer for Kirk Douglas. This was a mistake, as he turned out to have a wife and son – 'I vos in marriage' – though he suggested they were only staying together because his mother had a weak heart. One reason I have never thought wedding rings for men provided much protection for females is that the Finns wear them – he did – but they take them off. I can't remember how we met, but the anglophile club I was running did have links with the Army: they were a jovial lot, drank a lot of *yallovin*, which was wood alcohol (some joker said there were big differences between the different kinds – to do with whether they'd been made from round wood or planked wood). One depressing sight I remember was once when the *yallovin* had run dry and the officers were ordering liqueurs not by taste or colour but alcohol content alone.

We had our Christmas party in the officers' mess; speeches, coffee, games – I can't remember if we had drinks but I think we must have done. They gave me a lovely watch for a present. I organised the party; in fact I organised almost everything, though my successors, I gather, operated with a strong and helpful committee. The people who were technically in charge of the club had actually lost interest in it and it was hard to get them even to show up; the ones who *were* keen didn't have any official standing. And since I was the first teacher-secretary they'd had, nobody knew what should be done any more than I did. It was the first time I'd completely run my own show. Getting thirty or forty serious Finns to run about playing silly games to improve their English gives you a great sense of power; not to mention putting on scenes from *The Beggar's Opera*, which they adored.

I didn't learn much Finnish, since I was there mainly to talk English. The Finns I taught mostly knew a good deal of written English, but didn't know how it sounded, and having been occupied by the Germans, they were apt to use German constructions: phrases like 'Won't you take place?' meaning 'Won't you sit down?' or 'a self-made cake', meaning 'home-baked'. I taught small groups of half a dozen or so, and I was allowed to give paid private tutorials. One woman I taught privately was a delightful English teacher who knew far more English grammar than I did: among the valuable things she taught me was the existence of a whole new tense, the present perfect – important in English English, since you can't correctly say, for instance, 'I already said that' as in American English you can. The other thing she taught me was the marvellous combination of digestive biscuits and blue cheese. Which is the only food lesson I took away from Finland. No doubt it's better now, but their food then was dreadful: only two words in the language, I was told, for cooking methods: one for boiled, one for 'cooked any other way'. And there was a grim pudding I mentally called 'Pond', apparently made from fruit and cornflour, which was the consistency and usually the colour of mucus.

Everything at that time was pretty basic, since Finland,

having been on the wrong side during the war, had only just stopped paying off its reparations. This meant that their houses were beautifully spare, cheered only by an abundance of indoor plants; and the fundamentals of Finnish life were tough too. You wore wool stockings; they told cautionary tales of girls who had worn nylons and had them frozen to their legs. If you didn't have a fur coat you had multiple linings to your cloth one. The roads weren't metalled because tarmac wouldn't survive the frosts, trains looked like something of out of the film of *Anna Karenina*, they burned wood and didn't hurry. Once Martti and I were going to Helsinki, but had a row after the train had started and he simply got off – I was appalled, but it was going so slowly he was fine.

I didn't mind leaving Finland because by then I knew the next year was going to be America. But I made staunch friends with Liisi and Lilja and Aune, with whom I had lodged, and I am in touch with them to this day. After the stagnation of London, that strange bracing year in Finland opened a world of possibilities again; and even the Martti thing was perhaps not wholly crude. For he always said that when I went, he would give me his knife – his treasured *pukko*, a highly symbolic thing for Finnish men. We'd split long before and I'd thought nothing more about it; but a few days before I left, a soldier turned up with a package. No message, no signature: just the knife.

A WIDER WORLD: AMERICA

My first experience of an American train was a sleeping-car attendant waking me in the morning as we neared Ithaca in upstate New York with the words: 'Hell, you look awful.' I didn't care: America looked wonderful.

It was the shining El Dorado of all our wishes, in the fifties. We who had read Dorothy Parker and Thurber and Ogden Nash, who had seen extravagant musicals and movies with the ideals of *High Noon* and *Mr Deeds Goes to Town*, we all longed to go there. But in those days you had to have a reason and a hard-to-get visa. So in my case it involved persuading my dons at Cambridge that maybe I should be an academic after all, getting a scholarship from the English Speaking Union and a Fulbright travel grant and pitching in any savings I had; finally joining the *Queen Elizabeth* and sailing to New York, spending a few days marvelling at it, taking the train to Ithaca, where Cornell is located.

America hit me between the eyes with a force I can scarcely describe. Everyone nowadays has seen the approach to New York a hundred times, but I was an innocent. I even somehow thought the Statue of Liberty was outside Philadelphia, so didn't realise, when it hove into view, that we were nearly there, and suddenly saw the New York seafront for the first time – it was *beautiful*.

As was so much else: it was autumn; no one had told me about the attractiveness of American domestic architecture; the excellence of the clothes you could buy – Britain had still hardly started; about supermarkets, at that time unknown to me; or the ordered ease even of picnics. I sent a photo to my parents of me sitting on a picnic bench; they were mainly staggered by the *size* of the banana I was eating. Pat, the eldest of my five housemates, had a car, a 1953 Studebaker, a streamlined lovely. There was frozen custard, there were sandwiches to die for (I could write a thesis on the decline of the Great American Sandwich).

But it wasn't only the luxuriousness. I had met an Englishman called Colin Leys, the son of my mother's oldest friend, on the *Queen Elizabeth* (you didn't fly in those days at our sort of level), and there was a lot going between us. He was on some form of scholarship at Princeton and I visited him there; I spent Christmas with him in Toronto, with relations of his; he gave me *white skates* for a Christmas present and I thought happiness could hardly go further. I learned to skate properly on Lake Cayuga, where they cleared the snow near a restaurant, and there are pictures of me gliding with one leg in the air, and reversing in a crouching position with one leg stretched – I wish I could do it now. We went on to ski – at which I was hopeless – in Saint Sauveur. Finnish skiing had been gentle, but this hurtling downhill was dreadful, you crashed down, you fell over – did you get any sympathy? No – you were supposed to be up and doing it again immediately – not my thing at all. But Colin was, or so I thought.

During the Cornell spring break, we drove down through the South; we camped on a sandy beach, we admired the houses in Charleston; on one exceptionally cold night (the peach trees in Georgia froze that year), we had to sleep inside the car, keeping going on 65-cent New York wine (resolving between mouth-withering gulps to spring for the 75-cent Californian next time). A slightly drunk black youth banged on the windows and asked what we were up to – well, nothing, actually – and eventually stumbled off. Next morning he re-appeared, very chastened; his mother said, would we come up for breakfast? Our teeth chattering, we made our grateful way to a simple cabin with a big fridge on the porch outside; she gave us coffee and hamburger; as we thawed out and we thanked her delightedly, she said simply, 'It's de Lord's work.'

So much of what I admired that year in the States was an illusion, I now realise. I saw factories surrounded by the huge cars of the ordinary workers: it seemed my socialist paradise come true. I relished my kindly Southern blacks without any real idea of the discrimination still going on: it was decades before I read Toni Morrison and Maya Angelou. But it did seem a freer, happier place: I remember riding into New York once on a bus, and falling in with a stranger, and wandering around Times Square with him after midnight – it didn't occur to me that it might be risky. And what was not an illusion, is real still: the sheer fact of the constitution, the ideals; the memorials in Washington – to Lincoln, to Jefferson – had me as bowled over as any ten-year-old from Crossroads, Iowa. Jimmy Carter said: 'America didn't invent human rights; in a very real sense, human rights invented America'. I'm still inclined to agree. And I still think that America has a remarkable ability to cure its own ills; I just wish it would grasp how hopeless it is at curing the ills of other countries.

When I got to Cornell I was housed in the wing of an old museum, the Helen M. White House, with five other postgraduates: Maija Kesä from Finland, Lali Lim from the Philippines, Josie Chen who was American but of Chinese origin; plus Americans Joan Rafaj and Pat Rowland, older than the rest of us. We each had a room, and there was what the authorities called 'a very simple kitchen'; it had a refrigerator bigger than most cupboards I'd ever seen – it didn't seem simple to me. This was only one of the extreme contrasts I was to meet between America, now firmly over any wartime shortages it had experienced, and Britain, still not out of austerity, let alone Finland.

We agreed to cook communally, two a week, on a given budget; after a few weeks the only rule was that the Finn and I should never in any circumstances be allowed to cook together – she being inclined to lament the absence of fish heads in the supermarket and suggest insane substitutions ('No cornstarch? We will use cement' – well, perhaps not quite), and I didn't know anything about it anyway. But three of the others were Home Economists and knew a great deal, and it was from them that I learned enough of the rudiments of cooking to enable me, much later, to tackle *Cooking in a Bedsitter*. This gang of girls immediately bonded so firmly that except for Pat, who died a few years ago, we are all still in touch; but we couldn't have been more different.

Maija was a farmer, still is (we discovered halfway through the year that she thought people had sex like cows, could only conceive during oestrus); she had a loud voice and an hourglass figure and was extremely attractive to men. She had a boyfriend in Mexico to whom she spoke so loudly when he rang up that Pat said: 'Why doesn't she use the telephone?'

Lali was the daughter of a general, the first Filipino to graduate from West Point, her mother the first woman to graduate summa cum laude in Manila. Her father had been killed by the Japanese when they overran Manila, but she and her mother had been in the States at the time, seeking treatment for her polio, from the aftermath of which she still needed crutches. She was pretty and frilly and silly on the surface; years later when I visited her in the Philippines I was told that she was now a tough businesswoman running Tupperware – but this tiger of Tupperware was still pretty and frilly. Filipino women, who manage huge amounts of Filipino life, never seem to feel the need to appear anything but highly feminine.

Josie was neat and precise and bossy and organised and very necessary to our slightly scatty ménage. Her boyfriend and family were all Chinese; when she got married at the end of our year, she wore a conventional white wedding dress for the

Episcopalian ceremony and then changed for the reception into a fabulous crimson Chinese dress with a dragon all the way down it.

Joan was a historian; the daughter of a Lutheran Pastor in Scranton, Pennsylvania, she was a bit of a pedant at that time, but has eased up wonderfully since and is married to an extremely interesting physicist. We all spent Thanksgiving with her family, and went shopping with her, persuading her, to the disgust of her regular sales assistants, to abandon the rather dreary pastels with which they immediately bore down on her.

And Pat held us all together, stopped us being idiotic whenever she could; den mother was the sort of role she had. She was the eldest of a large Catholic family in California; she was tall but had been immensely fat: she had been in one of the armed forces and had always been 'good old Pat', everybody's friend and nobody's love. But at some point she had had enough of that, and by the time we met her she had become tall and slim and elegant – but still nearly thirty and unmarried – a state she had remedied by the end of the year.

We had a reunion thirty years later. We were all contentedly married with children – except Lali, who has an American steady but always rightly reckoned she'd have a far more fulfilling life as a powerful businesswoman in a large and loving family in Manila than as a housewife in a New York apartment.

I was supposed to be in America for academic reasons; I was that curious hybrid, a graduate assistant, supposed to be studying American literature, which I did, a bit, and writing a thesis on William Faulkner, which never actually got written, while at the same time teaching basic English – grammar, expressing yourself, spelling – to seventeen-year-olds. Cornell had, and has, a great tradition of teaching a whole lot of subjects other than routine liberal arts, and the aggies, as the agricultural students were called, came to college at sixteen and needed a certain amount of basic grounding.

I did various odd jobs to augment the scholarship money, which was fairly sparse: the first one was cleaning house for a woman who paid me just under the going rate and followed me around pointing out every speck of dust. The second job was for one of the women who ran the student employment bureau. She paid me slightly over the odds and praised me to the skies – so when she said could I clean the windows I eagerly said yes (there's a lesson there somewhere). But after a bit I discovered that if you asked for a job in the men's bureau it paid far better, and worked as a gardener, a job which included holding on to a blind cord hanging out of a window in order to shave the face of a bush with a huge electric trimmer – well, it seemed a good idea at the time.

We were allowed to work for extra money while our academic work was going on, but we were all on the sort of visa which absolutely precluded our staying on to work; we were told that if we even enquired how we might possibly do this, we would be deemed to have breached the terms of our visitor's visa and be deported. So picture my feelings when I wrote to the student employment bureau in Berkeley, California, asking about summer jobs, and to the visa authorities asking for permission (about which there was no problem anyway) to pay a visit to Canada – and put them in the wrong envelopes. When I realised what had happened (the Berkeley people sent back the visa letter in some bewilderment), I wrote again to the visa people explaining that I *had* been thinking of doing more work there in the summer . . . blah blah . . . that I thought I'd need more money, but now wouldn't because Cornell had increased my grant – true, but it had happened weeks before – so I didn't need . . .

I received a puzzled reply thanking me for keeping them abreast of my plans. I was darn lucky to get away with it, and I still think it was quite something to have had both that kind of visa and, before I was through, a Social Security number.

I have to admit that not just the illusory thesis on Faulkner, but even the classes, got skimped on occasion, when kind faculty members would take them over to enable me to See America. This mostly meant trips to Princeton to see Colin but also included a weird journey to Mexico in the company of a friend of British friends: an artistic con man – I'm not being unkind – called Carlton Smith. He was the nominal boss of an outfit called the National Arts Foundation, run from Bement, Illinois, which consisted of just about nothing and no one but him; but he had done some surprising things, including getting Haydn's head back from the other side of the Iron Curtain.

He asked me to go to Mexico with him, the girl he had hoped to take having fallen through; he described her as a Mayan princess, though closer questioning suggested that she was simply a girl from Phoenix, Arizona, who looked like one. I wasn't going to pass up such a chance, the more so as I wasn't required to do anything more compromising than rub wintergreen into his bad shoulder.

We went first to Yucatán, which seemed unbelievably exotic; we visited temples; he hired a small plane to fly to Palenque, where we had to spend the night, much to the pilot's fury, because Carlton hadn't got us back to the plane before it was too dark to fly. Then to Tampico, where I saw real dugout canoes still in use, and on to Mexico City on a plane which he caught, with confidence, half an hour late: the only time I've ever seen an air hostess in curlers. In Mexico City I was increasingly racked by a badly upset stomach and the squits, and was taking decreasing amounts of notice of, or interest in, what was going on, which was a pity because we actually met Diego Rivera. Carlton Smith had no difficulty accessing him and other luminaries, simply because the National Arts Foundation sounded so respectable and grand.

And so back to Cornell, and the world of classes, and dates – you simply had to have a date on a Saturday night: if any of us didn't, we would drive thirty miles to a neighbouring town to cover our shame. Having come from Cambridge, where in my time there wasn't any special emphasis on Saturday evenings and girls who got engaged before they came down were distinctly in a minority, I was slightly appalled to be told that if American college girls weren't 'pinned' (the halfway stage to becoming engaged) by their sophomore year, and engaged by their senior year, they would probably be seeing a shrink. Years later I entirely failed to persuade Marilyn French (she of *The Women's Room*) that educated European girls didn't experience the same pressures as the Americans. The American women had been pushed far more firmly back into the kitchen by the noble soldiers returning from war; Rosie the Riveter was now Carol the Cook or Mary the Mom, and girls used to say quite cheerfully that they were at college for a 'MRS degree'.

Of course we British girls all yearned for love; most of us read and reread Nancy Mitford's *The Pursuit of Love*, but this endless pressure to be married by a certain date seemed to me to be positively cruel. Other cultures in which marriage is compulsory do give the girls a bit of help, whether it's matchmakers, parental involvement, or arranged marriages in the relaxed Japanese or the rigid Muslim mode; but here the girls had to do it all themselves. When it came, a decade later, the women's movement didn't take me by surprise, since I knew exactly what crippling patterns it was up against.

We Europeans might have had a longer hunting season in which to find our mates, but marriage was what we were all going for in those days; and the big question was always Is He the One? – in this case Colin. The situation was complicated, for me, by the fact that I'd by no means broken with Jack: Jack, brilliant, loving, kind, amusing; in so many ways the ideal mate for me but absolutely not the romantic lover I hoped for. I know some people think you can't very well have both, and that a close and enduring companionship is a better bet in the long run, and sometimes I would think I was being unrealistic in not settling for that – though I'm quite sure, now, that if I had married Jack I'd have led him a pretty dance. I remember that year once getting up at three in the morning to walk through the woods and think my way to a conclusion about it – I suppose this must have been early spring – but conclusions weren't easy or immediately necessary.

What tipped the scales was a letter from my father, who almost never offered personal advice; he knew Colin and I were thinking of driving across America when the academic year ended, wrote that he 'knew what a strain it can be on a young man', and suggested we get married. I could think of other ways of easing the strain on a young man well short of the altar, but the letter forced me to realise that yes, I would dearly like that; and I realised Colin probably wouldn't. Anyway, off we set in his old Buick when the semester ended, and drove across America, bathing in the salt lake of Utah, discovering that if a desert place is lonely enough you are actually delighted to find empty Coca-Cola bottles littering the way – it proves someone else has been that way at least once. We discovered, too, that it's amazing how far you can go with a leaking water tank, if you're prepared to stop every now and then to let the engine cool off.

We had a few weeks in Aspen, Colorado, when it was only just beginning to become smart; we were staying with Norman Singer and Geoffrey Charlesworth, a gay couple who remained my friends. Colin worked as a dredger for the firm that had made Liberace's piano-shaped swimming pool, I got a job cooking the breakfasts in a bowling-alley coffee shop – which is how I know what happens when you fail to grease a waffle iron: you spend the next three hours scraping tiny bits out of its runnels with a knife. By this time I suppose I knew that Colin wasn't going to propose, and actually I can see his point, now. He was very young for his age (though twenty-four he was often refused drinks, embarrassingly, in American bars); probably it's not a good idea for a too innocent man to marry the experienced girl who has dealt with that problem. I think I broadened his outlook quite a bit, from his fairly uncomplicated left-wing academic stance; but anyway it was no go. I got to interview Walter Paepcke, who was more or less the founding father of Aspen; we bought me a Royal typewriter for $20 in the Church Aid shop (rather like the Hussar buying the discarded girl a little milliner's shop, I later thought) and I resolved to become a journalist.

Why a journalist? I suppose I'd enjoyed such writing as I'd done – essays, blurbs, occasional articles for magazines – though I'd never worked on a newspaper. But it also seemed a good idea because I so liked an unsettled life: of the seven summers since Cambridge, I'd succeeded in not working through five of them; at that rate, I thought, if I didn't get into an unsettled trade I'd never get anywhere at all. But it wasn't an overwhelming call, a vocation; only later when I was firmly ensconced did I realise that this was where I absolutely belonged.

It was embarrassing, I suppose, for my parents that all this was happening with someone they more or less knew; but my mother wrote a limerick to cheer me up at this time. It went:

> There was a young man so obsessed
> He didn't like women undressed.
> He'd a mother fixation
> And spent his vacation
> In sailing from Bosham to Brest.

So Colin sailed back to Britain from San Francisco, and I applied for jobs via the ads in a San Francisco paper, and went upstate to work as a waitress in the Feather River Inn in Johnsville. I learned to carry a tray on one hand. On my day off, I rode a horse into the wooded hills and a chipmunk explored my lunch box – it was far too hot for the horse to do anything alarming like hurry, and the western saddle has a stout pommel to hold on to; when I tried to rise and fall in the saddle in the approved British way the horseman laughed so much he swallowed his gum the wrong way and had to be thumped on the back by the hands. On the inn's Gala nights, the staff too wore fancy dress, so I served dinner for thirty in my Chinese pyjamas. We went down to Reno to bet our wages; I got hold of the others' winnings and hung on to them when they, crazed with failure, wanted to get them back and lose them along with the rest: at the end it was 'Gee, thanks, Katy – you're a pal.'

I earned enough to pay my fare back to the East Coast and subsist for several more weeks; I stayed with Pat and her new husband in Washington, went back via New York, spent the crossing gloomily writing Colin The Letter, which everyone who has ever broken up with a lover is tempted to write; all about how it was, and what I meant, and what went wrong, and what perhaps still . . .

I finally posted the letter when I was at home in England, and it crossed in the post with a short note from Colin saying he was marrying a Danish girl he had met on the boat coming home. I rang him up, to tell him not to read my letter; he said OK he wouldn't. 'Be happy,' I said in strangled tones, and rang off.

But I didn't want him to be happy. I wanted him to be deeply miserable. Not much of a tribute to my sentimental education if he was, of course.

PART 3

INTO JOURNALISM

I spent a damp and gloomy term in the winter of 1955 living with my parents in Marlborough and filling in for an absent teacher in a nearby school; I was down on the timetable as biology, but as I didn't know any I was allowed to teach English, of a sort, and the trade cycle, and bits of logic and almost anything else that might keep them quiet, which it often didn't. The only training I ever had was contained in the single sentence: 'Never turn your back on a class'. My experience of teaching adults was no help at all, and I was lousy at it. But I had to get together a bit of money to go to London and try to get a job as a journalist.

By this time one or two of my Cambridge friends had found some sort of niche in the media, so they could pass me on to people who had – or might have – jobs to offer. I had an introduction to a literary agent, who asked me unenthusiastically what I wanted to write. Maybe articles for women's magazines? She was in the middle of explaining, crushingly, that mostly these were done by people on the staff, when her phone rang. By sheer good luck it was the editor of *Home Notes*, who had just had to let someone go, and did Jean know of anyone . . .?

'There's this girl in my office now,' she said without enthusiasm. I went over immediately, and was hired.

Home Notes was a tiny magazine apparently printed on loo paper. My main job was to subedit the 'Real Life Love Stories'. These were not, of course, real life, but colourful dramas dreamed up by hardened professionals; they arrived in batches of six and I had to compose the strapline across the top of the page – things like 'I said I could never forgive him but it was only my pride speaking'. They were illustrated with posed photographs; if the picture happened to feature a tall dark girl where the text said a small fair one, you changed the text – that didn't cost any extra, and what did it matter anyway?

It was a cosy little office; I particularly remember Chrissie, a pretty blonde girl who did the Horoscopes. She would go round the office: 'What's your sign, dear?' You would tell her, and she would ask: 'What would *you* like to have happen to you this week?'

Of course nowadays the people who do horoscopes are experts with charts and calculations and big salaries; but I've known too many journalists who have had to make them up one way or another to have any respect for them – even if it were to seem even remotely credible that our lives should be governed by the shapes that some Greek shepherds, hundreds and hundreds of years ago, thought the stars vaguely resembled. I am not saying that it is totally impossible for events in outer space to affect our lives in some way – radiation and all that; but the idea that we might have it all systematised into something like the Zodiac is, to me, like saying you can have a functioning 13-amp ring main when all you actually know about electricity is what you get by looking at lightning. And as for deciding what to do on the strength of such things . . . well, Claud Cockburn answered the question of what was, for him, the worst moment of the war with this: it was when a general's wife rang him up on the *Daily Express* on a Saturday to ask if he could tell her next day's horoscope, as her husband wished to plan a battle.

Before I got the job, I had a huge stroke of luck when I came to London and needed somewhere to live. I had a friend, Sheila Gibson, whom I'd met during the useless architectural term, and I knew she had a sister who owned a flat. So I rang her up to ask whether the sister ever let it.

'No,' said Sheila, 'I'm living in it.'

'Oh well, never mind.'

'But my flatmate leaves for Australia on Saturday and I'm looking for another.'

And there I lived till I left to marry Gavin.

It was a tiny flat, but we managed never to scrap, more or less bought food when we needed it and reckoned it would even out – though it was all a bit haphazard. One evening we had people to dinner and someone spilt red wine down my friend Anna Bostock's brand-new, deadly expensive white suit; we put salt on it and all was well; but five minutes before the shops shut we hadn't *had* any salt – I'd had to race out to get some. Thank goodness my good luck has often taken the form of mitigating the awful effects of bad luck.

Sheila was a most remarkable woman. She grew up in Ireland but was so puny and frail she was not expected to grow up at all – 'You'll never rear that one,' said the village biddies. And so she wasn't sent to school; the one time they tried it she instantly caught all the childhood diseases and never went back. During the war the family lived in Bath, and she had some kind of job in the Admiralty there; and at the end of the war she said: 'I want to be an architect.' Her father said: 'It'll kill you', and everyone else said: 'But you don't know any mathematics at all!' Which she didn't, but reckoned she could learn. The first teacher she went to said it was hopeless, but the second said: 'Get a slide rule and I'll teach you how to use it.' After a summer learning maths, she went to the Architectural Association School of Architecture in Bedford Square, which was where I got to know her.

She did indeed get pneumonia, twice, during the course; but at the end of it emerged with flying colours and a travelling scholarship which took her all round the Mediterranean. She just about invented the art of meticulously envisaging what an excavated building would have been like when it was up, rather than making do with just a general hopeful impression, and became a favourite of Nikolaus Pevsner – but all that was later. In 1956 she became a partner in the architectural firm of Carden & Godfrey, though already making punishing trips to Turkey and Libya, eating dreadful food as she was diabetic – nothing much but hard-boiled eggs for a month – and always toiling off to a Catholic service if there was one going on any-where near.

Sheila never married; the one person she would have con-sidered was divorced, and she felt, apart from anything else, she couldn't inflict that on her Catholic family. But she had a life she relished: she said once about her work, 'This is what I am *for*.' Her last years were spent in Oxford, continuing to draw even after several eye operations. Only when pneumonia was added to renal failure was the frail child, who once climbed a huge tree to see how the roof of her home was made, finally, in her eighties, brought to earth.

You could say that Sheila was only one of a kind of woman who did marvellously well as the twentieth century progressed; people like her, and my treasured aunt Margaret, and so many others were freed from what had been an almost automatic assumption about women: that only marriage and child-rearing were what they were for. Of course there'd been pioneers before, and there were plenty even in the sixties who would still assume that single women had simply failed to get married. But I grew up with career women all around me. A friend of mine once said: 'You were so lucky to have Margaret, you knew you didn't *have* to get married.'

Sheila's life, and those of her sisters, were so different from those of their single aunts, none of whom ever worked, and had to fall back on being interesting eccentrics: one went to bed for two years for no very clear reason, another was given to singing, 'I'll take you home again, Kathleen' in a cracked tenor at inappropriate moments. But Sheila was this excellent architect; her sister Thea was a teacher; Joanna became a stage manager, beginning in the Birmingham rep clutching a couple of books on electricity and hoping for the best (headline the following week: 'Birmingham Rep Blacked Out'); her sister Patricia was an ace rider in dressage events.

A few years ago Margaret and I were staying near Berwick; an old pupil of hers had found that her grandmother's family home, Marshall Meadows, was now a country-house hotel, so we went up there to wander round and look at gravestones. At one point we'd left the main road to explore a chain bridge; there were people on horses coming over it. We fell into conversation and I asked them if they knew Patricia.

'Yes, indeed – and she still rides – she's fine once they get her into the saddle.'

At which point Margaret remembered an ancient Countess of Salisbury who had to be tied into her saddle: 'And she would come to the back of her private chapel in her wheelchair; when they got to the bit where Adam said "The woman tempted me and I did eat", the Countess would boom: "Shabby fellow!"'

Margaret is a seriously happy single woman (and not, I suppose it needs to be said, lesbian). She always reckons she had a remarkably lucky life, completely different from the shallow stereotype of the sad frustrated spinster. The adored baby sister in a family of five, she was half brought up by my mother. Once, when she was a baby, an inept nursemaid was bouncing her up and down to get her to stop crying; the ten-year-old Edith said scornfully: 'You'll never get her to stop that way', and the nursemaid, at the end of her tether, said: 'Well, you take her then!' and shoved her into Edith's arms. And from then on, Edith took over as much as she could.

Margaret had an idyllically happy childhood: long holidays in the Highlands and pleasant schools; she loved her brothers and sisters and especially cats – at her sister Kitty's wedding she was carrying flowers during the service but by the time they were taking the pictures she'd swapped her bouquet for a cat.

She went up to Newnham in 1932; at the end of her time there the one thing she didn't want to do was become a teacher and be bundled off to teacher training. 'I want to go to America,' she said, and a sympathetic don managed to put in an application at the eleventh hour to get her a scholarship to Smith College. But a teacher she did become; she was headmistress first of Skinners' Company's School for Girls in north London, and later head of Godolphin and Latymer in Hammersmith. She instigated and ran a bursary fund when the school went independent; and in 2006 they named a building after her.

I sometimes feel that if half the people I meet have been taught by my father, the other half have been taught by Margaret; she was certainly a beacon in the lives of extraordinarily large numbers of girls. She knew, for a start, how to listen – which was why girls came to see her with all sorts of problems. But she could be forceful when it mattered. There was a celebrated occasion when Penguin Books had been putting on a display around the school, and it suddenly became apparent that some of the books were getting nicked. 'Oh, but they're such nice girls!' said the indulgent Penguin people. Margaret wasn't having any of that. She got the school bell rung, had them all into assembly and said: 'There comes a time when people have to decide what they owe to a community . . .' and much more. The books were all back by lunchtime, and one child even came weeping to her office to confess.

I may have admired these splendid single women, but I had no wish to emulate them, and in the winter of 1956, when I was beginning to be a journalist, I seemed to get a good deal of male attention. There's nothing like a broken heart – all that emotion floating around with nowhere to go – to attract men, plus the confidence of feeling that I was actually doing the right job at last. Not so much at *Home Notes* alone, as I was soon plotting my next move.

I had done one or two bits of freelancing while all this was going on, and was beginning to meet more journalists; at one party I met Gordon Watkins, who worked for *Picture Post*, for which I longed to work – I had practically grown up admiring it – and said so. He asked me, with barely concealed disdain, what I thought I knew about picture journalism; the true answer was 'Nothing', but I said something bright about pictures telling a different or contrapuntal story from the text, and it was apparently the right answer; he said he'd explore possibilities.

At the same time I asked Victor Anant, who was a tenant of my friend Anna Bostock's and also worked for *Picture Post*, if he could help. He said he wouldn't recommend me himself as he thought (rightly) that he was on the way out and it wouldn't do me any good, but he would introduce me to the great photographer Bert Hardy. Bert would do anything for a good picture, was famous, and also criticised for a picture of a little gypsy girl with her pants hanging down; he was a rough diamond in many ways. He was fairly stingy with money, gruff to talk to, but had a perfect eye for what would make not just a good shot, but part of a good feature.

Bert used me as his model in a feature about girls being lonely in the big city, posing me with a suitcase at Waterloo looking lost or gazing sadly into my gas fire – such was Bert's photography that you could almost hear the gas fire popping. Then he went back to the office and gave me a good press, said I could think intelligently about pictures, and I was one step nearer joining.

Those pictures by Bert Hardy have followed me about ever since: they went into the Hulton Picture Library from which people hired them for all sorts of purposes: the first time round it was for a Lucozade ad and I got paid £5 for a big poster of me sitting bleakly by the fire; it carried the caption 'Feels like crying but all she needs is energy DRINK LUCOZADE'. The next time it was for what was then called the Council for the Unmarried Mother and Her Child, and I said no. After that, nobody asked my permission but the pictures cropped up from time to time for years, culminating in a cover for a book called *Martin Sloane* which also became a poster in the Undergound – but the humiliating thing was that so many years had passed that no one except my own son recognised me.

PICTURE POST: *A RIP-ROARING TIME*

The telegram to my parents said: 'HAVE GOT JOB ON PICTURE POST WHICH I WANTED MORE THAN HEAVEN.'

The magazine was housed in an old-fashioned building in Shoe Lane, off Fleet Street, and even then it was dominated by the giants of its past: Tom Hopkinson who had edited it, Sylvain Mangeot, the great sleeping journalist – legend had it that he had gone to sleep in a Kremlin briefing and wakened up to highly confidential information being divulged above him, which made his name. Lionel Birch – Bobby – was editor; he was good at editing but even more practised at getting married. The trouble was that he usually got his decree absolute from the previous marriage just about the time he'd begun to go off the one who had caused the split; he would then marry her, and start another disastrous liaison with someone else.

A stalwart older woman, Monica, who had been Sylvain's secretary, was the mother hen who coped with all of us chicks. Once she was inveighing against Bobby Birch when the renowned photographer Inge Morath wandered into the room. '*Really*, that Bobby . . .' Monica began; at the end of her tirade Inge agreed: 'Oh I know, my dear, I was married to him one time.'

What made *Picture Post* a great place to train was that you were always working with a photographer. If you think about it, a lone reporter is rather like a learner motorcyclist: where is the white-knuckled instructor? The *Picture Post* photographers were masters of their craft. They would think in terms of how each picture might fit onto a page: 'We need another vertical' or 'should have him full face as well'. Many of them were veterans who had worked their way up from being darkroom boys, had maybe, even, grabbed a Leica off a dead German in the war years; so beginners like us were taught by people like Thurston Hopkins and Slim Hewitt and Bert Hardy. And they didn't just know about pictures either: they knew how to approach a doctor to get the 'real word' on a patient they'd had no luck with, or how to win round someone who didn't want to talk. They were pros all round.

The relationship between the photographer and the journalist was, I think, peculiar to *Picture Post*: the two worked totally in tandem in a way that they don't now and didn't elsewhere even then. You acted as a pair: if he came back with the wrong pictures the journalist was in as much trouble as the photographer, and, equally, the photographer worried that the journalist should get the right story.

You didn't know till you returned to the office if the text was to be a thousand words or just captions – but the captions were considered as important as any text. Indeed, after *Picture Post* folded I got my next job, on *Woman's Own*, by virtue of a caption: it was about two tigresses who had lived with one male tiger and then eaten him. The caption ran: 'His wounds were mortal, his trouble immortal. He tried to live with two females at once and it killed him.'

Picture Post was heady stuff for so many different reasons. The pace of it – you never knew, when you went in to work in the morning, if you'd end up at a posh press conference, a dress show, getting on a train to track down some newspaper story in Sheffield or climbing into the photographer Frank Pocklington's sports car for a seven-hour ride to Falmouth to interview a couple who were taking their baby round the world on a ketch. I'd be off to interview footballers' wives in Manchester on a bank holiday Monday (even then, the dullest job on the planet), a film star the next; I kept a leather bag permanently packed with my own stuff as well as, I used to say, everything a photographer had ever wanted except a blonde. My first task, though, was editing the letters page, and I still have a stern letter from Gordon Watkins telling me not to let the tiny success of my first feature go to my head, that in the long run Reliability Was Vital.

The sheer fact, for us cubs, of working with people who were absolutely the best at what they did – not just the photographers but that master of constructive cynicism Trevor Philpot, or Denzil Batchelor, dedicated professionals such as Gordon Watkins and Robert Muller (Bob was gastronomic editor for a bit, but said it was like being the sauce chef in a snack-bar) – made us feel that we were privileged, special, fortunate beyond the normal.

But it was more than that: you had the feeling that I guess anarchist cells have, of a sort of ribald underworld that knew more about the way the world was going than other people. We shared the gossip that didn't get printed, the inside stories we knew – or thought we knew; we relished the fact that we could cover a grand occasion or a rough scuffle at a workingmen's protest, a fashion show or a strip joint, while belonging to none of it, and the quite unjustified feeling of being outside the system, but for that very reason superior to it. It went with a marvellous camaraderie, in bars at unseemly times of night, back in the office sometimes, kicking around on the job anywhere and at any old time. Small wonder if you tended to see less and less of any friends who weren't prepared for you to break a date at half an hour's notice or turn up two hours late.

This was the world in which I got to know one of the newest recruits, Gavin Lyall. He was involved with a girl, I had my complications; we were mates. We would sit around in bars, I would grab Gavin as a fill-in if an assignment needed a well set up bloke, we would head for a drink when our masters ground us down. There were affectionate meetings: I remember our tossing coins off Westminster Bridge once, and his putting an arm round my shoulder and saying: 'That was a very long-term wish', and the first time he kissed me was on the top of a bus, as he left after we'd been seeing *Friendly Persuasion*, a film about Quakers – he was one. I suppose we both had a speculative eye on each other – as for heaven's sake you did have in your twenties, if you knew or even suspected that what you were currently tying yourself into knots about wouldn't, or at any rate shouldn't, last.

EDWARD AND OTHERS

Considering how totally suited Gavin and I ended up feeling we were to one another, one might have thought that obviously I would have wanted him from the start, that marrying him would have been a foregone conclusion. Actually it was anything but. At the time we met I was assuaging a frantic passion for an unavailable married man with someone else, an old friend who had become much more: Edward Behr.

Edward was a journalist who was also one of the right-hand men of Jean Monnet, he of what was then the Coal and Steel Community, forerunner of the Common Market. He later went to work for *Time* magazine in Paris, and much later wrote the book *The Last Emperor* and one about being a foreign correspondent called *Anyone Here Been Raped and Speaks English?*.

Edward was bilingual, which was very useful to me. This was because when Lionel Birch was fired as editor of *Picture Post*, the only other girl on the paper took off with him to the South of France, and I was told to cover the Paris collections. I knew nothing whatever about fashion, which didn't worry me; what did, though, was whether an unknown like me would be able to get the all-important couture *carte* without which you weren't admitted to the shows. Edward fixed it for me.

'Marvellous – how on earth did you do it?'

'I pretended to be the *rédacteur en chef* of *Picture Post*,' he said.

'What's *rédacteur en chef*?' I asked innocently.

'Editor.'

I was stunned.

'To catch the atmosphere of the Paris collections,' I wrote, 'you must lock yourself in a hot cupboard with a bottle of spilled scent and a champagne hangover.' In those days, apart from guarding the doors of the overheated salons rather better than if they had been the vaults of the Bank of England, the dress houses like Dior and Lanvin and Balmain had rules that were strict to the point of paranoia, aimed to stop their designs being copied on the high street. If you were caught drawing you were thrown out and barred from all other shows; just one or two pictures were released immediately after the shows, and only the daily press, not magazines, were allowed to take photographs in fashion week itself. Mere magazines had to come back to do theirs some weeks later. In an atmosphere of frantic drama, screeching phone calls and roof-raising tantrums, the fashion editors would choose which clothes they wanted to photograph, book the model girls, make it all fit a timetable and then, if you were a magazine, you went back to London.

So I chose clothes and girls, and decided to have them photographed with the beautiful statues in the Musée Rodin; this too Edward managed to arrange through an influential friend from his Monnet days, Georges Berthoin. His postcard said: 'Berthoin has phoned the Beaux Arts man who has

phoned the Rodin man who will presumably phone the statues to see if they agree too.' And then it was time to go back
to Paris; *Picture Post* had commissioned a photographer, and
he was supposed to meet me there – only he didn't.

Desperate phone calls to his agency raised nothing (made
harder because I was staying in the Hotel Récamier, a folksy
little place on the left bank recommended by Edward, where
madame on the switchboard got quite upset if anyone wanted
several phone calls in a row). No photographer. Now what? Go
back to *Picture Post* and say I hadn't been able to . . .? Never.

Fortunately I had fallen in with a photographer on the plane
from London who had made a pass at me; I had his coordinates,
got in touch, asked could he do it? No, he said, not his sort of
thing; better try Magnum, the renowned photo agency, and see
what they could do. Which I did, and they gave me Frank
Horvat; he later became a world-famous fashion photographer,
but I believe this was his very first fashion assignment. (He is also
the author of the perfect definition of seductiveness in clothes:
not a come-hither look, but 'a fortress imperfectly defended'.)
Then I told the office about the non-appearance of their man.
'Seek another photographer at Magnum,' they telegraphed;
and I'll admit that one of my proudest moments was wiring
back: 'HAVE ALREADY FOUND PHOTOGRAPHER AT
MAGNUM.'

But we'd lost a day with all this; so it all had to be set up
again: extra Saturday permission at the Musée Rodin, and
some of the girls I'd booked couldn't do Saturday; so other
girls had to be booked. But they were different sizes, so there
had to be different clothes . . . Of such is fashion journalism.
But at the end of days like that, you feel you've conquered
Everest and invented a cure for polio on the side. Absurd.

I was with Edward throughout the winter of 1956–7, though

he was mostly in Paris; but before that we had a strange holiday in Morocco. We drove down through Spain, skipped Tangier because he hated it and ended up in Rabat, where he spent days interviewing people and I, bored, kept having my hair dyed more and more blonde. The effect was extraordinary. Photographers I hardly knew whinnied knowingly down the back of my neck; messenger boys whistled even when I was wearing gumboots and inherited tweeds; a playwright I tried to interview on 'Some Trends in the Modern Theatre' thought I was trying to get a part in the show.

There was a fetching picture of me on a balcony in Casablanca, but I haven't got it now. Years later I asked a man called Diz Disley, jazz musician and artist, who made a speciality of drawing from photographs, to do a drawing of me as a present for Gavin. I gave him my entire 'Kath in Action' file, with the Casablanca picture, me interviewing Arthur Miller and such – and never saw any of it again, or the drawing. A year after that, I happened to see Disley in Bond Street. Furiously, I pulled his little Acker Bilk hat down round his ears and started to berate him . . .

The only trouble was, it wasn't him.

However, the little hat was no coincidence – it was the jazz hat of the time – and when the man knew who I had thought he was, he was entirely sympathetic and said he'd have done the same himself.

Parkinson's Law states, I think, that moving to a glossy new building is often a sign of a business on the way out; and so it was with *Picture Post*. We juniors weren't aware of most of it, of course; but some of the desperate measures to save it did impact even on us, cheerily seated at our sunny desks in the new building. They kept appointing new editorial people who rarely agreed with each other; we soon learned to do nothing they told us to do without checking with Trevor Philpot, wily and experienced deputy editor, who knew what might actually make it into the magazine.

What killed *Picture Post?* There was a lot of talk about its being killed off by television, and certainly its attempts to be up-to-the minute and in colour were pathetic: it made a great fuss, for example, about getting colour pictures of the Grace Kelly and Prince Rainier wedding only *two weeks* after it happened, whereas newspaper and TV photos had been around from just hours after the event. But other, similar, magazines – *Life, Paris Match* – lasted far longer, and I think the real trouble was that it completely lost its sense of who it was aiming at. It would have a showbiz feature of great triviality on one page (I did the captions on a Marilyn Monroe feature in which I entirely forgot actually to mention her name, and didn't get fired – that shows how far they'd lost their grip); then there would be two thousand heavy words about a political situation abroad. The two pieces simply didn't fit. Of course you can – should – have lighteners in even the most serious of publications, but this was a very uneasy mix and it didn't work.

PART 4

AN END AND A BEGINNING

IN PURSUIT OF LOVE

I remember with great vividness the day *Picture Post* folded. Gavin Lyall and I had been to a presentation in a grand Park Lane hotel to promote some species of tinned fish called Norway sild. We had all been told to be back at the office by two o'clock because there was to be an important announcement; I think we all knew it was the end. But I had another problem as well. I sat in the park with Gavin and told him that Edward was taking me to Paris that evening and I thought he was going to ask me to marry him; what on earth was I to do? Gavin said I shouldn't expect him to be entirely disinterested.

'No, but what do you *think*?'

'I think,' he said carefully, 'that you're a girl in her late twenties who wants to get married, but . . . *but* . . .'

And we went back to the office and received the fatal news.

In the event the dreaded proposal didn't quite happen, because when Edward and I got to the airport that evening I found I hadn't got my passport, and had to go back and get it and fly to Paris the following day, and Edward was so fed up with such behaviour that he thought better of the idea, at least for the time being. But then – I'm still surprised I was so clear-sighted – I did a very sensible thing. I said I thought we should call it a day. If I had no job, I thought, I would be inescapably too tied up with Edward and dependent on him.

'Would it make any difference if I asked you to marry me?' he asked.

'No, I don't think it would – because the kind of person you want me to be is not the kind of person I want to be.'

What he admired was the dash-about, independent, self-sufficient journalist girl; he detested what he called my do-gooding side – which I thought was something I actually should have more of. Later, much later, Gavin took the opposite view: I had a big heart, he said, and he just hoped there was a place in it for him.

There followed a strange limbo, that summer, while *Picture Post* was wound up and we thought about the unknown future: we were mostly offered jobs on other Hulton publications – I was offered *Housewife* – and there were various farewell parties. But we were paid off handsomely, and Gavin, who'd hardly been abroad except occasionally on assignment, was all for travelling around Europe for a bit. (He'd been on a film trip to Libya on which he'd become the only man to beat Sophia Loren at ping-pong – because, he said ruefully, he was the only man fool enough to keep his eye on the *ball*.) With one of my rare and excruciating efforts at silence – they are few enough for me to count them – I didn't ask if I could come too, I waited till he asked me, which eventually he did.

But I didn't want Gavin to trail along, with me taking the lead. He was younger than me, I'd lived abroad and kicked about Europe before; it seemed important that he should tackle the business of roaming around Europe on his own. I didn't want to be telling him how things were done, being the bossy one – not if anything serious was to develop between us. We arranged that I would go through Paris, to see friends, and Luxembourg, to pick up currency (at that time you were only allowed to take £50 out of the country), while Gavin would join some Cambridge friends who were water-skiing on – and frequently in – the Mediterranean. We would then meet – where? At that moment inspiration struck: 'The whale in the Monte Carlo museum.' And there we did meet – but we very nearly didn't.

I took my time in Paris, and had a few silly outings with a bunch of French journalists who worked for *Cinémonde*. One afternoon they took me to a *foire des vedettes* in the suburbs. A fair of starlets it might have been, but actually there were very few; someone asked for *my* signature, I asked them what name they'd like me to sign. My happy idiots then decided I should actually *be* a film star. They thought I looked a bit like Simone Signoret, so they started telling everybody I was Simone MacWhitehorn, '*qui tourne actuellement un film en Bretagne*' all about Breton autonomy; but they had to be careful, it was too like Algeria, very sensitive. They took photos of me with a Breton crêpe-maker, then actually printed all this nonsense in their magazine.

While I was in Paris I got a long letter from Edward, who was in Algeria by then. He tried to explain, as he never had when we were together, about himself, and us; his inhibitions and his reserve; he said he was somewhat like the character in Camus's book *L'Étranger*. After a weepy evening very nearly in the arms of Stan Karnow of *Time* magazine (ye gods), I boarded a train to Marseilles with a copy of *L'Étranger*, and read it to the end, in French, in a day; and if I had had any way of getting in touch with Gavin to call off the whale, I would have got on a boat and joined Edward in Algeria. Which would have been a disaster: I'd have been miserable, Gavin would probably have married someone else, and I would never have had the life I've had . . . it doesn't bear thinking about.

The whale: an august nineteenth-century skeleton in a quiet room lined with books. And coming through the door at the far end a gangling figure in a wide-brimmed hat. We took it from there.

We boarded a train into Italy, spent a week or more around Lerici, staying in a modest *pensione*. High above in the cliffs there was what seemed to be a sort of vast open room, not quite square; we couldn't make out what on earth it was, and our non-existent Italian wasn't up to asking. It was high summer, it was hot; the only way we could get up there involved setting off at four a.m. Which we did, and discovered that what we had seen the day before were marble mines, the massive slabs being lowered directly over the cliff, presumably into boats. We were both rather proud of having actually got up that early, and wrote about it in our letters home. But we realised that it was going to give both sets of parents an entirely wrong idea. Each being absolutely certain their own little chick was totally averse to four a.m. in any form (except possibly as a continuation of twelve midnight), each would naturally assume the *other* was a red-hot keen athletic early riser.

It was Florence next, which is, I suppose you could say, where we fell in love – except we didn't, really – we *grew* in love. It was a deliciously slow process; we shared a room for economy's sake long before we were sharing it for any other reason. I'd have happily gone to bed with him quite early on, but Gavin thought it was all too important to be rushed, to risk its being just another affair.

From Florence to Rome, where we disagreed about the ceiling of the Sistine Chapel – later on in life we used to congratulate ourselves that we never quarrelled about our own ceilings as we'd quarrelled over that one – and then on to Naples. The way we got a room on these journeys was to ask at the station bureau for such things, so in Naples we wound up, heaven knows how, in some joint at the top of a vast marble Mussolini office building. I remember – with incredulity, now – finding an ancient typewriter and writing to Olly Lednicer, an old friend in America, that I was going round Europe with a nice young man – 'But I don't think anything much will come of him.' (That seems, in retrospect, extraordinary – not least because the letters had worn off the typewriter keys and yet I was still able to type. Me, who had resolutely refused to learn touch-typing, since in those days if a girl could type she never got to do anything else.)

We left Italy, crossed to Greece and spent a day in Athens in the sort of café where, if you haven't ordered anything more after an hour or so, they think you might be thirsty – and bring you another glass of water. Peace in a dozen ways grew round us.

We set off again one sunset for the island that seemed to have least in the guidebook to attract tourists: Sifnos. As we stepped, wobbling, on to the quay in the morning, we were met by a man saying he was the Sifnos tourism representative; our hearts sank. But it turned out he was the local schoolmaster and that was just about all the English he knew. He directed us to a retired sea captain (Greece was full of retired sailors who spoke a bit of English) who rented us a room: whitewashed, bare, cool from the August heat. And there, finally, we got it together.

We swam in the warm sea; we made love on a flat rock

when the Greeks were reliably at lunch; I finally said 'I love
you' up to my shoulders in the sea. We went for our meals to a
local café, where the food was – well, it was useful to be blissfully happy. The Greeks seemed not to carve their meat in
any very predictable way, in fact it didn't seem carved so much
as torn apart. At one point there were some distant bangs and
crumps from the mountainside where they were, I suppose,
blasting rock.

'What on earth is that?' I asked.

'It's just them dynamiting the goats,' Gavin reassured me.

There was then a curious hiatus. I didn't want us to leave
the island until Gavin had actually asked me to marry him
(we'd already decided on the wedding date); but he, since I'd
said 'Don't propose in bed or what do we tell the children?',
had resolved to propose at Delphi. At dawn. And he did.

As dawns go, it lacked a good deal: Gavin had envisaged
shafts of first light but the dawn, in most places, just gets
lighter, especially if the place you're at doesn't face east.
However, the deed was done, and we had a magnificent breakfast in a hotel with real French coffee and proper croissants to
celebrate.

Then we had to write and tell our folks the glad news. It's
not easy trying to describe the person you're about to marry to
your apprehensive parents. 'Tell them,' said Gavin, 'that I'm
three yards high and two inches wide, and that I've got the
chest of a boy of fourteen and the lungs of a man of ninety' (I
didn't). He was tall, certainly, with auburn hair – it had been
flaming red as a child; he had long sensitive fingers for
stroking cats and me; a mind of which I then had hardly
glimpsed a fraction, a wicked sense of humour, and a temperament that made him refuse ever to be hurried or bounced
into anything.

After a few more days in Athens, Gavin made his way home with all deliberate speed to find work, as men about to marry are supposed to; and I took my time, thinking the future secure, as women do. I crossed back to Italy on the deck of an overnight boat, sharing my knapsack pillow with a tramp in a hairnet, and made my way to Venice, there to reflect for a week on what I had agreed to; what I had done.

I was staying in a nun-run hostel, and from there June and George Grun collected me to drive me back to Britain. They arrived before I was up; I directed them to meet me at a café under the Accademia Bridge, and there told them the happy news: that I had finally found the right man, that he was terrific and that we'd be getting married on 4 January. George's immediate reaction was 'That's splendid! I'm delighted! *And don't let anything happen before January 4th!*' Oh well; he'd seen me through plenty of false starts; he was as pleased as anyone that this wasn't going to be one of them.

I think we were lucky to have had that long summer to find each other, out of reach of the cynicism of our Fleet Street mates, some of whom, once we got back, thought it was hilarious. It was a summer entirely on our own terms, with Gavin increasingly confident, the pair of us finally sure of what we were doing. Of course we had to buckle down to the business of finding new jobs, finding somewhere to live, getting ready for the wedding; but the sure and certain base was there; the rest was detail. I do remember, though, the tense moment when, not having seen him since Greece, I was to collect Gavin from Savernake station to come and meet my parents. Naturally, I was a bit nervous; I took a lot of trouble with dress, make-up and so on, and carefully sprayed my hair with hair lacquer – except it wasn't, it was the insect repellent we'd used in Greece. I suppose, at least, I must have smelt familiar.

Then I had to write to Jack to tell him that I was getting married to someone else. By then I suppose he realised I was never going to marry him; but the deep connection between us remained; though not anything for Gavin to feel jealous of, ever – in fact he came to value Jack as I did. I still have Jack's letters from around that time, and am humbled by the stoic charity with which he planned my future. He wrote:

I start from this point, that I want us to stick together, in some sense, in some mode, never mind how the dice fall. This is big stuff that we are engaged in . . . For here is the trouble: here you are, footloose and off the reins, looking for the man who fixes and justifies, since you think (as I do) that the devotion between man and woman is what matters the most. Looking for the not impossible he, lands you in patches of trouble, for the way it goes is that rank outsiders come up to scratch and love you variously, vehemently and, in short, in vain; while hot favourites have a habit of straying off the course or have a leg missing . . . I can see that we shall come to no good unless you are happy. You must contrive to make a go of it, and this means in your case that you must become married . . . the vital point for you to fix is to come to terms with some man who has wisdom and charity. No wisdom, and you will not respect him for more than a summer; no charity, it is really hopeless, for there has to be kindness between men and women, and you are not strong on kindness . . . we are both hard towards those who love us in vain . . . so the he we are talking about is someone who is going to put his wits to understanding you, while at the same time matching up to your justifiable wish for a man with gaiety, go and plenty of hair on his head.

So I had found that man. And Jack continued to belong, ultimately, to all of us.

GAVIN LYALL

Who was this Gavin? He grew up in Bournville, near Birmingham. His father, a Scot, was an accountant; he mainly audited accounts for such firms as Rowntree and Morelands, Quaker firms both. Ann, his mother, was a complete Quaker; Joe, his father, what they call an 'attender', which seemed to mean someone who never actually attended but was fully in sympathy. They had a small house with the usual arrangement of a fire in the sitting-room and sometimes in the dining-room, but no heating at all upstairs unless you were really ill. It was an amiable suburb: the boys played in the road, yelling 'Car coming!' if one did, and all going inside to listen to *Dick Barton*. There was an area of rough ground nearby, where a neighbour had dumped an old bath; delightedly the children of Cob Lane fetched newts from a pond and kept them in it.

Gavin went to an excellent nursery school, a prep school he didn't think much of, and finally King Edward's, Birmingham, where he had a great time. He was popular and successful at school; he was never, I think, the life and soul of the party – but neither was he a loner. Someone shrewdly said once that he was the man sitting happily reading a book by himself – but in the corner of a *crowded* bar. And not always with a book, either. He lived so completely inside his head that all his life he could often sit, in an airport for example, quite contently doing nothing but think, while some of us would even reread the small ads in the back of *Car Hire Gazette* rather than just sit there with nothing.

He got the Poetry Prize and the Painting Prize, he was in the first fifteen and the first eleven. He left King Edward's at the ripe old age of nineteen; there were fingernail scratches down the walls of the school where they'd had to drag him away, he said. As Red Lyall (he had masses of red hair then) on drums, with Martin Davison he formed his own jazz band. It was initially called the Canal Street Four because, to start with, 'Canal Street Blues' was the only tune they knew. While he was a schoolboy Gavin had often drawn posters for a musical instrument shop, which paid him in kind. Martin remembers that they got both a clarinet and a trumpet; Gavin tried the clarinet and Martin the trumpet, but it was soon clear that at least it would be better the other way round. Martin plays the clarinet brilliantly to this day, but Gavin, admitting that he had a tin ear, had to stick to drums.

He also recalled his parents being bombed while they were eating what turned out to be the last banana of the war; Gavin thought it indicative of their characters that though his mother's half was lost for ever, his father had prudently pocketed his in time. During the war they had an air-raid shelter. Family legend has it that when the siren went, they could move Gavin down there without ever waking him up, propping him against the banisters if they had to pause for breath. They kept hens, which his sister Barbara was able to eat with relish, tears streaming down her face – 'Poor Chirpy, poor Chirpy . . . yes, more please' – gulp. They grew and stored potatoes, not too successfully – Gavin remembered them uncovering the spud pile and mice exploding from it in all directions, their cat too bemused to take any action.

Both children had been offered a refuge in America by Quakers there, and – so typical of Quakers – they had asked eight-year-old Gavin whether he wanted to go. Gavin said only if Barbara could go too and he could meet Walt Disney, and as neither condition could be met (Barbara was too young) he stayed in Birmingham.

He thought it was a great place to grow up; but while most of his friends headed for Birmingham jobs or Birmingham University, Gavin set his sights on Cambridge. First, though, in 1950, there was National Service, and he went into the RAF; because of Korea, they were once again training pilots, and that was what Gavin became.

He loved the Air Force. He'd been terrified he'd be turned down on medical grounds because he had a sort of goitre, but apparently managed to tuck it under his chin sufficiently to pass. (He had it removed in the early sixties at a time when the people in the flat below us were medical students; they took an evil delight in showing me – with pictures – exactly how the operation could have gone wrong and left him speechless. Ghouls.) Like most other conscripts, he became adept at avoiding doing what he didn't want to do. The best trick was going round with a couple of dustbin lids ostensibly checking that their numbers matched those on the bins (they invariably didn't). 'What are you doing, airman?'

'I'm just checking these lids, sir – the officer told me to.'

'Which officer?'

'I don't know, sir, an officer, sir, I don't know *which* officer . . .'

He was fascinated by flying and remained so all his life; but he didn't want to become a civil pilot, and having flown Meteors (at a time when they were killing one in ten of the pilots in training) was never interested in flying small aircraft. He once told me he was scared stiff, even to the point of nearly chucking it in. So he should have been, our younger son Jake said in his speech at Gavin's memorial service: 'A pilot who has not been terrified has either too little experience or no comprehension of the gravity of his situation.' As it was, he spent his last summer before demob instructing the young on Tiger Moths. Grounded he may have been, but the flying scenes in his early books were outstanding, and what he first became known for; even non-flyers like me could feel the sensation of flying into a cliff of cloud or looking into a whole round rainbow from above.

From the RAF he went to Cambridge; and after the RAF, the rules imposed by his college seemed juvenile and footling. He went into Hall one day and they were throwing bread rolls at each other . . . he had as little to do with Pembroke as possible. Relations between him and it – or at least Professor William Camps, its Master – were further soured when he started spending most of his time writing for *Varsity* magazine. Camps found out that a certain undergraduate was gay, and banished him to a lodging on the outskirts of Cambridge, where he became intolerably lonely and committed suicide. Camps replied to press queries with 'A happy well-adjusted chap. No idea why he did it . . . popular with all . . .', and called Gavin in, hoping that *Varsity* would be discreet about it all. But Gavin, furious at the way the lad had been treated and with the full consent of the boy's distraught parents, printed the whole story.

Gavin read English, but not with much diligence: there were more interesting things to do. He wandered around Cambridge in items of discarded American Army uniform, he and some mates made a film, and when one of his supervisors said that the two things that spoiled a man's chances of a good degree were rowing and an unconsummated love affair, Gavin was able to reassure him that he was not involved in either. He eventually became editor of *Varsity* – a job which involved not only editing, but going outside Cambridge to the printer's to see it to bed. At that point he realised that he, as editor, would be personally vulnerable if it went under financially, which it often – indeed, usually – showed urgent signs of doing. So he got his father to help him change it into a limited company. He did a cartoon strip about a lackadaisical student called Ollie, which made him pretty well known around Cambridge – indeed, when he got engaged to me, one or two people seemed to be congratulating me on becoming engaged to Ollie.

He might have become a cartoonist rather than a journalist, except that he didn't want to be stuck in a back room. He wanted to be out where the action was. The irony, of course, was that he wound up writing books – stuck in a back room.

'You're Shirley Burt, aren't you?' was a question I was often asked; Shirley Burt was the worthy, slightly homespun second lead of Gavin's first book, *The Wrong Side of the Sky*. To which the answer usually was 'Dear God, I hope not.' But maybe there were resonances of me in the books, here and there. There was a scene, for example, in *The Crocus List* where Agnes says, with controlled venom, 'I can't stand a man who can't handle me.' Gavin knew that was one thing I couldn't stand either, and had found in a majority of the chaps I'd been involved with before. He, Gavin, could handle me, and knew it. If I was getting up a pointless head of steam about something totally irrelevant to whatever we were talking about, to whatever actually mattered, Gavin could talk me down off my stupid inflated cloud almost without trying. Under his benign wing, I sometimes even felt guilty about what I had put other men through. It was odd, really. With only one exception – Colin – everyone else I'd ever been involved with was more experienced, older, ought to have been better able to cope with me; but only Gavin actually could. One possible explanation was that, during those courting months, he didn't need me the way some of the others had done. I remember vividly an occasion when he said – sometime, I suppose, during what my mother sardonically called our Nuptial Flight – 'I don't need you. I need this', pointing to his glass, 'and this', the cigarette, 'and the occasional nurse. I don't *need* you. But I want you along.'

Absolutely compelling.

So why did he want me along? He found me amusing, I suppose, but he also wanted, I think, someone with her own sense of direction; he once said sadly of an earlier girlfriend that she had unfortunately married 'before she knew who she really was' – he reckoned I did know. He never got on with dumb women, valued long, serious conversations and liked my writing; wanted, in fact, an equal partnership. I once, writing about marriage contracts spoken or unspoken, said that mine included the condition that my husband should 'laugh at my jokes and bring me sherry in my bath' – I marvel that I must, at that time, have liked sherry.

WEDDING BELLS

After that summer, I imagine a man writing this might move on to say simply: 'So we got married.' A woman is conscious of the nearly endless kerfuffle: the planning and the decisions, the clothes and flowers and bridesmaids and my trousseau, for which, through all my parents' scrapes and financial worries, my mother had guarded the money; the where and what time and . . . and . . . and, only some of which is of the slightest interest to anyone but the bride and her mother. Some parts of it do stand out, though.

Sheila Gibson and Gavin's sister Barbara were to be brides-maids, the reception was to be in the Adderley, a lovely room in Marlborough College. The wedding itself was not to be in the school chapel, which had apparently been designed mainly to allow the masters to keep an eye on six hundred boys at once and would have entailed a half-mile walk up the aisle; so we wanted the attractive small parish church at nearby Preshute. Gavin, however, was a Quaker, and Quakers don't christen – they wait till you're old enough to know your own mind. Could he, therefore, be married in an Anglican church? He certainly wasn't going to be christened just for the ceremony. (Years later, a local vicar offered to do the chris-tening of one of our sons; Gavin politely explained that Quakers didn't, whereat the man offered 'a simple naming ceremony – it doesn't have to *mean* anything' – say that to a Quaker and flames start coming out of his ears.) The Preshute vicar sorted it for us, however, because before prudently departing on a skiing holiday, he dug up some ancient statute, designed presumably for missionaries in the field, which per-mitted a Christian to marry an unbaptised heathen provided the heathen 'knew the meaning of Christian matrimony'. As my father said, 'He doesn't have to like it, he just has to know what it is.'

So we were married on a cold January day – it even snowed; my dress was white velvet, with a rose at the back – since that was what they were mostly going to look at. We had Thurston Hopkins to take terrific *Picture Post*-style pictures of every-thing – in those days couples usually had only one stiff row of the carefully posed. Martin Davison was the best man, and as they stood waiting for me to arrive he alerted Gavin to the

music, which I'd scored for the organist without giving the
title. It was from the song:

> A man can grow old
> In the dust of the prairie;
> But a man can't grow old
> Where there's women and gold.

Anything to make the trembling groom feel a bit better.

It all went off beautifully, and we left for our honeymoon in
my father's car, having hidden it in a remote garage to protect
it from the attentions of Gavin's ribald friends. It was in the
dark of the garage that I had my single moment of doubt about
the whole thing: 'What on earth have I let myself in for?' I
thought. Then, and never again.

We had the bridal suite, that night; my bouquet in the basin,
a sense of wondrous disbelief as I looked at the wedding ring on
my finger. 'I feel it's on me too,' said Gavin. It had actually happened, we were together for good. We had a dreamy, quiet week
after all the rush and fuss of getting ready for the wedding, much
of it in Hardy country – Gavin bought me a copy of *The Return
of the Native* – 'For the days on Egdon Heath'. We stayed at the
Miners' Arms for some of it, and some at the Castle Hotel in
Taunton, less grand than it is now. And then back to the flat.

The flat was only half furnished. The excitement and drama
of getting married was over. It was still January. The hot water
wasn't working. We were nastier to each other in that week
than ever before or later. There was a lot of 'Chrissake, why are
you being so difficult?' and 'Well you knew what I was like
before you married me . . .' And then the hot water came on
again, and we shook back into real life; it was *still* January, but
everything was fine.

LIFE AS A WIFE

We rented the attic flat of a large Victorian house uphill from Swiss Cottage. When we moved in it was pretty bare. In the kitchen there was a table and two chairs and the stern Ideal gas stove on its resolute little iron legs that we'd bought off the outgoing tenants for a fiver; we had a bed, a present from my brother John and his wife Jo; certain built-in cupboards and not much else. We had to put a floor in the hall, ignore one room which for a couple of years became a foetid dump for everything we didn't know what to do with; which left us with the one big room that was to be our living-room.

It needed a hell of a lot done to it. At the beginning, I almost despaired, almost wept; while Gavin simply got us started on one particular thing: making a mosaic hearth for our gas fire. That somehow reduced the whole thing to a series of tasks, and the fear went out of it. He knew how to handle us. But he didn't always know how to handle the DIY. There was, under the eaves of this attic room, a wooden corner cupboard, papered and painted over for generations. Gavin set to work to get all that off, so that we could have a lovely stripped-pine cupboard there, and after about two months he achieved it. Only, when he put varnish on this fine pale wood, uncovered as a virgin on her wedding night, it turned a dark orange (do many virgins do that?). At which point Gavin's patience gave out; he chopped the whole thing down, went out and bought some boards, and in less than a day had recreated it in fresh pine.

It was an attractive room, in the decor of its day. We had an extraordinary cane sofa in the corner in the shape of a fish, bought with an income tax rebate of – eleven pounds! Walls with different wallpapers – well, this was nearly the sixties – and a Heal's table that I was sorry to part with twenty-five years later. When Gavin's parents finally saw the room they said, 'It's like something in a magazine!' and it was.

The kitchen and bathroom, however, were not. They were carved out of the one room, with a flimsy partition between them; it had a round hole in it through which you could see whether your egg or your bath was boiling over. No lavatory – that was downstairs – so I installed a serviceable Victorian commode. I bought this in the Portobello Road and brought it home on the bus. 'Oh how lovely,' fellow passengers said, thinking of plant stands. 'What are you going to put in it?'

I didn't write at a desk, or even a table; it amazes me now to think that all my articles until 1965 were written sitting on our bed with a typewriter, mostly to the sound of 78 rpm gramophone records playing on the side. The record-player had a contraption for piling up the records so that they let themselves down one by one, in a stream of continuous music – which is why, in my mind, dozens of symphonies and concertos run together in a way that would have their composers – not to mention my violinist daughter-in-law – whimpering with pain. I suppose even when I had a job I thought, then as now, that offices are fun for the social interaction, for gossip and for getting the latest lowdown on the higher-ups; but they're no place actually to get any work done. Not writing work, anyway.

PART 5

ON — AND OFF — WITH THE JOB

WOMAN'S OWN

But when we married, I wasn't writing much. I was working for *Woman's Own*, ostensibly as an assistant editor, to replace Irene Linden when she went off to have a baby. It was a weird place. It was run by Jimmy Drawbell, the managing director, and one or two male acolytes. In order (I supposed) to appease their sense of offended masculinity for running a women's magazine at all, they tried to instil a sense of urgency and high drama into what, given that it was pretty untopical, ought to have been a perfectly tranquil affair – as indeed its rival, the always slightly more successful *Woman* run by Mary Grant, succeeded perfectly well in being. Drawbell liked to appoint two people to one job and see who won; he was good at sacking people – I later discovered that half the best women journalists in Fleet Street had done their grim stint on *Woman's Own*. The editor was Eileen Ashcroft, a pleasant woman who once went so far off-message as to say: 'I can't think why they go on about only children and childless marriages so much – I was an only child and I'm married without children, and I've been happy as Larry in both situations.'

I managed all right by not paying too much attention to the prevailing hysteria; and the production editor, a slightly faded elegant lady named Ira Morris, was never fazed by any of it. 'What's the headline?' I would ask. '"Why Every Girl Needs A Little Red Dress",' she said. 'Or if the colourway comes up blue, "Why Every Girl Needs A Little Blue Dress".' When I once enquired about some giveaway item of scent that was described as being about to please the British woman 'with a never-before beauty', she said, 'It means that this perfume, which smells like an open cesspit, has never been thrust on the unsuspecting public before.' Joan Chapman, who was part of what was regarded as the *Brighton Evening Argos* mafia, took it all in her stride: 'Come on, shipmates,' she'd say, 'messenger goes in ten minutes.' And somehow the flapping around would calm down enough for the copy to get away on time.

There was a medical column, allegedly written by 'Dr Roderick Wimpole', who could not answer readers' queries – small wonder, since it was actually written by a woman with a medical dictionary who had once lived for six months with a gynaecologist. Knitting was important, and I was sternly told not to jeer at it. '*You* make a mistake,' said the knitting editor, 'and all you have to do is apologise. *I* make a mistake, and cardigans have one sleeve longer than the other all over Britain.' There were the normal features on clothes and cook-ing and decoration, but not bathrooms: it was reckoned, even in 1959, that not enough of our readers had them. And there was the all-important 'Evelyn Home' advice column. No such column has ever been written without value judgements, and the ethos of this one was clear: it was supposed to reinforce women in their role as wives and mothers, cheer them up and enable them to carry on. So if a woman complained of, say, a wandering husband, the answer would not be 'Yes, he's a rat, try putting too much salt in his food and starch in his collars.' No, it must, surely, be your fault: you haven't been loving enough, you haven't responded to his needs, you've been coming down to breakfast in your curlers.

This would have the comforting effect of letting any woman reading it think, Yes, it's because *she's* been silly; I wouldn't behave like that so it won't happen to me. Gavin said that it was exactly the same reaction as pilots feel when a plane crashes: they want to believe that it's pilot error because then they can reassure themselves they wouldn't make such a mistake. But if the wings fell off, or if you said: 'Tough – a blonde got him', well, that might happen to me next time, the pilots would feel; just as any wife reading the column might feel a shiver of unease.

It was assumed that nice girls didn't let their chaps Go Too Far – and even that 'if he really loved you, he wouldn't ask you to'. It was not so long, after all, since one such agony aunt had deleted a recommendation to some woman to spend a trial weekend with her lover, for fear of being prosecuted for obscenity.

I suppose it is this sort of thing that has given the fifties their reputation for prissiness; for what actually went on was nothing like so prim. In wartime, after all, it's known that people are far more uninhibited, and women didn't suddenly put a padlock on their pants at the signing of the armistice. There was also an enormous amount of what was known as Heavy Petting, by which an awful lot of crunch decisions could be avoided. What was assumed, at least in the magazine, was that it was the ambition of every woman – and almost the only ambition – to be a good wife and mother; and there was a lot of sensible stuff about how to do the job. What they put in was not so bad; it was what they left out that was so limiting.

There was a further restriction on what was advised. *Woman's Own* had no separate Irish edition, and it didn't want to get banned in Ireland. So it did its best not to provoke the Catholic censors across the water. There was often a small item at the end where the actual query was not printed; the answer might be 'What you describe is not unusual and few would consider it wrong.' We would all rush to look at the original letter – *what* wasn't unusual? Masturbation, we learned. But you couldn't actually mention it.

'The Weekly Sex,' I called the article when I wrote about it all later in the *Observer*. I wondered how much more subtle damage was done by cutting out not just words but ideas that presented a difficulty:

> Year after year the sub-editors cross out 'sex' and write in 'romance', and imply that emotions can be tidied up as easily as kitchen cupboards. Husbands will stay at home if women only comb their hair and give up their careers; the nastiest of houses can be transformed by a little crochet and wrought iron; a face like the back of a bus can be made lovely by a little rouge in the right places. Everything will be all right if you just talk it over calmly with your husband, your doctor or your mother.

There were stories, of course, though not written in the office. Usually they were about a girl and a not very thrilling boy-next-door; along would come someone richer and more exciting and for a time she'd be dazzled by him. Sooner or later he would prove to be a rat, he would let her down or disappear or turn out to be married; she would see through him and return to good old patient Tom-next-door. And I suppose it was hoped that, thus encouraged, the girl readers would do the same and their mothers be reassured that they would.

I never felt that I got my head round the job at all, and mostly other people were whipping away what I was supposed to be doing, so it wasn't getting any better; worse, if anything. So after six months, with Gavin's entire agreement, I resigned. And was called into Drawbell's office:

'But Katy – so disloyal ; why, why? What would you *like* to be doing?'

'Part-time feature writer,' I mumbled, and that, for a time, he made me.

I inhabited a small room down a corridor shared with James Leasor, later better known as a novelist, and Correlli Barnett, later a distinguished military historian – heaven knows what he was doing there. There was also a rather glamorous secretary, Frances, that they would take out to lunch alternately or together. Bill – which was how Correlli was addressed – would get through the tedious days by fantasising about seeing Drawbell making out in the Strand Palace Hotel, on to whose windows ours looked out: 'It's him! I know it's him, because he's got "Warm and Sincere" tattooed on his left buttock!'

I was required, among other things, to write a series called 'Undiscovered British Beauties'. Choosing them wasn't difficult; one drove around factories and so on and the only two girls without frizzy perms looked so much better than the others that of course you chose them. Making their lives sound interesting was far harder. We of the chattering classes might feel that we'd made our decisions, had been directing our own lives, for quite a while; not so these docile girls working on the production line. Their stories were deeply boring: in the end I

used to time myself to see how quickly I could get the assignment done – though I didn't at that point even aspire to A. J.
Liebling's claim that he 'could write faster than anyone who
could write better and better than anyone who could write
faster'.

My copy, obviously, was not dainty enough; and in
November Drawbell called me into his office and fired me with
five hours' notice and a week's pay. They could do that in those
days.

I rang Gavin in tears; back to square one, look for another
job. Gavin was pretty gloomy, too: his job, directing BBC television's *Tonight* programme, wasn't working out either. And if
you fell foul of Donald Baverstock, who ran it, no one, in that
desperately cliquey atmosphere, would drink with you in the
bar. Grace Wyndham Goldie, the boss above Baverstock, is
now widely acknowledged to have been particularly foul to
Gavin, refusing to give him an interview when he wanted to
discuss whether he had a future with the BBC; and for quite a
while he was bitter about the corporation. He turned it into a
decent anecdote, though. While their hitmen, he said, were
seeking him through the corridors of Shepherds Bush in order
to fire him, he was trying, for his part, to resign. But every
time he stormed in and banged on the desk, 'I'm not standing
for this any longer!', the man behind it would say, 'Not me, old
boy; try Room 48 along the corridor.' In the end he just lapsed,
and quietly ceased to be there.

What had happened to 'We're Gavin and Kath, we can do
anything?' Bright hopes seemed distinctly dimmed. But who
knows – maybe it was all for the best. Gavin started to write his
first fiction in deserted rooms in the BBC studios at Lime
Grove, and began to work for the *Sunday Times* one or two days
a week. About this time a friend asked me to a party where I

might, he thought, meet someone who'd give me a job – I turned it down because it was the twentieth anniversary of George Grun coming to Britain, and I felt I couldn't miss that. But at George's I met Peter Lovell Davis, their close friend, who asked me to another party where I met Alan Brien, who edited the back pages of the *Spectator*. There was a column called 'Roundabout' which was three hundred words of jokey reportage. 'Could I, please,' I asked, 'do the cat show?' No, but he gave me something else: and by the summer I had taken over the column completely and got a job on the staff.

BOOKS AND COOKING

A lot had happened in the meantime. Gavin's casual job on the *Sunday Times* built up till he was taken on the staff, ultimately as Air Correspondent. A man called Tony Facer, who worked for the publishers McGibbon & Kee, had an idea for a cookery book aimed at all his friends who tried to cook on one ring. All cookery books – even the ones for beginners – were in those days written for people with proper kitchens, which was exactly what students and people starting out in one cheap room did not have: they had a gas ring, an inadequate cupboard and probably no water nearer than the shared bathroom at the end of a corridor. So I set out to write a book for them, and in three and a half months I had written *Cooking in a Bedsitter*, remembered by a whole lot of people who have never read a word of my journalism – and a fixture, as she herself once told me, on the shelf of Delia Smith.

How did I know what to write? I was no great shakes as a cook, though I had learned a certain amount about cooking from my housemates in America. But for this book, ignorance was almost an asset. Starting in much the same place as the inexperienced reader helped me to understand what had to be explained – what couldn't be taken for granted. Most cookery books assumed you knew the meaning of terms like 'braising' or 'stock' or 'browning meat' ('Does it actually go brown – it looks more grey?') and basics like how to make a white sauce.

What I did was to trawl through a lot of cookery books – particularly one by Marian Tracey called *Casserole Cookery* since casseroles are cooked in one pot – and adapt the recipes to a single ring. This meant working out, for example, how to make a Welsh rarebit without a grill simply by pouring the cheese mixture over the toast (and putting an egg in it to stop it curdling). I pointed out that when you'd burnt the toast and scraped off the burn, the thing to do was to turn it over and bang it burnt side down. In fact, predicting the mistakes, which I'd usually made myself, was half the battle: even simple things like overcooking lamb – since 'we all have a tendency to go into a butcher's with high hopes and come out with lamb chops'. In America I'd encountered supermarkets, but in Britain we didn't yet have them, so you had to face a proper butcher. I sympathised with readers who had seen the 'planned cow' in other cookery books, with dotted lines showing where the different cuts came from, since it was no help at all when it came to choosing the actual red bits on the slab. There was far less frozen food, and just about nothing you could describe as 'fast' except fish and chips in a bit of greasy paper – I actually included a way of making pizza in a frying pan in the early editions (a mistake – it was highly likely to explode) because you couldn't yet buy them on every street corner.

It wasn't, I said, just the problem of cooking on one ring. It was not having any water to hand; it was the problem of finding somewhere to put down the fork while you took the lid off the saucepan, somewhere to put the butter where it wouldn't get mixed up with your razor or your comb: 'It is cooking at floor level, in a hurry, with nowhere to put the salad but the washing-up bowl, which in any case is full of socks.'

I put in a pretty comprehensive Beginner's Index which explained what stock was, how long different items should be cooked, how to keep down the smells; how to thicken a sauce and keep things hot in a thermos. I urged readers not to buy a dinky little pan in Woolworth's but to think in terms of a big pan to match their big appetite. Some things seem bizarre now: that I had to explain what an avocado was, or yoghurt; that I had to urge teabags on them; and we didn't know then that an asbestos mat was a very bad idea.

A few of the recipes I made up, such as Toucan Mash, which came out of two cans; there was a dessert called 'veiled country lass' in Scandinavia – I said she was better known in this country as Cold Charlotte. And I shared with the readers The Dish, which was – is – almost foolproof; we left it on all night once and it still made a good ragout. That had evolved from my proudly buying steak for a friend's birthday in America; it was nice and red but my housemates pointed out that it was actually the wrong sort of steak for grilling, so I had to turn it into a casserole; which by sheer luck got me, for one evening only, a reputation as a good cook.

The book was in print for forty years, but if anyone thinks I made a fortune out of it, they're wrong. The wretched hardback publisher, who printed about eight copies and kept it in print for a year or so, continued to take 50 per cent of my Penguin paperback royalties for the next twenty years – that's what comes of not having an agent.

Penguin and I revised it from time to time, and we did a particularly big one in 1990 because the eating habits of the people I was writing for had changed so much. For one thing, they were more health-conscious and wanted more salads and similar. For another, housing had changed: fewer were living in a single room and more were sharing flats; so we needed a chapter for those 'no richer or fussier than you are', called 'Your Turn to Cook'. But even more significantly, horizons had vastly expanded. People still ask if the book could be reprinted again; but the conditions in which it was written were so totally different from the scene now, with infinitely more ready-made food, microwaves, woks, a dozen different cuisines absolutely standard, that it wouldn't make sense.

At the time I was writing it, British cooking was slowly moving out of one era and into another: away from both the obligatory meat and two veg of tradition and from valiant wartime attempts to make too little go a long way. And it's staggering to think that at the beginning of the fifties 38 per cent of women cooked – *cooked* – three meals every day. One forgets how circumscribed cooking had been in the days when people didn't have fridges – you had to eat food up in a day or two, even with meat safes for hanging outside windows and ter- racotta milk-coolers.

But the scene was opening up. People were discovering European food again, realising that spaghetti didn't have to come out of a horrible tin, that there was more than one kind of rice. Elizabeth David's books about French and Italian cook- ing were changing our whole perception of food, even if she had to tell her readers that you *could* get olive oil – at Boots, in little bottles designed for the relief of earache. What I was doing, much of the time, was adapting standard recipes – or at least recipes standard in other countries, like goulash or Greek lamb casserole or Chicken Maryland or Jamaican spiced fishcakes – to top-of-the-stove treatment, and doing it all on one ring. It took a lot of juggling and some sleight of hand, but it was surprising how much could actually be achieved.

Before the book went out of print it found a few audiences I hadn't expected: pensioners on their own who knew how to cook but didn't know their quantities for one. (I was reminded of my mother, trying after the war to convert her schoolmaster's-wife recipes for sixty into recipes for us four — easy enough to divide the pounds and ounces of meat and potatoes, but 'one cup of salt'? Some students of Trinity College, Cambridge, actually wrote a play based on the book, which was performed at the Edinburgh Festival. And once when Gavin and I were invited, by a dining club which had the admiral in charge of Portsmouth among its members, to visit the Navy there, I was accosted by two gnarled old sea-dogs covered in gold braid who thanked me for saving their lives.

'But I've not been to sea . . .?'

'When we are sent on a course we're given a pan and a spoon and a copy of your book, without which we would have starved.'

During that spring of 1959 I also, rather incongruously, taught in a charm school for a couple of months.

'You *what*?' said my brother John. 'What on earth do you teach?'

'Colours,' I said defensively. 'We put the girls in front of a mirror and drape them in fabric, to try to get them to realise that "I like this colour" and "This colour suits me" are not the same thing. And I teach them Deportment.'

'But you walk like a duck, dear!' said John, incredulous.

Towards the summer of that year, the charm school folded (not from my ineptitude, but because the backer skipped the country). I was doing a little freelancing and the small 'Roundabout' column but not much else. Gavin, by then working mostly for the *Sunday Times*, decided this could not go on.

It was, I recall, the act of baking my own bread that finally made him crack: I suppose I was still so brainwashed by the women's magazines that I thought domesticity was what was mainly required of me. But a docile slipper-warmer was *not* what Gavin thought he'd married.

He took me up to the top of Hampstead by the Whitestone Pond; in those days there was a bench, on which he sat me down, and donkeys, which he ignored. What he said, in effect, was: 'This nonsense must now cease; for God's sake get a proper job.' Actually I was, or so I desperately hoped, on the very brink of getting a job at the *Spectator*; and indeed, very shortly after, it came up. Many years later I asked him, reflectively, why, when it had taken him so long to consent to a child, a house, a second child, he had so cheerfully gone ahead and married me? He said: 'I never saw you as a liability.' But he must, I suppose, have had some nasty moments before that scene by the pond.

TWO TYPEWRITERS ON THE GO

When we had been married twenty-five years, Gavin's sister, an ace cake-maker, made us a cake in the form of a typewriter, all the keys correct; she flanked it with two toothbrushes. Why *toothbrushes*? 'I thought it was time you had two,' she said – all this in memory of an occasion when we had shown up in Paris with two typewriters and one toothbrush, a neat symbol of what we were and were not prepared to share.

We were both writers, though later Gavin was mainly writing books; and that had enormous advantages, in that we could and always did read and comment on each other's work. The things I suggested for his writing tended to be on the lines of

Left: The Gray family (clockwise): Kitty, Arthur, Edith and Marcus with their mother, Mamie, before Margaret was born

Right: My mother, Edith Gray, as a young woman

My parents, Alan and Edith, never looked at their most cheerful on formal occasions

Left: Dr Herbert Gray, my grandfather: founder of the Marriage Guidance Council in the thirties

Right: Stout infant Katharine and intent older brother John

Above: On a Scottish loch in an inflatable boat (John's burst and he dragged it to shore to return it to the makers)

Left: After my pigtails were cut off – much to my father's regret

My housemates in America (from left): Pat Rowland, Lali Lim, Maija Kesä, Joan Rafaj; in front, me and Josie Chen

Skating on Lake Cayuga, near Cornell – *backwards*

My brother John, in his years as Overseas Director of the CBI

Professor Jack Gallagher of Trinity College, Cambridge: my guru and greatest friend ever

rging from the church with Gavin, eshute, near Marlborough

Gavin's parents, Ann and Joe Lyall, arriving for our wedding

One of the publicity photos for my debut as fashion editor for the *Observer*

At a Paris couture show in the early sixties – I'm the one in the squared skirt

Gavin, with one of the
innumerable aeroplanes
he made – in the days
when our kitchen was
painted a military green

George Seddon, wh
masterminded my
writing for the Obs
and launched the
'unisex' women's pa
which became com
worldwide

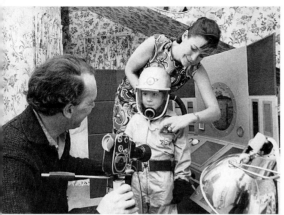

Getting small Jake ready
for his starring role in
some space movie
dreamed up by Gavin

h my father, Alan, in the early seventies,
r we'd been to Greece together

General Bernard Lyall instructs Private
Jake Lyall for some manoeuvre crucial to
the filmed battle in which they are starring

Gavin in the early eighties with one of his highly successful
Major Maxim books

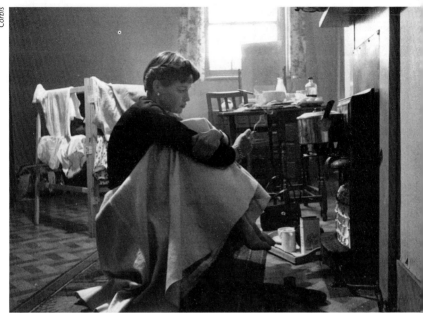

Bert Hardy took this photograph for a feature on 'Lonely in London', which helped get on to *Picture Post*

Gavin with a favoured cat, Dolly Gray

...dora, our second boat, named after Gavin's aunt, on the river Thames where we were ...essly happy

...ve: Our sons, Bernard and Jake

Right: Nancy, Bernard's wife,
with Megan and Ruby

Gavin at seventy – he never stopped
smoking

My youngest and best-loved aunt Marga
still going strong in her nineties

My favourite pictu
of Gavin, my husb
for forty-five years

The way I look now

'She'd *say* something at that point, not just unbutton her blouse', or 'I don't understand his motives here – he's got to look more noble than the man he's fighting', or 'That scene has gone on for eight pages but it only makes one plot point.' What he did for mine greatly concerned clarity, or style – he once said of something that was too loosely written 'It's knitted with too big needles.' He could often take a thought one stage further, say when it got dull or turgid; or occasionally flatly disagree with my point of view, in which case we'd argue it till nearly deadline. My columns usually provoked one of three responses: 'That's good', 'That's fine but you need to correct this or that' or, worst, 'Just what are you trying to say?' But decades later he once said, as I handed him my copy: 'You know, even after all this time I still think, Good, I've got something by Kath to read.'

The downside to us both being writers, though, was that we were both competing, as it were, in the same field – and a public one where we were both vulnerable. It could be excruciating, especially during the years when Gavin was slowly switching from one style of book to another, when people would recognise me but not him, or call him Mr Whitehorn by mistake. Gavin thought he shouldn't mind about this, that a newspaper had more readers than a book; and he had always, and genuinely, wanted an equal partnership and just about insisted that I did the best I could. Quakers have always believed that women are in charge of their own destinies and Gavin felt very strongly that I was not to waste my abilities; but it would have been easier if one or other of us had been in a less visible profession.

From about the beginning of the sixties, though, we had no such problems: both of us were increasingly finding our feet and doing well. We had a great time, as an unencumbered couple, making friends in our own line of work, having enough money at last, meeting for the odd meal out or a drink in a pub after work. It set a pattern we tried to keep up later on when we had the children: we would have a regular babysitter one day a week, simply to make sure we didn't go out together only when it was to a party or other invitation. Gavin used to say, later, that he was glad we'd had a chance to get to know each other really well for six years before there were any children – Bernard was born in 1964. That meant they could never play one of us off against the other, we knew each other too well.

Gavin's involvement with the *Sunday Times* was growing; he covered the Queen's tour of India and Nepal in 1960 before he evolved into Air Correspondent, and he started to write a thriller. We enjoyed doing things to the flat, we had jobs, we had each other; we also, it turned out, had cats. I had no idea I'd married into cats, but I ought to have been warned by the affecting pictures of Gavin as a little boy with a kitten peeping out of his Hamlet-type shirt. The first was called Kilroy, who never forgave us for bringing in cat two, Algernon Aubrey St John Fishbreath (always known as Sid), who was a gent. After that there was a succession, including Sindy, who provided Gavin with a party trick: he would throw a scrunched-up cigarette packet into the air, she would leap to catch it (but if it was going to fall short of her she assessed the trajectory and didn't try). Gavin was incredibly gentle and good with cats, but his affection for them sometimes led to bedtime conversations such as:

'What are you doing with that cat in the bed?'

'Cat? Cat? What cat?'

'If there isn't a cat why is your bottom purring?'

He also went in for cat psychology. When, much later, we had an agreeable and friendly kitten, Betsy, who turned into a bag of nerves when the older cat died and we got a new kitten, Gavin said fondly: 'She just wasn't ready to be the Senior Cat.' He occasionally wrote entries for a non-existent column called 'Dear Auntie Mog', to which cats were supposed to bring their little problems.

I think we thought that cats would one day be an easy way of introducing our children to the facts of life; but in the event it got complicated:

'Oh look, there's Flannel Foot talking to her father, isn't that nice?'

Pause.

'Mummy, what is he doing to her?'

'Er . . .'

For years we bred the cats and spent a lot of time finding homes for the kittens. Unsuspecting girls who came to deliver typing, say, would find to their bewilderment that they'd apparently wanted a kitten for years.

We were both away every now and then on journalistic assignments, and sometimes I missed Gavin dreadfully. I once asked my mother-in-law Ann how she had managed when her husband was away all week, when he did the audit for firms such as Clarks or Rowntree. She wrote that Mondays were bad, but she did the washing and she liked that; on Wednesdays she went into Birmingham and met her sister for lunch; on Thursdays she began to look forward to the weekend and on Friday Joe came home. 'Other women,' she wrote, 'didn't have those awful Mondays. But they didn't have those Fridays either.' I knew what she meant.

It was as Air Correspondent that Gavin first went to America, on a tour of air bases, but he had been fascinated by it since his schooldays. As I mentioned earlier, he went around Cambridge in old bits of American Army uniform; he adored Dashiell Hammett and – at least at first – Raymond Chandler, and was passionate and knowledgeable about the West. 'The American West was won by the American East; the means used were the Colt 53 and canned baked beans,' he began one article. He had stacks of paperback Westerns, and in the first flush of love I even read all the way through Elliott Arnold's *Blood Brother* – it was a long, long trail. And, of course, movies – in those days there were no videos, and we had to traipse across half London to see, for example, *Winchester '73* for what seemed like the seventy-third time. I remember writing a slightly sour article saying that it wasn't that when you'd seen one Western you'd seen the lot, but that when you'd seen the lot you felt as if you'd seen one.

In fact in quite a lot of things our tastes were entirely different: ties, for example. He liked them colourful – too colourful, to my way of thinking.

I once said: 'Did you *buy* that tie?'

'Of course I did – how do you think I got it?'

'I assumed it had been given away free with something.'

He was passionately fond of jazz – Count Basie, Duke Ellington among others. I liked classics. Our musical tastes met only in the Inkspots, in the Modern Jazz Quartet and particularly in negro spirituals. Once when our second son Jake and I were giving a decent burial to some baby blackbirds knocked off by the cats, and the child, having helped me plant bulbs in the autumn, innocently asked, 'When will these birds come up?' Gavin said I'd missed a trick by not replying: 'On de great gettin'-up mornin'.' But that was later – much later.

A COLUMN ON THE SPECTATOR

When in July 1959 I was taken on to the staff of the *Spectator* to write the column called 'Roundabout', which was an extended form of the small one I had been doing before. I knew exactly what I wanted to do with it. It was to start with a report on something – a book, an event, a trend – and then make a thoughtful, or ribald, point from it, so that it was not just reportage. This was the forerunner of the column I later did for the *Observer*.

I could write about more or less anything – marriage bureaux, for example: 'The most marriageable man in Britain is probably a tall Roman Catholic, a white-collar worker of forty-three, with hair.' Or Christmas, and what men should give a girl: not a bottle, because 'either she drinks it with you (unfair) or with another man (dead loss from your point of view) or else gets quietly sloshed with the girls, with great risk of Telling All'. I urged teachers to strike for the sake of the future of the profession, now that the increasing number of working mothers would make such a strike a serious inconvenience: 'Teachers will not go on being too good for their salaries. They will soon be bad enough . . . to deserve no more.' I wrote about Applied Motoring, which is all the things that go on in a car besides driving, such as 'finding the way, losing the matches, knitting, radio-twiddling and singing'. I didn't yet know that I should have added responding forty times an hour to "Are we nearly there yet?" from the back seat. I explained that the main point of camping was to remind one why they invented the house . . . The articles were light, but not, on the whole, as lightweight as they seemed.

What was novel about it, I suppose, was that on the whole columns then were either specialist ones about cricket or foreign policy or cars or fashion, or they were firmly designated Funny – and except for subjects like fashion they weren't usually written by women. I was one of the first to bridge the divide between women's writing and what I suppose the blokes would have called serious writing. What I did on the *Spectator* was fairly inconsequential, but it attracted the eye of George Seddon of the *Observer*, who more than anyone else felt that the subjects that were not work or politics or business or sport – male preoccupations – merited just as much serious attention and just as good writing as they did. But it was Brian Inglis on the *Spectator* who started me off.

I was also to edit the back three pages: the consumer column written under the name Leslie Adrian, the wine column, and the design one, written by Kenneth Robinson. It was a marvellous place to be. The *Spectator* was enjoying its one radical moment; it had Brian Inglis as editor, Bernard Levin creating a whole new style of parliamentary ringside commentary under the name of Taper, and Cyril Ray doing, among other things, wine.

Brian Inglis, the man who invented the phrase 'fringe medicine', had plucked Bernard from the magazine *Truth*, where he was doing theatre criticism. Our happy band included Alan Brien who was arts editor and Karl Miller on books. Alan and Bernard often found it convenient to meet in Karl's office, which was between theirs, Karl's impotent fury at their antics being half the fun. The atmosphere was slightly that of a rather rowdy school at break time: I would sometimes hear someone say, 'Why, you rotten little under-sized Jewish idiot . . .' and look round in horror, only to find it was either Ray addressing Levin or Levin addressing Ray. In fact they were all incredibly rude to each other, and I thought I couldn't reckon I was accepted until they were equally rude to me; but with females, it was the opposite – an unbelievably fulsome gallantry.

Most of us youngsters were headily conscious of having enough money (not from the *Spectator* alone, I need hardly say), in some cases for the first time. We would take ourselves out to lunch in Charlotte Street or the pub, passing as we did so the Royal Ear Hospital, whereat we would shout, 'Wot abaht the workin' class ear?' But it wasn't all high jinks: Bernard waged a long, sometimes tedious but ultimately effective campaign to free five Bahrainis wrongly imprisoned on St Helena; it remained one of his proudest achievements.

Cyril Ray, with whom I shared an office, was older than the rest of us; he had been a distinguished foreign correspondent for the *Sunday Times* in Moscow; he had been a war correspondent for the BBC, had made the Arnhem landings and personally liberated the best local hotel. He recalled with relish the keen and frightened young American soldiers in camouflage with black on their faces arriving at the hotel, to find Ray sitting on the terrace drinking champagne. He said a shooting-stick was a good accessory for watching a war, and when he was seconded to General Patton he was identified by an aide as 'that man with a red beret on his head and a stick up his arse'.

Ray and I scrapped amicably for several years. About once a month we would have a row about frozen peas or, occasionally, frozen concentrated orange juice, which I rejoiced in as being better than tinned, while he denounced it for not being as good as fresh. I only once had the upper hand on that one. Gavin and I, in a fit of total madness at the high water-mark of our financial folly, stayed at our own expense for over a week in the Gritti Hotel in Venice (in the days when it *was* the Gritti, before it was taken over by a chain), and there they discussed whether the juice was from this year's oranges or last year's: Ray hadn't thought of that one.

He was an intensely quarrelsome man, had in fact quarrelled with most of his previous employers, usually on a point of principle; he managed to combine extremely left-wing opinions with a taste for gourmet cooking, fine wines and aristocratic accoutrements. An oculist's son and a graduate of Manchester Grammar School, he had started on the *Manchester Guardian*, but even when he was only earning their normal pittance had a taste for hand-made shirts and expensive shoes; later in life he belonged to Brooks's, had a set in Albany and sent his son to Eton, while still proclaiming the most radical views. Somehow one saw it as a lovable eccentricity, not a piece of hypocrisy at all; he said his ambition was 'to have a bottle of first-growth claret on the table of every trade union leader in the country'. (Little did he know that was exactly what they ultimately had – but it wasn't the triumph of the working man so much as greed and boss-hood springing eternal.)

When not actually disapproving of you, he was the most amusing company in the world. When he got a house in the country, he complained that they 'needed two of everything including the baby'; when his house in the country – a bigger one – burned down and his kind neighbours took his things in to keep till he found somewhere else, he would complain that all his shirts were in one house two miles away, all his ties in another, three miles in the other direction: 'It takes so long to get dressed in the morning.' And he wrote limericks. As a wine writer, he wearily once penned in a French bar:

I would if I could but I can't
See one more bottling plant.

I would rather by far
Sit here in this bar
Writing this with *la plume de ma tante*.

Brian Inglis was a very good editor indeed. He knew how to leave things alone to develop, instead of picking nervously at them too soon; a favourite phrase was 'Leave it for three months.' And when he took on someone new he didn't, like most editors, just hire a good political writer to do political writing. For example, he'd see a good TV critic and think, He'd be good at theatre; see someone doing theatre – like Bernard – and think, How about Parliament as theatre? Consumer-consciousness was just beginning to invade journalism; Brian chose the name 'Leslie Adrian' for his consumer column because he figured that most people took advice more readily from one sex or the other, so let's leave it unclear which the writer was. Actually it was an amalgam of himself, James Bredin, Jean Robertson, occasionally me and anyone else who had something to say, but written not from an expert point of view – 'I *know*, listen to me' – but as a newcomer: 'I didn't know, but this is what I found out and it's interesting.'

On press day, Wednesday, the theory was that we were too busy to go out to lunch, so one of us – often me – would go and get stuff from a delicatessen and the office cellar would be opened. In practice it took twice as long, of course, and often included luminaries from politics or other papers, plus contributors such as David Cairns or James Bredin, Peter Forster, Bamber Gascoigne, Clive Barnes. They later had to move the weekly event to Thursday to get the paper out at all.

At that time the *Spectator*'s viewpoint was much more pink than blue. Levin as a student had been pretty left-wing. Once someone came to the LSE to harangue them about the joys of capitalism, and was telling the story of the birth of M&S – how a man started humbly with a market stall, and then two, and then a shop . . . 'And the name of that man was Marks! And the name of his partner was—'

Voice from the back of the hall: 'Engels!' It was Bernard, of course.

The proprietor was Ian Gilmour, liberal in such things as his opposition to capital punishment and the Suez escapade, but in 1960 he announced that he was going to stand as a Conservative MP. This pulled the ideological rug from under us; for we were mostly lefties disillusioned with some of the results of leftism; no way were we suddenly going to become conventional Conservatives. Within a year, we had all left, Ray and I for the *Observer*, Inglis for TV and books; Alan Brien had already become theatre critic of the *Sunday Telegraph*. Bernard was covering the theatre for the *Express*; he later moved to the *Daily Mail* and then to *The Times*, believing that 'you should put all the bits back in the bag and give it a shake from time to time'.

When Brian Inglis left as editor he was replaced by Iain Hamilton, to whom I owe the one really hurtful act of discrimination of my career. When Bernard left, there was to be a farewell lunch, so I turned up in my best red suit soon after twelve. At about half past Hamilton said: 'Well, I'm sorry, Katharine, we're going to lunch.'

'Well yes,' I said, 'that's why I'm here.' But he had booked it at the Garrick, which as he well knew did not at that time admit women at lunchtime. The others were horrified, for we had been as close a set as ever soldiers were in battle or actors in a production; and Hamilton was an incoming outsider. Bernard and Alan took me off and poured champagne into me, making Bernard forty minutes late for his own farewell lunch; but I was hardly soothed. And when, some time later, I handed in my notice, I relished every minute of Hamilton's increasingly desperate attempts to get me to stay.

The reason he was so keen for me not to go was that, by the time I left, most of his stars had already gone; I had stayed on because there was a possibility that I might have to settle a libel action. I had accused journalist Willi Frischauer – not by name, but identifiably – of writing an 'Inside Germany' column during the war based simply on guesses about what was probably happening. (Paul Johnson is supposed to have said in front of witnesses: 'But you know you did, Willi', but Paul wouldn't testify on my behalf.) Journalists don't usually have to pay their own libel damages – they couldn't – but another journalist who was currently being sued had written his little libel unashamedly from sheer malice, and there was talk of his being made to pay up as a punishment; so I feared I might have to as well. Finally I learned that the sum involved would be £500 if I did get stuck with it; I rang someone I knew on the *Daily Mail* and asked, could I write something for the paper? So I produced a three-parter which paid enough to cover the £500. Poor Gavin, who happened to be flying back from Australia, casually opened the *Mail* to see his wife's name in headlines and wondered what the hell had happened. Nothing had, except that I was now free to leave the *Spectator*.

By this time Gavin was on the *Sunday Times*, and the *Observer* when I joined became bothered at the idea of a husband on the rival paper. They offered him a job, which he didn't take as they didn't seem to know what they wanted him to do; they just knew he was an OK guy. This highlighted in a way one difference between the *Sunday Times* and the *Observer*. The *Sunday Times* told you what views were or were not acceptable for the paper, but they didn't care, and didn't ask, what your private views were (Gavin suspected that *they* suspected young journalists were all Communists). When he was sent to cover the Queen's tour, they said: 'We don't know what you think of the monarchy but our readers think it's great.' The *Observer*, on the other hand, reckoned you could write what you liked and they'd support your integrity – *but* they only hired people of the same mind as them in the first place. Which policy gives the journalist more real freedom was a matter for debate – especially after the sixth jar in a Fleet Street pub.

GAVIN: FROM JOURNALISM TO THRILLERS

Gavin had started to write his first book while he was coming unstuck from the BBC, and finished it while he was at the *Sunday Times*. Its hero was the pilot of a small plane, and it stood out from the ranks of other thrillers mainly by the descriptions of flying – gut-wrenching encounters with a weather front, cliffs of cloud – that had even non-flyers like me gasping. I read *The Wrong Side of the Sky* once it was seriously advanced, and I was, luckily, near enough to my publisher's reader days to recognise its quality, so it was easy to say it was good and mean it. There was a certain amount of Chandler-esque wisecracking, and maybe his characters weren't as deep as they later became; but it was obviously gripping. It would be the first of many. (The title came from a remark of my mother's: on seeing my brother John off to the RAF she said, in parody of any mother sending a little boy off to school: 'Now remember always to wear your winter woollies and don't fly on the wrong side of the sky.')

By the mid-sixties it was clear that Gavin was a thriller

writer, and a very good one. He was awarded the Crime Writers' Association Silver Dagger twice, film options tended to be bought on the books, and his publishers loved him; he was Chairman of the CWA in 1967–8. He had made clear to me before we married that he was *not* going to write a novel – was that understood? And I'd reminded him with some irritation that it was his previous girlfriend who'd kept on at him to write books. *I* didn't care; as far as I was concerned he was a journalist. Ho ho. It is only now, trying to write this, that I fully realise how different the two things are: for a book, you need serious slabs of time and no interruptions – there's none of this five-hundred-words-by-lunchtime stuff. No wonder that when our small son Bernard was hanging on the safety gate at the bottom of the stairs yelling: 'Daddy come down! Daddy don't work!' he used to come out of his attic study and say: 'Someone take that child *away*!' If writing about facts is hard enough, creating people and monsters, gunfights and emotions, out of thin air must be twice as difficult.

I suppose when you get married you think that quite soon you will 'understand' the person you married. I doubt if I ever explored at all fully the extraordinary hidden caves and tunnels and secret passages of the Aladdin's cave of Gavin's mind; it couldn't be done. People always ask a writer: 'How do you think up your plots?' and there's rarely a good answer, since creative processes are unfathomable, often even to their creators. Gavin loved doing the research – there were maps and reference books everywhere, endless postcards of places, accounts of visits to experts, old magazines; he would never have dreamed of setting a book in a place he hadn't visited, like Harry Keating writing about Inspector Ghote before he'd ever been to India. He put people's quirks and habits into his characters – my schoolmaster father was the prototype for the Harrow master in *Blame the Dead*, Chuck Korr for the eager Joe College CIA man in *The Crocus List*; the great slug of a Master of the college in *The Secret Servant* was Rab Butler – but they never spotted themselves. At that time he and a few other writers would use each other's names, too – Kingsley Amis had a certain Father Lyall killed in horrible circumstances in *The Alteration* in retaliation for some jokey insult of Gavin's, and Henri Bernard (Levin's first names) met an equally revolting end in Gavin's *Venus with Pistol*.

The respect of other writers brought Gavin some excellent friends. Mary Stewart and he met on a publicity tour; she took him to lunch at the Connaught, and when the waiter started unctuously with 'We find the ladies prefer a sweeter wine', she said firmly: 'In matters of wine I am no lady', and ordered a first-growth claret. Later on we met her and her geologist husband Sir Fred Stewart, often in the Highlands; he not only took the boys fishing, but very nearly succeeded in persuading them that the reason for the conservation ban on fishing on Sundays was so that the fish could go to church. He introduced our son Jake to the fishing shop at Dalmally, too, where the man who ran it, Mr Church, memorably commented: 'If fishing had more than ten per cent to do with actually catching fish, it would be illegal.'

THE OBSERVER WOMEN'S PAGE

My time at the *Spectator* overlapped with the *Observer*, in a curious and ultimately unsatisfactory way. The *Observer* had been looking for a women's editor, had advertised the post; half London had applied, me included, whereupon we had been asked to write two trial pieces: one on tipping, and one on whether mothers should work. This process, though, didn't in the end actually produce what they wanted. They moved on to the idea that there should be two women: one to do the fashion, which in those days was the Queen Bee job of the women's pages, and another to do the heavy stuff, the editor David Astor not thinking that anyone who could do fashion could have the gravitas needed for the rest. Finally he decided that Anne Scott-James, a heroine of mine, author of *In the Mink* and outstanding women's editor of the *Sunday Express*, was to do the fashion; and George Seddon, having read my *Spectator* column and gone back over the applications, wanted me to do the gravitas bit. But I was having far too good a time at the *Spectator* to leave, and said no.

Then Anne Scott-James changed her mind about accepting, and George said to me: 'What about you doing fashion?' We thought I could do that without giving up my *Spectator* column. I didn't know much about it, of course, but I had done the Paris collections for *Picture Post* and once for the *Sunday Dispatch*, and I'd taught at the ill-fated charm school. So we thought, Let's give it a go.

It was agreed that I would take over from Alison Settle in July 1960. And at that exact moment Gavin got a half-frozen face: Bell's palsy. There was a lot of euphemistic chat about having sat in a draught; what I suspected was that he was a bit shattered by my being offered a prestigious job like that – he wasn't yet Air Correspondent – and I worriedly asked Cyril Ray if he thought I should back out. His reply was crisp: 'If he's got a frozen face because you've been offered it, he'll be paralysed all down one side if you turn it down.'

During that spring *Queen* magazine thought it would be fun, seeing that I had something large and definite looming up in my future, to wheel me around assorted fortune tellers, astrologers and palmists to see if any of them spotted it. None of them did, which increased my already sizeable scepticism about their claims. More: Gavin and I were in the middle of a serious falling-out about the purchase of a car, which we could now afford. Gavin wanted a sports car, and I went along with that, on the grounds that he was younger than me and it would, I thought, be a great mistake to have him miss out on any aspect of his youth. But Gavin being Gavin, the Lyall caution kicked in, and the sports car he said he wanted was a dismal little thing called a Sprite. Not much up from a pram with a big engine, it seemed to me to be too mere to count, and I urged him, if he wanted a sports car, to get a real roaring monster. I even gave the globe-gazers a clue by mentioning a car, but they all swept it aside: couldn't be important, a car. So they weren't even much good at picking up the vibes from the psyche.

In the end I got fed up with the whole subject of the car and stopped talking about it, and Gavin in the unaccustomed silence realised he didn't actually want a sports car at all, and we bought an unremarkable Ford which served us fine. At least, it did while we lived in Nutley Terrace, halfway up the steep hill of Fitzjohn's Avenue towards Hampstead, because when the battery was flat (which it often was, usually owing to us having left the lights on), we simply pushed it round the corner and got it started on the hill. When we moved to Provost Road in Chalk Farm, which was flat, we had to get a better car. (Gavin always identified the years by what car we had and what book he was writing – I don't know if this is a secondary sex characteristic or just what happens if you're an author – whereas I identified them by what ages the children were and where we went for the summer holiday.)

Before I actually became fashion editor, I was invited to the big summer party the *Observer* held for its staff and their families at Cliveden, owned by Bill Astor, David's brother. I didn't know whether it was a chic garden party (chiffon dresses, high heels) or more of a picnic occasion (jeans and T-shirts), so I asked the only other person on the paper I knew, Mark Arnold-Forster, what he was wearing. 'My second-worst pair of grey flannels,' he said, which didn't help much; worse, the word was going round the paper that the new fashionista had asked Mark for advice, he being unquestionably the worst dressed man in Fleet Street. They cancelled that garden party in 1963, and we all said 'Mean old *Observer*!' But then the Profumo scandal broke, and we realised that it had been exceedingly prudent to cancel, or the *Daily Mirror* would have been able to get pictures of *Observer* children gambolling around the infamous swimming-pool. Only later did we discover they actually had cancelled for reasons of economy after all.

As fashion editor I didn't know much, but I was filled with a burning – and, as I now think, wholly daft – crusading zeal to improve the British woman and get her out of that limp cardigan at all costs. At least, cardigans as then worn. British women, I said, don't actually see them, any more than Americans see boxes of Kleenex or the people watching a Japanese play are supposed to see the little black-gloved helpers who flit about the stage. My idea was that my articles should be about clothes, not just Fashion. Egged on by George, I would discuss winter woollies under the title 'Clothes for Other People's Houses': I urged people to work out who they were trying to impress with any particular outfit – employer? lover? other women? potential mother-in-law? I got into bad trouble with the advertisers for showing nifty little numbers from C & A when they wanted me to plug expensive places like Harrods and Marshall & Snelgrove, who placed ads with us. We published a small spiteful item called 'Is This Your Problem?', with a Colin Spencer cartoon showing someone's awful get-up and an analysis of how it got that way and what, if anything, could be done about it. And one article, called 'Trousseaux for Him', suggested that men might please try and rustle up a few new things before the great day, rather than arriving with a pile of half-clean socks and a bag of old sports clothes. We had a lot of fun, George's mantra always being that if a piece was too long, where possible you should cut the facts and leave in the jokes.

What was new about the kind of fashion writing I was doing was that I wanted to relate it to all sorts of other things: I wanted to talk about real clothes, not just about the latest hemline and godets and fabrics. And apart from dragging other subjects into the column, I tried not to take fashion too seriously. I remember dividing hats into three categories: offensive hats, defensive hats and shrapnel (meaning the kind of frilly bits that seem to have landed by accident on the heads of wedding guests); and decades later, a friend of mine bought a hat which actually had that quotation built into a small panel in the front of it.

George's insistence that the subjects on the women's page should be as thoughtful, amusing and all-round readable as anything else in the paper lifted barriers for all of us: we were bridging an immemorial gap between male writing and female. It was jokingly said about David Astor, who believed fervently in the importance of women, that he found it rather hard to hire them – because if they were single and childless they were not typical of, and certainly not good for, our readers; but if they had children, why weren't they at home looking after them? So he had squared the circle by hiring George, who had been married, had children but was a brilliant homosexual. In fact, though, I doubt if David knew this when he hired him; he just knew he was an excellent journalist.

George, dead now these many years, doesn't get the credit he deserves for having just about invented these women's pages that aren't women's pages, that were soon to be found the world over, with titles like 'Currents' or 'Trends' or 'Outlook' (we used to call them the 'Look, Stop and Listen' pages, after the kerbside instruction given to small children). He was marvellous to work for. He was meticulous about grammar and spelling, but he would always leave your copy alone in other respects, especially if he thought that changing it, though improving it this time, might demoralise you and so make it worse next time. There are two kinds of editor, those who make you want to kill them (and, as it's said of some sub-editors, 'won't see a joke without an appointment'), and those who make you feel so understood and appreciated that you positively want to do what they're asking. Even Gavin, who knew George only slightly as a person, admired him immensely as a professional and as co-editor of my work – which made a stir, I think, just because it bridged that gap between male writing and female. Of course, there were plenty of highly respected women journalists – war correspondents, reporters, leader writers (and there were women reporters even in the nineteenth century) – but if they were writing on the serious pages, they were expected to write in the same way as men, not to add anything that would only occur to a woman. We were still a long way from people like Libby Purves, Carol Sarler, Polly Toynbee and Janet Daley, who can write quite as seriously as any male, but in a way that is essentially their own – and female.

*

One way and another, what I was doing on the *Observer* got noticed and talked about, and as the sixties wore on I started being asked to do other things. I was on *Any Questions?* a lot – that went on for decades; I did *The Critics* on radio, and on TV I remember appearing on *The Eamonn Andrews Show*, which was considered a plum. When I was hugely pregnant and draped in a vast green silk evening coat, Andrews made some footballing crack which provoked me to say I didn't actually see my pregnancy as converting a try – he thought that was hilarious. I wasn't always much good on TV; Gavin once tactfully said that I was usually good in print, often good on radio and *sometimes* good on television, which was about it. But programmes like *Call My Bluff* were huge fun and tended to get me known; I was once recognised in a restaurant by a Beatle, who said 'Hullo, Katharine' and I had to whisper 'Who *is* that young man?'

An advantage of all this was often the people I met. Showbiz autobiographies always seem to me to get boring once they've arrived at the stage of 'and then we went down to Larry Olivier's' or 'my very dear friend Bette Davis', so I rather hesitate to say so, but a journalist does first and last cross the path of a good many outstanding people. It's not surprising that I got to have lunch with Bocuse, the great chef at the Connaught (he liked the rice pudding, of all things), or to interview people like Mrs Thatcher when she became Minister for Education (halfway through I realised the tape recorder wasn't working, didn't dare say so, and had to go back and say the interview hadn't worked out). Nor that I eventually found myself drinking with Betty Friedan in New York. And I once shared, or tried to share, a spliff in the company of Paul Bowles, to whom I had an introduction in Tangier – surely even Gavin couldn't disapprove of that? But although Bowles and his boyfriend were eating cannabis out of a jar like brown sugar, they said as I'd never had it before, I must smoke it. Only I couldn't and can't inhale, so I choked ignominiously and felt sick, and that was the first and last time.

Rather more revealing was being at a conference in Wisconsin with Robert McNamara a good deal later, when Mrs Thatcher was Prime Minister. He spent his time saying how absolutely wrong he had been about the trickle-down theory, having noticed at last that money mainly trickled into dictators' Swiss bank accounts. At that conference Shirley Williams and I were the only Brits – and I think the only women. By the end of the three days everyone was saying: 'Why isn't *she* your Prime Minister?' Why indeed.

There was another side to being known about: I was asked to be on the Latey Committee on the Age of Majority, which brought it down from twenty-one to eighteen. We laboured over the evidence, taking note of the fact that twenty-one had been the age of majority only because it was thought in the eleventh century that was the age at which a man could manage the weight of armour; and, in search of hard evidence for the earlier maturity of children nowadays, fastened with relief on the appearance of sanitary bins in primary schools. I wrote and rewrote a good deal of the report and got my photo on the front page of the *Daily Mail*. I also turned down an OBE. For forty years I didn't mention this, as it's considered bad form, but as *The Times* printed the names of all the refuseniks a year or two ago, I suppose I can now. The point was that if I'd said yes, everyone would have simply seen me as a journalist who had Sold Out. One of the others on the committee was Geoffrey Howe, later Mrs Thatcher's Chancellor of the Exchequer, who has stayed a friend. He and John Stebbings, later President of the Law Society, disagreed with the majority report about the age for marriage without parental consent, and wrote a dissenting minority one; it struck me as very unfair that we had laboured for months and months over the wording of the majority report, and he and Stebbings wrote the minority one quite successfully in one night.

The irony, as I see it now, was that one major element in our feeling that the young could make a valid contract, perhaps better than their elders, was that the young in the mid-sixties, blessed with free secondary education, were often far more clued up than their seniors, who had left school at fourteen, yet still had to be the guarantors of the debts and contracts of the young. The argument that the young are better educated than their parents would hardly stand up today.

But my main job remained writing for the *Observer*. Under George, we felt able to lark about. David Astor could tolerate a readable eccentricity both in the prose and in the lives of his writers: people like Jock Fergusson, who kept the Prime Minister of Malta waiting for ten minutes while he tried to get a ladybird out of his typewriter without hurting it; or Patrick O'Donovan, who passed his hip flask to the stranger in the next seat on an aeroplane with the words: 'I believe in God but I also believe in metal fatigue.' David had a maxim: 'If it isn't fun to write, it won't be fun to read.' This didn't actually mean all that much on the serious side of the paper, but it certainly worked for us.

We liked getting the readers to contribute: they were very responsive, and once when I'd used the phrase 'fills a long-felt want' and said it sounded like an animal, I got one sent to me – a draught-excluder in the shape of a yard-long red felt dachs-hund. We asked readers one December for their family Christmas traditions, and printed ones such as the family who rang a handbell through the house for Christmas Day to begin, the farmer's family who had to milk the cows come what may but then had a picnic dinner on the beach, and the family that spent most of Advent making a Christmas Dragon.

Occasionally we would have an idiotic competition, with the prize a bottle of champagne (people who would never lift a finger for, say, twenty quid will bust a gut for a bottle of champagne – they can *see* that in their mind's eye).

One of the most successful was the ghost game. It all sprang from a silly kids' story about a traveller lodging at an inn, who went to his room and saw a five pound note on the table, but when he went to pocket it, a sepulchral voice said:

> I am the ghost of Aunty Mabel,
> That five pound note stays on the table.

The story ends with Davy Crockett taking the room, and retorting:

> I am the ghost of Davy Crockett,
> That five pound note goes in my pocket.

So we had:

> I am the ghost of Mary Whitehouse,
> What filthy mind designed that lighthouse? (Gwyneth Barker)

> I am the ghost of David Frost,
> Super to see you, now get lost. (David Nathan)

> I am the ghost of Oedipus Rex,
> Since my mother, I'm right off sex. (Ivor Johns)

I am the ghost of Robin Day,
I always let you have *my* say. (Mrs M. C. Marsland)

I am the ghost of Christmas Past,
In those days ghosts were built to last. (Ian Macrae)

OK, great poetry it was not, but it hit a spot with the readers, a bit like the clerihew craze – for about five minutes.

When, later on, George Seddon and Shirley Conran were running the page together – it was called 'Hers' at that moment – they used to put snippets of information into little boxes, which Shirley would spice up. Gavin said it was like the Frost Fairy in Disney's *Fantasia*, touching everything with a wand and making it sparkle. The jokes were often slightly suggestive, at least by the standards of the time; it was the only time when the macho compositors in the print room actually read the women's page. There's a poignancy to the reason that particular embellishment came to an end: for each box, a block had to be made, so every time they had to cut or add a line, it meant a new box, which took time and expense, so finally it had to be given up. But nowadays, of course, with modern methods, changing such a thing would be a matter of seconds.

OBSERVATIONS FROM A COLUMN

It was in 1963 that I gave up fashion; after two miscarriages (which I shall come to later) it was clear I must slow down a bit.

I could now shop just for myself. It was heaven [I wrote] merely asking if they had a garment in my size, not arguing about whether it comes in enough sizes for the readers; and to wear an old favourite without being raked by those all-knowing dress-trade eyes that can put a date, a brand label and price tag on everything you have on.

'You look so modern in your sixteen-shilling hat,' the hatmaker Oscar Lucas once said to me. 'Twenty-nine and eleven, please!' I said, affronted. 'No,' he said,' 'I mean to make.'

I then started the general column. which I simply transferred from the *Spectator*, though by that time the format was rather different: it wasn't always based on a specific event or occasion, though it was often provoked by something in the news that week. It would be about a thousand words long, and I usually wrote it on a Thursday; when, much later, an over-fussy page editor insisted I do it on the Tuesday, it became far more difficult to write – it was too early in the week to write on the pulse of the moment and there just aren't fifty-two timeless subjects in a year. I think I was the first woman to be allowed to write a personal column of quite that sort, though soon afterwards Anne Scott-James was doing one for the *Mail* and Jilly Cooper a more light-hearted one for the *Sunday Times*.

My *Observer* columns, though personal, always – well, almost always – used the personal to lead in to something more general: they did have a point. Nowadays, of course, 'lifestyle' columns are everywhere, and a lot of them are pretty aimless, which is fine when they're funny, often futile when they're not. There's another problem, too, which is not always overcome. If you're reporting an event or writing a considered opinion about Russia or climate change or hockey, it doesn't matter whether you're Bill Deedes who is over ninety and apparently immortal, or the latest sharp graduate. But if it's a question of inducing the reader to say, 'Oh, God yes, that's me, don't I know it?', which is what lifestyle columns do, the busy housewife in Lancashire or the retired teacher in Scotland is going to be totally uninterested in the unemptied waste bins of a pot smoker in Islington – and vice versa. However, we didn't have to worry about any of that in those days.

The first book of my reprinted columns, *Roundabout*, contained *Spectator* articles and *Observer* ones as well. Gavin wrote a heart-melting preface in which he described me as a great journalist, but complained about having me scramble over him to get to the telephone so as to plead with some editor for more time. Plainly, the Gordon Watkins reproof about reliability had not at that point truly sunk in. But being on time, pretty important for most journalism, is vital for a columnist: 'I don't want it good I want it Toosday' is the rule of the game, for the alternative is a blank space. Patrick Campbell, who wrote a witty column for the *Sunday Times* for years, having started on the *Irish Times*, had a recurrent dream in which he woke to find his space in the paper completely blank, except for the one sentence: 'He couldn't think what to put.' But by the beginning of the seventies, George was saying with relief that I turned the stuff in 'Always on time! And always the right length!'

People have a lot of misconceptions about columnists. They think a Sunday columnist writes late on Saturday afternoon, which only those reporting Saturday afternoon matches are allowed to do – our deadlines are much earlier in the week. People also think columns take only a few hours to write, and they totally discount the question of actually finding something to say. This means trawling through all sorts of stuff – meetings, articles, visits, interviews – that may yield nothing at all; the hope is that it all composts down and something, come the hour, does emerge.

I think most columnists would agree that it's a question of having enough intake for the outgoing sentences; but the relationship isn't direct. Things have to happen to you: views, phrases, thoughts, indignations derive from all sorts of different things, and not just from what you're supposed to be writing about directly. You go abroad, you report a meeting, you have a baby, you make a new friend, you get involved in a cause or a tiresome fight or a road accident or a speed-reading class: it matters less than you might think what it actually is – the point is that *something* must give the mind a stir, or nothing is there to come out.

'What's your column *about*?' strangers would ask, and it was always hard to say; the only real answer was 'Almost anything.' The ones that were based on an event, a person or something in the news that week, like the old 'Roundabout' ones, were easier to write, but somehow a lot less memorable than ones that concerned some wider trend or controversy. I enjoyed casting a jaundiced eye, for example, on the natural-childbirth lobby's insistence that it could – should – all be painless, and on their spending months and months, when they could be teaching women how to be decent parents, teaching them how to breathe for twenty-four hours. I explored the fact that we always tend to think extreme religious views are more moral than our more liberal ones – If I Was a Better Person I Wouldn't Divorce, for example – and suggested that it was quite wrong to think that toeing the Catholic line on birth control was more moral: in quite a few circumstances it was plain wicked. It seems amazing now that saying that seemed rather brave at the time.

But the times were indeed a-changing – and so was George. When he joined in the late 1950s he was a shambling figure in the shapeless grey flannels of the *Manchester Guardian*, but he gradually grew more camp as the sixties progressed, with his flowing white hair, his white suits and pink shirts – which did not necessarily endear him to the more staid current affairs people. But all his journalistic standards were as high as theirs: he was meticulous about both grammar and humanity – one star journalist, Linda Blandford, pronounced herself 'morally immature' until she worked under Astor and Seddon. George was a genius, and the women to whom he gave a voice – myself among them – adored him.

At the time I joined, the *Observer* was still in Tudor Street but George's little empire and one or two other offices were down a nearby side road in a building with somewhat ramshackle adaptations. He and I shared a lovely secretary, Julia Marlowe, and she told me many years later that all the secretaries, who wore them, were affronted by my great attack on cardigans. She also told me that on Saturdays at noon they would all pack into one secretary's room which had a thin partition between it and the office of Kenneth Harris. He had a pompous sense of his own importance even then (though it got worse when he became the saviour of the paper and R. O. Anderson's right hand man after ARCO – Atlantic Richfield Oil Corporation – took it over. But on Saturday he would ring up his dogs. Presumably there must have been a dog-sitter to take the phone off the hook, and then he would say: 'How are you, my little darlings? Are you all right? Oh good! Woof, woof!'

CHANGING TIMES FOR WOMEN

The first general column I wrote for the *Observer* was about Betty Friedan's *The Feminine Mystique*, just published in Britain, in which she quoted from men who said: 'Oh you don't believe all that old stuff about women and careers, do you?' I suppose I naively thought that battle had been won long ago. I was amazed as well as angry; I think my feminism must have been of a pre-war kind. Still, I had a good time rubbishing the reasons men gave for keeping women out of the action; and for a lot of women – girls, anyway – who read our columns or who had to listen to us giving talks at their schools, we were the ones who were opening up new horizons for them. I've had letters from women years later who said they'd never before met any women who *didn't* think getting married and having families was all that women did. So it was liberating and new when I wrote suggesting, for example, that it was a bad idea ever to put society's pressure on women to be mothers since, apart from anything else, that would never be how you got the best mothers – any more than you would get good pilots by insisting the entire ground crew should take to the air.

I wasn't alone; anything but. Jilly Cooper was soon writing a hilarious personal column in the *Sunday Times*, Felicity Green was making the *Mirror*'s fashion pages amazingly more fun and interesting to men ('Could we have lingerie again next week?'). In the mid-sixties there was quite a lot of writing rebelling against the required perfection the magazines used to plug. Edna LeShan wrote *How to Survive Parenthood*, and an American publisher put out a series of 'Awful' books – the *Awful Dressmaker's Guide*, the *Awful Handyman's Guide* — telling you how to cope when it had all gone wrong; Peg Bracken wrote her *I Hate to Cook*, followed by *I Hate to Housekeep*. One of her best ideas is with me still – that you should do household chores in the order in which your *not* having done them will be discovered. So you start by putting a jug of Martinis in the fridge and make the bed more or less last.

But even as this mood, this growing realisation that women weren't built simply to breed and bake, that they could do anything, began to gather momentum, there were already some women writing about what a mistake it all was, and how much happier women were if they just stayed at home with the children. The woman who voices this opinion has always been someone I would like to throw down a steep flight of stairs, because of the hypocrisy of it. I always felt that if she didn't have children, you could forget it; if she'd had them and they were now grown she'd forgotten it, and if she actually had young children around she'd at least got away from them long enough to write an article saying other women shouldn't. She was *not* stuck in a steamy kitchen with no one to talk to but toddlers. One of my particular *bêtes noires* in this respect was – is – the famous Arianna Stassinopoulos who, though herself the second woman President of the Cambridge Union, made her name with a book called *The Female Woman*, which alleges that domestic women are far the happiest. Not that *she* confined herself to that life, then or ever.

BLASTING THE BANKS

One of the most blistering rows the column got itself into concerned an article I wrote about banks in the early sixties. It's hard to remember nowadays, when many banks are open till five p.m., not three, when you can get money out of cash dispensers round the clock, when instead of being patronised by a headmasterly figure in a waistcoat you deal with an Indian girl in a call centre, just exactly how irritating, and worse than irritating – frightening – the old banks used to be. In my piece I aired all the grievances shared in those days by just about every cowed depositor: inconvenient opening hours, a loan policy that was completely arbitrary, their making mistakes and not acknowledging them, charges that varied according to who you were, and particularly the demeaning way they treated women.

One example I cited was of a man who opened two accounts for his niece. He paid into one of them, and his wife or the nanny into the other. The bank was always charming to him, but after three months the women refused to go into the bank because they were treated so badly. I'd left a bank once, because when I was trying to cash a cheque with a male signature they asked me what it was for – I reckoned it was none of their damn business, even if I had slept for it; but it was the 'Now, now, little lady' attitude that infuriated me.

The uproar the article caused was loud enough to provoke another article. Then, soon after, a Royal Commission on banks made just about all the points that I'd made. I received masses of letters from ordinary readers giving instances of how badly they were treated. The only bank that got a good press was the Co-op, which paid interest on current accounts, had a flat and predictable rate of charges and allowed you to cash cheques in Co-op shops during normal shopping hours.

But there was an absolute explosion of rage from the banks. One 'wouldn't advance me ten shillings if I expected to make my living as a journalist', another accused me of the 'naiveté and complete immaturity of extreme youth' – I was thirty-five at the time. One of the letters made my point for me by deploring 'the arrogant assumption that bank services should be suited to her personal requirements'! Well so they darn well should: it was, after all, *my money*. And nowadays they do pay much more attention to what their customers want – not through any protest of mine, but because the competition of good building societies drove them to it. Even old Natwest, when it started to require a special extra pin number if you rang them up, had the wit to give the over-sixties another number to ring with a real person answering; and no press 1, press 2 at all.

But as late as the eighties, when I became a non-executive director of Nationwide, women were still furious that the statement for a joint account was sent to the man, not to both – and the row became more pointed when payments began to be made on the demutualisation of one society or another, which would also go to the first-named person of a joint account. Women couldn't normally get mortgages without a male guarantor, nor for ages money for a commercial venture – though at the moment the start-up businesses that *don't* go bust in the first few years are, interestingly, more often the ones started by women. The theory is that they have to psych themselves up harder and for longer before taking the plunge, so are less inclined to rush into hopeless schemes.

Considering that women have to do most of the day-to-day juggling with money in most households, it's puzzling how this idea of their fluffiness with money persists. Maybe men like to admit to having a spendthrift wife for the same reason that they like having handmade shoes or a big car: as in Thorstein Veblen's theory of conspicuous waste, to complain about your spendthrift wife implies that you can *afford* such an expensive luxury.

PART 6

STARTING A FAMILY

BABIES

We had agreed when we married that we didn't want to think about children for a couple of years. Gavin felt he was only just starting out on his career, he was not yet thirty; we could enjoy being just us for a year or two. But in the event it was a good deal longer than that before we started a family..

The first hurdle was Gavin's reluctance. Once, in Paris, well over the two-year mark, we were about to make love when I asked if I could leave off my thingummy; he said no. We went ahead anyway and afterwards, in the bath, I wondered for a few minutes whether I would leave him if he wouldn't agree to have babies. This was the only time in forty-five years I ever entertained such a thought, but it did, I suppose, show I really wanted them.

Then when we did start, I had a miscarriage. It wasn't dire – it was very early; I had it in New End Hospital up the hill in Hampstead; an interesting time in itself. There was one girl there who was hauled back home by her husband far too soon because he was sick of looking after their other kids; she didn't seem to mind but went off laughing. And in the next bed was Norelle Kiddy, a sculptor, who designed big pieces for the sides of buildings; she had fallen off a ladder and lost a much wanted baby. We became quite good friends and later on she began sculpting a head of me; it was mostly an excuse for going on talking, and as she carved away the face got smaller and smaller; but the hair stayed the same, so it seemed as if the clay hair was *growing*. Then she found a new lover, lost interest in talking; the head dried out and fell off its stand and I didn't see her again.

While I was in hospital Bernard Levin sent me a cheer-up hamper of the sort that figures in Victorian children's stories: *pâté de fois gras* and out-of-season fruit, a little bottle of champagne and a new novel and so on. He was also very kind to Gavin who, then as ever, was upset by anything medical. Bernard took him home and cooked him a steak, and Gavin, who almost always had some intriguing daft project on the go – making a model, photographing something weird, recording something odd – played him a tape he was making of various sounds produced by quite ordinary objects to sound like something else. One, for instance, was made by flapping a paperback about so that it sounded like 'the flapping of the wings of a Giant Green Poisonous Bat from Saturn'. Bernard was greatly tickled by this, and kept on bringing it into his columns; Gavin claimed copyright, and decided in revenge to make him such a bat. It was a truly horrible creature, with red bloodshot eyes and a trickle of gooey saliva (made of glue, I suppose) hanging from its cruel beak. When we finally presented it to Bernard, he said it was the most revolting artefact he had ever seen in his life; it ended up in the conservatory of one of his girlfriends, where I imagine it must have caused quite a jolt to anyone who didn't know its history; but the children were rather sad to see the bat go.

Keen to be under medical care before the third month, which was when the NHS clinic would have started to see me, when I was pregnant again I enrolled with Tony Woolf, a young doctor then at University College Hospital. He lived near us and would drop in on his way home for, as he put it, 'a Scotch and a smear'. But in spite of his concern I had another miscarriage at four and a half months, and this one was miserable. There wasn't nearly so much written, then, about the chances of women in their thirties not managing to have babies, but I was worried enough. The miscarriage itself was disagreeable, and I was quite ill; Tony later said that the event caused him to alter his teaching and no longer to tell his students, if you please, that every septic abortion was a deliberate abortion.

Third time lucky – and at least we seemed able to conceive at the drop of a cap. Finally in 1964 came our first son. I went to all the antenatal classes and believed – not having yet had a baby – in all the natural childbirth theory, was even slightly shocked when Tony tapped the huge mound of my stomach and said to remember that what actually mattered was *that*, the baby. When the birth was about a week late, Tony decided it had better be induced. So I went in to University College Hospital, was scrubbed and measured and so on; the induction was to take place the following morning. Then Tony said, 'Right, that's all we can do – why don't you get Gavin to take you out to dinner?' So we had a stupendous meal at L'Etoile in Charlotte Street – our last night of freedom, as it were.

Back at UCH, I woke up at six a.m. feeling frightful; a visit to the loo didn't seem to help. And then there in a canary-coloured sweater was Tony, who'd been up for another delivery, saying: 'Don't you see? – you've started!' He then turned to the nurse and remarked: 'Isn't it funny how few of my inductions ever need to be done?' Get her in the right frame of mind – encourage her to have a blow-out and *maybe* . . . a sight nicer to be induced by Château Gruaud-Larose 1953 than by the method generally then in use at UCH, which involved a continuous injection through the arm.

I was given pethidine, and heard through the mists Tony and another doctor discussing whether a donation the hospital had been given should be spent on research or on more beds; I remember thinking with total clarity: 'Idiotic – they ought to spend it on *more time between contractions*' – that's pethidine for you. Gavin was around, but none of us wanted him there at the finish and he was only too relieved to be let off. But to everyone's surprise I did my breathing OK, though I had to apologise later for the language I'd used, and the baby was born by eleven a.m. My brother John said simply: 'You have babies the way you do everything else – late, and extremely fast.'

I had hoped for a red-headed boy, and that was what I got; that day was the single happiest day of my life; I was too happy even to read. I don't mean that having children was the thing that has made me happiest; but almost never does one go straight from uncertainty and worry, at one swoop, into bliss.

A few days later, though, it was another story. I had been breast-feeding Bernard sitting on a chair by the bed, with the baby on a pillow on my lap. When we'd finished I got up and carefully laid him and the pillow on the bed while I sorted myself; but the pillow had been slightly flattened on one side by his weight and he rolled off the high hospital bed on to the floor – unquestionably the worst day in both our lives. Mercifully the paediatricians who checked him out with extreme thoroughness found no damage had been done.

We called him Bernard James. He wasn't exactly called after Bernard Levin, but Levin became his 'musical adviser', since Quakers don't have godparents. And once, when I was singing to Bernard in his bath, he said: 'Stop that noise I want to listen to the lavatory', so I was able to ring Levin to assure him that his namesake's musical sense was coming along fine.

The birth of our second son Jake was very different. By the time I was having him, in 1967, Tony Woolf had moved to Hackney, which seemed dauntingly far away, so I had Jake in the Royal Northern Hospital in the Holloway Road, in a private room. They wanted to induce him on my birthday, but I said that would be too complicated by half, and anyway there was a Crime Writers' Panel in Madame Tussaud's Chamber of Horrors that day, with Gavin taking part; I think we both thought that ought to be enough to bring on the birth, but it wasn't. This time I was all for anaesthetics, as it was a rather painful induction; and I desperately hoped for a girl. But it was a boy, and the next morning I wept as I looked forward to a long daughterless future.

Jake knows this, but he also knows that with hindsight I think I should have been delighted. I think I would have been a lousy mother for a girl – for a teenage girl, anyway. Most girls have a scratchy relationship with their mothers at that age, though boys don't, necessarily; I think I would have handled a girl extremely badly, probably been jealous of Gavin's affection for her, probably tried to run her life for her. It was somehow always easy to assume that boys were a different species, and if they and Gavin were doing things that seemed to me pointless or incomprehensible, that was just the way things were for males and I didn't have to worry about it. Our boys certainly had their own problems, but I am now certain I was lucky to have them.

HELP AT HOME

I was exceptionally fortunate, as I now realise, to be able to go on working *and* stay at home with the children much of the time: for nine years I didn't even have a desk at the *Observer*. This was in large part due to the help I had. When I was hailed on *Desert Island Discs* as one of the first women to 'have it all', and asked how I managed, I said I had masses of help, listing mother's helps, a daily cleaner, my mother and so on. But somehow only my mother made it through to the final broadcast – maybe Sue Lawley thought it sounded more democratic. But my mother, though devoted, was plainly not there all the time, and others were: particularly Trude.

Trude – pronounced to rhyme with Judy, not Jude – had grown up in Austria during the war, hiding fearfully from soldiers as it ended. She had come to Britain as an au pair girl and was disgracefully exploited, being left in the country in sole charge of several children during the week, doing all the cooking and washing, including sheets, for parents who only visited at weekends. By the time she came to us as a cleaner she was married, with a son at school; she came every day from ten till three. In the seventeen years she was with us she missed only one day, and as soon as there was Bernard it became clear she was marvellous with babies and small children.

When he was of an age to be pushed round the park we recruited Rossie. Mrs Ross, a spry seventy-year-old, got the job over the languid heads of half a dozen limp twenty-year-olds and became a sort of honorary grandmother. Eventually we moved on to live-in mother's helps, sixteen-year-olds who had left school but couldn't begin training to be nannies till they were seventeen. We reckoned this was OK because Gavin worked at home, so there was a grown-up there in case of fire or a broken arm. We never had au pairs, because before I had a baby of my own I'd researched au pairs for an article, and come to the conclusion that the system only worked really well when the mother was around to share conversation and chores, which was exactly what I didn't want to do. When I think of women like my stalwart daughter-in-law, who has no help at all except the occasional babysitter, I realise how lucky I was.

WRITER AND FATHER

Gavin saw quite soon that given one decent night's sleep a week I could cope, and took Sunday mornings, even unto the dirty nappy, from quite early on (and brought me breakfast in bed every Sunday ever after). Working from home, Gavin was a secure back-up to our arrangements with the helpers; but he was much more than a minder to the boys. He would make films of them – but not running along a beach or coyly posed with the cat, but more likely dressed up as Sherlock and Watson or spacemen or gangsters. When Bernard was about four Gavin made a film in France with Bernard as a bailed-out pilot and himself as a Gestapo officer complete with foul little moustache; and at one point he involved his sister's family the Drinkwaters, me and his parents too in a film called *The Logan Brothers* – the two red-heads, Bernard and his cousin Colin. He turned his parents' garage in Birmingham into a Western bar, and filmed the final shoot-out among the trees of the Lickey Woods. Jake, aged about four, was the sheriff. No wonder Bernard described Gavin as a real English eccentric.

Gavin was always making something – a new book-holder for his desk, an underwater scene in a small tank; endless model aeroplanes. He would even sew – things like a fake

leather waistcoat for a three-year-old playing a cowboy –
though not the buttons on his own shirts, ever. He made a
doll's-house for Bernard when he was about four, admitting he
made it because he liked making things. He gave it the same
wallpapers and furniture as our own house, and was never
allowed to forget that when Bernard saw it he put the Mummy
doll behind the desk and the Daddy doll in front of the TV.

I kept it for my grandchildren, and when the little girls
found that there was a high chair, they complained there was
no baby; I said Gavin would model one, and he did. It turned
out to be a very tiresome commission: made of plaster of Paris,
wearing a yellow garment of some sort, and with stuck-on flowers at the kids' request. When he gave it to the satisfied small
girls, he said wearily: 'Of the two ways of making a baby I
know, I prefer the other one.'

Most of Gavin's models, other than a succession of aeroplanes, were made to be photographed, and built only to be
seen from one side. He was meticulous about them; once, for
example, he had our New York lawyer friend Sol Glushak up
on the roof of his building counting the windows in a distant
skyscraper, so that Gavin could get the detail – the hardly visible detail – *exactly* right for his model of a volcanic eruption in
Central Park. People looking at the framed photographs of
these dramas and accidents couldn't believe that they were
only photographs of models, and that the incredibly realistic
dust from an earthquake or smoke from an explosion, say, had
been effected by my blowing down a tube on to a hidden cache
of Johnson's baby powder.

Donald Westlake, renowned thriller-writer, once asked
bemusedly: 'Why is Gavin so *serious* about all that?' I said: 'He
plays like a child – children are serious about what they make.'
I used to say: 'He writes like an angel, he plays like a child, and

he shops like a woman.' He did. Men mostly only like to go out determinedly to buy something in particular, but Gavin actually enjoyed shopping; he would drift round shops for hours, happy even when he bought nothing. Once when he was heading into a toyshop in search of model cars or cranes I reminded him that he did have (by then) grandchildren. 'Girls,' he said scornfully, heading firmly towards the tanks. Tanks fascinated him, and a picture of his best model tank appeared on the cover of *Uncle Target*, which was mainly about tanks – the last of his Major Maxim books.

What always puzzled people about Gavin, the central paradox, you might say, was that he was a Quaker obsessed with military things. He certainly revelled in the intricacies and mechanisms of guns, tanks, bombers; but also in the order of it all – the formalities, the uniforms, the taboos of military life. For years his bedside reading was either *The Caine Mutiny* or *From Here to Eternity* – it was a world he could lose himself in. He was fascinated by how things worked, including organisations: at one point he was even intrigued, for example, by people like Albert Speer and the top ranks of Nazism – 'the senior management of Hell'.

Maybe it was his Quaker side which made his characters' attitudes to violence so complex. They kill people; they fight them, but even the soldiers in his books, inured to violence, have their dilemmas – dilemmas which worked themselves out endlessly inside Gavin's own head.

There's a theory that writers don't write about what they do, but what they dream of doing: I don't know. Gavin wasn't violent himself, though I suppose he may have felt he could be. There was one deplorable occasion when he – or, to be frank, we – got into a fight. We were in a nightclub where George Melly was singing, and a drunk American was being loudly and disgustingly rude about him. I told him to shut up because George's pregnant wife was sitting there; he told me to fuck off. I retaliated, and he threw me down three small steps. Gavin turned round, saw someone manhandling his wife, and unhesitatingly broke a bottle of red wine over his head.

Our hosts were amazed ('usually such a quiet couple!'), though not too upset – after all, this was the sixties; all the same, they ushered us out. After an hour or two I was inclined to regard the whole thing as hilarious, but I could see Gavin clouding over every time he thought about it, for days. No bad thing, possibly, for a crime writer to discover his own springs of violence, but that's the only instance so far as I know.

THE BOYS

I reckon I was a reasonably good mother of small babies: I breast-fed them both for three and a half months, which was considered the ration in those days; and quite a good mother of teenage boys, with whom it's mostly feeding and listening; but I was very bad at toddlers. The trouble was that I tried to do everything with words, which is not how it works. I remember with shame one time when Jake was in the bath, being unhelpful, and I said: 'Oh *why* won't you cooperate?' and Bernard, standing by, said: 'He doesn't know what the word means.' Of course not. I always did bath them myself, unless we were going out early; got them up and put them to bed. It took me a long time, though, to realise how tired they could get. Bernard always made a fuss about coming up for his bath, and another fuss about getting out of the bath – until one day I had to start the whole process early, and he sailed through it all. Belatedly

I grasped with how much weariness he must always have faced our endless flight of stairs. (Me too, come to that – until I started to have my gin before their bath, not after, wrote about it and was thanked for the advice by more than one mother with tears in her eyes.)

Bernard and Jake had – have – totally different characters. Bernard was slightly at odds with the world from the word go; he would on the whole do the opposite of what was suggested as soon as he was old enough to understand what the message was. If you told him on an escalator, for example, 'Don't put your feet too near the edge', he immediately put his feet near the edge. This was bad enough before Jake arrived, when Bernard was three; but then he added the usual elder-child fits of jealousy.

Jake was a huggable baby; he tended to be easily good at things; and since Bernard was occupying the awkward-child slot, Jake slid effortlessly into the good-boy one, and got praise and approval all the more. We sent them both to The Hall, a local prep school which had a very good junior school with female teachers and a modern and interesting look about it; its head, Raymond Cooper, is once said to have claimed: 'Yes, we're now as good as a state primary.' We didn't look hard enough at the senior school, which was a very different kettle of fish. It was run by masters; its stated aim was to get the boys into good public schools; it was keen on games and pretty uninterested in boys who weren't likely to do them credit.

Bernard never seemed to get good marks, and he wasn't good at games. On one occasion he was set to move a bench in preparation for sports day, dropped it on his foot and said 'Fuck!' in the hearing of parents; we got a stiff note about it. Gavin, always much better at fighting Bernard's corner than I was, sent an even stiffer letter back, saying Bernard might have

behaved better if he hadn't been kept out of games for the
previous *five* sessions while they groomed the high flyers. I
have a heartbreaking memory of Bernard, aged eleven, saying
during one late-evening session that he thought he might take
up tennis: 'I would *so* like to be good at something.' He bucked
up a lot when he got into University College School, and for
a time all was well.

　　Delighted about the children were, of course, all the grand-
parents. Gavin and I thought we were lucky that our
backgrounds were in many ways so similar. Both sets of parents
were basically left-wing – liberal or labour; nonconformist –
Quaker or Presbyterian; professional class – his father an
accountant, mine a schoolmaster. There was a Scottish element in both – Gavin's father had been at Glasgow High
School; both sets believed firmly in education (and for girls as
well). And both had – I didn't realise for a long time how rare
this was – an unshakable belief in the young running their
own lives. 'Made with the same tools', was Gavin's phrase for
it.

　　But there were big day-to-day differences between the two
households. What was so happy about Joe and Ann's home was
that it was relaxed, it was sunny; Ann was terrific with little
children; there was a constant atmosphere, at least until they
were quite old, of cheerful, bubbling amusement. Having
coped successfully with the schooldays in Birmingham of both
Barbara and Gavin, she was used to changes of plan, meals
being late, things going wrong. My parents, having lived all
their lives to the tyranny of school bells, were much more
uptight about such things. There were other differences: we
had always had water with every meal; Gavin's mother was teetotal, but you got a gin before the meal from Joe and made it
last. So the only place I drank gin right through a meal was in

this blameless Quaker household. Once when Gavin as a boy had had a fall and broken his bike, he managed to get to a telephone and ring Ann. She said she'd come out on the bus to meet him. 'I knew you'd think of something comforting, he said.'

The children loved going to stay with them, and they were delighted to have them. Once when Jake was out on his tricycle in the park near where they lived in Bournville he fell off, and splashed into the little lake, firmly holding his small trike up out of the water. When they got back, Ann stripped him down and put his wet clothes in the spin dryer; then she wondered why he was still standing there hopefully. He was waiting, it turned out, for *him* to be put in the spin dryer. She was fond of spin dryers, was Ann, and much later, when they had moved to the south coast to be near Barbara and her husband Dennis, who by then lived in Chichester, she mourned the death of the twin-tub culture: their dryer had tended to judder alarmingly round the room unless held down, so Ann would sit on it while it was running; it still bounced round the room with her on it, but less.

When the boys were very small, in the sixties, we had holidays in Grimaud in the South of France, at the end of May or early June when it was cheaper and not so hot; once they were at school it had to be August. And one holiday, the summer we spent in a borrowed house in Vallabrix, near Uzès, west of Avignon, was more memorable than I would have liked. The house itself, in that small village with one tiny shop, was pleasant enough from a grown-up point of view, but there was a distinct lack of local cafés. We drove less and less hopefully through villages like St-Quentin-la-Poterie and St-Hippolyte-de-Montaigu and St-Victor-des-Oules, eventually rechristening our village St-Jésus-les-Soifs. We bathed in a nearby river with a wide, safe swathe of shallow beach; but the children wanted to go to the sea. So go the three of us went, while Gavin worked – an hour and a quarter at least down a motorway, which made as little sense as staying in the Cotswolds so as to go to the beach at Bognor. The beach, when you got there, was ghastly, all endless sand and sun umbrellas, but they liked puddling about in the shallows, and I would swim out to do my statutory fifty strokes out and fifty back. On one occasion they'd moved a bit down the water's edge and out of sight; I lay down to sun myself dry and thought nothing of it, but when they hadn't appeared again after five or ten minutes I sat up and started to look for them: they were brought back shortly, crying, led by a kindly French hand.

Jake cheered up in a few minutes, but the effect on Bernard lasted, seriously, for some years. Even two years later if he looked up and you were out of sight he would break down – in Euston station stopping to look at something and falling behind his father, in the hairdresser's left there for only as long as it took me to buy a paper, he would look around, fail to see us and crumple.

I suppose nowadays one would never dare let one's children out of one's sight on a crowded beach for a moment, any more than I do my grandchildren in the park; but we weren't so hyped up about paedophiles in those days; it's only now that I can wake in the night and shudder to think what might have happened.

One beach experience, though, did somewhat vindicate our relatively firm way of raising the boys. We'd been lent a house in Exmouth, and been shown the short cut to the beach, which, without our realising it, bypassed large notices saying 'Dangerous Currents'. The boys had a small rubber boat, with which they were sloshing around while I swam. My matronly breaststrokes went well enough as I swam out, but when I turned to swim back, nothing happened. There was, luckily, a man nearby in a kayak with a large buoy attached to it; I asked for a tow, and the man, who was actually the beach lifeguard, put me down on the rocks and explained about the current.

But the rocks were some way from the sandy part of the beach, and they were covered with barnacles and I had bare feet; there was no way I could run back to warn the boys. So I shouted 'Go back! Go back!' And they did. Bernard's huff lasted all day, of course, and Jake cried; but if their little rubber boat had got into that current . . . In that much underestimated social document, Laura Ingalls Wilder's *Little House on the Prairie*, and its successors, there are frequent occasions when the family would simply not have survived if the children had not done exactly what they were told at some dangerous moment; permissive childcare and the laboured discussion of absolutely everything is, if you come to think of it, as much a privilege of affluence and safety as three meals a day and television.

MILITARY MATTERS

When the boys were quite small they enjoyed the huge bed-time joke of Gavin pretending to be a sergeant major. They had to stand by their beds, which, trembling with giggles, they would do, while he said in stentorian tones: 'Yer 'orrible! Yer disgusting! LOOK at that button!' (They would leave a pyjama button undone on purpose.) Or he would stand behind one of them and say: 'Am I 'urting you?'

'Sir, no Sir!'

'Well I oughta be 'cos I'm STANDIN' ON YOUR 'AIR!

Get it cut!' (Getting it cut was no joke, and in the photographs of that time it always looks rather long. They finally started wanting me to cut it – I suppose they were finding it hard to see out – and I said I would if they let me write about it; which I did.) I have an uneasy feeling that other Hampstead parents tutted that Gavin, the warmonger, actually *drilled* his children; but the boys loved it.

It got more grown-up during the seventies, when Gavin and Bernard played war games together; they played them very seriously indeed. They got themselves up in military gear; they had a warboard as big as a ping-pong table, with polystyrene hills, endless model tanks and soldiers and armoured cars; they even co-authored a book about it, called *Operation Warboard: How to Fight World War II Battles in Miniature*, and toured the country doing radio broadcasts to publicise it. Gavin was of Quaker stock, and Quakers are supposed to be dead against war; Bernard was brought up on war games and is now a pacifist. So it goes. And the question of war, peace, soldiers, the military has been a complex one for me for a long time.

The way my parents felt about war was part of a general revulsion at the horrors of the First World War; it even extended to my mother loathing the red, white and blue bathroom I jokingly decorated for the boys; to her, that sort of patriotism was exactly the trouble. But I remember two – maybe three – incidents relating to war that mapped my own feelings. The first was when I went to Downe House, was put in an annexe because I was thought to be 'difficult', and got into an argument with one or two of the others about conscientious objectors. They'd been brought up to think of them as cop-outs, only avoiding conscription out of fear. I was tearfully horrified at this dismissal of my own father, and when Auntie, as we called the housemother, came in to turn out the lights I appealed confidently to her as a grown-up – and she said: 'Conchies are cowards.' I didn't know how to cope with that at all.

As an evacuee in various places I hardly encountered any bombing; on the one occasion that I was in an air raid, in Glasgow, I remember quite clearly what most amazed me. As I heard the anti-aircraft guns booming, realised bombs were actually being dropped, I thought, Grown-ups are doing this. *Grown-ups*, the people supposed to be wise and knowing, are actually shooting at each other.

All the same, I had read Ernest Raymond's novel *Tell England* under the bedclothes and wept my way through to the mattress; I adored Rupert Brooke; it was only much later, after *Oh! What a Lovely War*, that I began to make distinctions between one war and another, and realise what a criminally bad war had been fought in Flanders, and that if ever a war needed to be fought the Second World War was the one.

Being married to Gavin made for some extremely complex adjustments. Though he was a Quaker and his father an objector too, he was not only happy to be called up and join the RAF, but absolutely fascinated by everything military, long before he made Major Maxim his hero. I think there's another paradox, for Gavin and a lot of other militarily inclined people. What can be very attractive about the military life is having ranks, and rules; even if you spend half your time figuring out how to break them, they are always *there*. Knowing what you have to do, to whom you are answerable, where you have to muster, what you have to do to your rifle, your aeroplane, knowing who are the people who give you orders and who the people beneath you – 'first the horses, then the men, only then the officers' – in a word, *order*.

Yet the result of any operation, or skirmish even, is total dis-
order: ruined villages, broken power lines, crops unharvested,
desolate families, absence of civilisation. I spent a lot of time
telling Gavin he didn't worry enough about what happened to
civilians, to the raped and displaced and hungry; that war
wasn't just about soldiers. He would tend to reply by citing the
awful ordeals – such as biting the tongue out of a dead man's
mouth as a test of toughness in Vietnam – that the soldiers had
to go through. I would say that was still man-to-man stuff and
not what I was talking about.

During the Bosnian upheavals we had endless arguments
and conversations about it, even resorted to writing out our
differing points of view. But I remember on one occasion when
we'd been arguing for an hour, and had reached stalemate, we
stood up and clutched each other frantically: 'This is too
important to disagree about.' It was.

He, plainly, was not a pacifist, and nor am I: we were both in
agreement about that. But the commonest argument or discussion or disagreement we had, not once but over and over
again, was where the individual conscience should, or should
not, override orders; and whether or not a soldier had any
right to have a view about which war was being fought.

The focus of this particular argument was, originally, a
bomber pilot who was asked at the time of Suez to set forth to
bomb Egyptian villages. He pulled up the undercarriage of his
bomber so that it couldn't fly. Gavin argued that he'd signed up
to obey orders, and if every soldier passed his orders through
the filter of his own convictions, no officer could ever get anything done right. I thought the pilot was right, and pointed out
we didn't let anyone off the hook at Nuremberg when they
said: 'We were only obeying orders.' The irony of this is that it
is Quakers who say that it is your own conscience, not what

anybody else tells you, that should be the only guide; and Gavin was the Quaker.

When he was in his late twenties, his mother, who worked part-time in the Friends' office in Bournville, said they were drawing up new membership lists and she had to know whether to transfer him or not. After a week or two brooding, Gavin said yes, he was a Quaker. She told me later she could perfectly well have transferred his name, but thought it was time he positively made up his mind.

Quakers are supposed to be austere, pacifist and teetotal; Gavin, it has to be said, was none of these things; but he had an appreciation of a woman as a human being – a Quaker characteristic – and, unlike so many good men (as opposed to seductive sharks), was superb at giving presents. He once carted my typewriter all over London to buy a case that would fit it *and* the various toiletries that one took round in those days. And once when we were opening our presents at Christmas he had Jake put on a record; I turned to rebuke him and then realised it was playing 'As Time Goes By'. Then Gavin passed me a full Martini glass with a tiny silver olive fork engraved with my initials, and said: 'Here's looking at you, kid.'

PART 7

CHOPPY WATERS

BOOKS AND BOATS

The Crime Writers' Association once held a festive lunch at the home of thriller writer Berkeley Mather. He had a lovely large house in the country, and as these people in their best bibs and tuckers wandered across the grass, I idled with the idea that one might stage a short story among such: which of the crime writers present might have committed the crime? And the answer actually was: none of them, for you never met a nicer, more friendly, cosier set of people in your life. They seemed almost entirely free from the savage ego-wars of the 'serious' novelists. Gavin's theory was that when someone reads a good thriller, and likes it, they then look for another thriller, so everyone's success helps everyone else.

Be that as it may, they were terrific people to be with. Gavin relished them, and adored his time as Chairman. There was a happy convention that you didn't say you'd read someone else's book – at least not where anyone could hear you. If you actually had read and admired one, you drew the author into a corner to whisper the compliment in their ear – a good idea, as obviously no one could have read everything. That way, there were no hard feelings.

We had John Bingham, who was thought to be the original of Le Carré's Smiley; we had Miles Tripp, who had a blameless day job as a Charity Commissioner. We became great friends with Michael Underwood, Office of Public Prosecutions by day, crime writer at the weekends. (I once did a story on 'What Bachelors Eat': when first Michael's parents and then his housekeeper died, he said he ate pears out of the tin standing by the draining-board most evenings, while a bought shepherd's pie heated up in the oven.)

Michael not only belonged to the Crime Writers' Association but set himself to revive the ailing Detection Club, which was almost dying on its feet. Founded by Dorothy L. Sayers and G. K. Chesterton, it had Agatha Christie as Chairman, but its rules at that time prevented anything but classical detection – what you might call body-in-the-library mysteries, which in the sixties were as rare as clues in Chapter Two. Michael and allies broadened the remit to include thrillers, and it became a sort of crime writers' top table. Christianna Brand, author of *Green for Danger*, was among that select band; she was a hilarious woman, even when she was dying of breast cancer writing us all amusing letters about it. She adored small Jake, 'though normally a keen member of the Herod society'. We used to see her swigging a small bottle of something strong before going into the Garrick Club to sample its discreet offerings of wine – 'No, dear, no good at all for me.'

But the greatest friends we made were Dick Francis and his wife Mary; we used to go and stay with them in their calm, friendly bungalow in Berkshire. Mary had had polio when she was carrying their first child, Merrick, and had spent some

time in an iron lung, an experience which informed one of
Dick's thrillers. All her movements were, perhaps because of
this, leisurely and measured; peace set in whenever we passed
through their doors. They were the only people we ever stayed
with who made the children feel that *they* were honoured
guests, not just the add-ons of the grown-ups who were the
really welcome ones (not that we were asked to stay much
anyway, though I doubt if our children were any more invasive
and tiresome than anybody else's).

The only problem with the Francises was that Dick was
totally conditioned to wake very early in the morning to ride
out, which usually meant that he was half asleep by ten p.m.,
which was about when Mary and I would start to argue. Gavin
complained: 'By the end of the evening Mary's a Fascist, Kath's
a Communist and Dick's asleep; and I have to keep the peace.'

They were welcoming; they were good company; but they
had another incalculable asset, and one which changed our
lives: they had a boat. This was a motor-cruiser on the Thames.
They'd called their house Penny Chase (because they had to
chase the pennies to get it); they called the boat the *Penny
Lark*, because it was a bit of lark. Later they got a camper-
van – a 'drawing-room on wheels' – for sheltering from the rain
at races; it was called *Halfpenny*, and when later they got a far
bigger boat, it was *Tenpenny*. They took us on *Penny Lark*, we
adored it; and not once, but twice, they lent it to us.

This was where we first learned of the endless patience of
lock-keepers; of the impossible way the Didcot cooling towers
start off on one side of you and end up on the other, when they
plainly can't have crossed the river; of the weird variety of
ducks. Gavin's theory was that bird books were the *Debrett's* of
ducks, as it were; who actually bred with whom was quite
another matter. When you saw a mallard female with seven

ducks of which one – only one – was bright yellow (and would later be white), you knew she'd had a fling with – not a wild lover, but a tame lover: a domestic duck.

This, too, was where we learned to loathe swans. They look lovely, day visitors coo over them, there is a picturesque swan-upping every year, and since the ones that don't belong to the Queen belong to the vintners, they are the answer to Omar Khayyam's speculation:

> I often wonder what the vintners buy
> One half so precious as the thing they sell.

But they hiss viciously if you don't feed them, they make a row pecking flies off the side of your boat at six a.m., and they can be strong enough to break your arm with a wing. Once they bit young Bernard when he was trying to offer them a bite of something. You can't hurt a swan, of course, it's against the rules and would send that dread missile, a Wrong Message, to the young. Gavin solved it by dribbling a tablespoonful of curried baked beans on to the swan's back. Enough to cheer the bitten child – not enough to hurt the swan but enough to annoy the hell out of it. Very satisfying.

The first time we had a sunny week on Dick and Mary's boat with our two little boys, it was idyllic. The second time it was a rainy fortnight with bigger boys; we spent a good deal of time playing bad-tempered poker below decks. On one occasion we moored in the lock cut, where the current is faster than in the main river; Jake tried to hunt for 'fishy-wishies' with a plastic bucket insecurely tied to a rope, and it was whisked away downstream. Whether we were crosser at the loss of the bucket or at the winsome phrase 'fishy-wishies' I don't know, but it was a pretty sour picnic we had on the bank; and passing the tray of lunch things back on board, we let a knife fall into the river.

We were appalled, as everything on board was part of a carefully matched set. But the knife had probably stuck in the mud of the steep bank . . . 'Why don't I get down and try and find it with my feet?' I suggested.

'Oh don't be ridiculous,' said Gavin crossly.

But I did: I got into a swimsuit, lowered myself down the ladder and got the knife up with my prehensile toes. That's the kind of triumph you remember.

Not triumphant at all, alas, was the matter of the mattress. There was a slight leak in the roof, which had wetted the vast mattress that was shaped to fill the whole bow area of the boat where Gavin and I slept. In the wide reach below Lechlade the sun came out; there was a fine drying wind, so I put the mattress on the deck to dry.

And of course it blew into the river. We spent the rest of the week trying to get it dry, sleeping on it anyway because we had to, and desperately worried because we knew Dick and Mary were taking the boat out for a week the day after we got back. But Mary, typically, got it dry with a smile by putting it in a hot summer house – and all was well.

Later, much later, we got our own boat; but I doubt if we would have thought of it if it hadn't been for Dick and Mary.

Gavin, through the sixties, had gone on working for the *Sunday Times*, until he felt he wasn't getting enough time for his books. His second, *The Most Dangerous Game* (published in 1963), was written after we went to Finland to research it; it's one of my own favourites and would, I think, have made a splendid film. But it was *Midnight Plus One* (1965), without aeroplanes, centring on a car journey across Europe, that nearly got made into one (it's recently been reprinted in a Classic Crime series). Then back to flying for *Shooting Script* (I thought up that title), followed by *Venus with Pistol* (1969), because he wanted to try writing a first-person character he didn't think was particularly sympathetic.

Around this time Gavin was taken over, as it were, by Booker Brothers: it was a device cooked up on the golf course by Ian Fleming and Booker's head Jock Campbell, that Booker should buy an author's output – or some of it – and pay him a salary. Gavin was one of the early ones, in 1966, and for a while it seemed a good idea. But without the wolf at the door he didn't seem to feel the need to keep at it quite so determinedly.

It was about now that Gavin began to cook and delivered his celebrated axiom: 'If you know you've always got plenty of it, you've just run out of it.' I wasn't always there to cook his lunch and he wasn't going to eat kids' food with the help. It was not long before he'd worked his way up from baked beans with a dash of chilli to grinding his own spices and saying you had to call it a pimento not a pepper – we had such arguments about this that it became known as The Vegetable that Dare Not Speak Its Name. He much preferred elaborate, time-consuming food – Chinese, curries, Mexican – anything that at some stage needed days of preparation. He decided to recreate Boston Baked Beans, for example, and also went through a dreadful pickling phase; dreadful because pickling, apparently, has a rigid timetable, so that you have to do a certain thing after exactly a certain number of days, even if one of them is Christmas Day – and one year it actually was. So the house was filled not with the enticing smell of roasting bird or even cheapo scent from nasally challenged friends but the disgusting scent of boiling vinegar.

'If you're cooking,' explained Gavin, 'you are Doing Good. No one can say you ought to be doing something else – like writing.' He had discovered, in other words, a particularly good form of what Donald Carroll, writer and editor, calls Work Avoidance Schemes. Without these no writer can be expected to get through the day – there's a limit, after all, to the number of footling telephone calls, cups of unwanted coffee and cutting of toenails that can go on, no matter how stuck is your plot. Even journalists can suffer from it: I once said, after a busy morning: 'I've done the wash, cleaned up the bulbs, rung your sister and tidied up the spare room.' Gavin, perceptively, replied: 'What ought you to have been doing?'

Maybe I didn't even know. It was about this time that things became distinctly tricky at the *Observer*. George Seddon was easily the most inventive editor around, but it's fair to say that the men who ran the serious side of the paper – or so they would have classified it – had no idea of what he was about, and decided that they ought to go back to a conventional women's editor (probably under pressure from the same blinkered ad men who had tried, when I was still doing fashion and highly popular with readers, to get me sacked because I didn't feature posh enough clothes).

So we started trawling for a women's editor, and finally Suzanne Puddefoot was settled upon (an old girlfriend of Gavin's, incidentally); but both George and I had thought very highly of a runner-up: the glamorous lass from TV, Linda Blandford, and kept in touch with her. And when Suzanne became ill shortly before she could take over, a solution was dreamed up consisting of George, me and Linda running the pages together.

'It won't work,' Gavin said.

'But we all like and admire each other so much!' I said.

'It won't work because divided command doesn't work,' said Gavin. He was proved dead right.

The most obvious problem was that George and I would agree on things before five o'clock; I would go home, and then he and Linda would hit some snag and everything would have to be changed, so in the morning I had the hassle of working it all out without the satisfaction of seeing things done as I wanted. The mere fact that Linda and I were not necessarily in the office at the right moment was one trouble, but there was also, you could say, a general lack of direction. Linda realised this quite quickly and moved out to edit 'Pendennis', working directly for David Astor, but I stayed involved longer – and regretted it; editing wasn't my forte and it didn't fit well with life at home.

Gavin thought I was doing too much; I began to think he wasn't working hard enough. We had several blazing rows about his not doing any work, apparently just writing to someone called Frank Hardman, a retired electrical engineer with whom he had struck up a correspondence. On one occasion the row got to the point where Gavin said 'Get fucked!' and I said 'But not by you!' and stormed off to the spare room to sleep – the only time I did (well, no, of course not the *only* time, but the only time from anger – the others were for unmemorable things like snoring or coughing).

But he and Frank had the last laugh: they wrote a script together for a film that actually got made. It was about – or supposed to be about – space travel when it had got to the beat-up-old-Dakota stage of grubby reality. They brought in Gavin's old friend Martin Davison, who knew something about science, and they sold *Moon Zero 2* for a surprising amount of money. The script was good, but the film, Gavin always thought, was terrible. The people who made it were dazzled by Kubrick's *2001* and couldn't resist trying to make it glossy and improbably perfect, the exact opposite of what the authors had intended; all the gritty realism was gone. When my hairdresser told me he was going out to Elstree to try the green wigs he'd made on the girls in the film, I should have feared the worst.

After that Gavin wrote *Blame the Dead*, set partly in Norway (his hero read in his guidebook about 'their morals, mountains, prices. All seemed high'); and then in 1975 *Judas Country* using the trips to the Middle East as background. *Judas* was in the same vein as his earlier books, but the tone was harsher, the wisecracks seemed more contrived (though one of his obituarists thought it his best book ever). Gavin was plainly discontented and ready for something different.

He tried one or two feature film ventures, but none actually made it; then he started TV scripts, but without too much result there either. One concerned an Army major, Harry Maxim, seconded to Whitehall to keep an eye on something dodgy; after a few months Gavin took me out to the Rossetti pub in Ordnance Hill – we tended to adjourn to a pub for any Really Important Conversation – sat me down and said: 'I want to do Maxim as a book.' I played devil's advocate: wouldn't it be too slick, too superficial, too telly? No, said Gavin, it would not. And in 1980 it became one of his absolutely best books ever, as *The Secret Servant*.

While Gavin was writing proper books, I started to write minibooks, sea-horses compared to his great sharks. It started with an article on behaviour for the *Observer* colour magazine; Methuen urged me to expand it, and it became *Whitehorn's Social Survival*. It was all about how you deal with a dropped brick; how you should behave when you stay with other people; how to get your guests to go when you're dropping with tiredness; how to avoid being classed as a persona non-starter by being a wet – (who always expects other people to ask them to do things) – or a snake (charming, but an evil gossip), or a social bulldozer who never stops talking. Not exactly etiquette – it was about behaviour. On the cover was a picture of me exhibiting a trick that Jeanette Norelle had taught me when we worked at the charm school: how you can leave a hand free for shaking hands while still holding a plate, a glass, a handbag – and a cigarette. You can almost tell when any picture was taken or movie made according to whether there's a cigarette in it or not; combining a fag with a drink and a plate of food didn't seem odd in 1968.

The book tackled hitherto unmentionable problems like realising you are about to make a rude smell or need to be sick, what to do if your knicker elastic fails, and the inadvisability of putting the used matches back in the box or scratching your ears at table. It had, I recall, a disastrous effect on my own social life, because people expected me to be expert in all the things I recommended. They were particularly good at passing me thing after thing in the hope that I would end up dropping the lot. And it was when the original article first appeared that I had the unenviable experience of sitting in an aeroplane behind a man who was reading it while I was desperately trying to stop my baby rubbing his shining bald head with a rusk.

It became the start of a series of 'Survival' mini-books, none longer than fifteen thousand words (there were collections of my articles before and later, but I didn't have to write anything extra for those). We had *How to Survive in Hospital*, in which I maintained that the perfect patient has the bladder of a camel, has only one illness at a time and does not call the nurses 'girl'. *How to Survive in the Kitchen* aimed mainly at helpless males suddenly confronted with a proper kitchen and three starving children, rather than the old bedsitter audience.

Then there was *How to Survive Children*, written from the view point of making their battered parents' lives easier and advising on how to fend off the patronising advice of the Jewish mother type – not necessarily Jewish, of course – who runs the house and her life entirely for the (supposed) benefit of the children; or exposing the professional father – usually an educationalist – who makes you feel a moral reptile if you don't read to your child for an hour at night, but has understandably taken refuge from his own brood in the arms of another woman – any fool can be a good parent one day a week. I think I gave a good deal of sensible pro-child advice in it, but it was illustrated with wickedly anti-child pictures by Bill Belcher. The purpose of children's parties was to remind you that there were children worse than your own, it also asserted, that parenthood is not what you ought to do, it's what you can stand.

Through all this, the column kept going. I remarked on how comfortable you feel with old machines if you know how to make them work, and suggested that much the same applies to people: 'Look at the savagery of early married rows; at that stage imperfections in one's mate are intolerable . . . later you just shrug; he – like the clock – only works on his side.' When I suggested that doing Christmas at the last minute was OK – 'Not only is it not too late . . . it is quite possibly too early', for this I was rebuked by the orderly Cyril Ray. But a reader wrote later to say that the phrase had inspired him to recontact an old love, and they were now happily together.

I spat at men who disparaged women in business, recalling a

pert salesman on a train who kindly explained that management consisted of getting people to do things and women were useless at that – so much for Aspasia and Lady Gregory and Diane de Poitiers, not to mention Marcia Williams, I thought. And I asked, testily, 'Did Metternich ever break off at the Congress of Vienna to persuade the Spanish Ambassador he wanted a ginger kitten, or Palmerston ever have to hurry home from the Foreign Office because the builder was expected hourly? I doubt it.'

The article Gavin most approved of, I think, was one defining the difference between A-work, which everyone understands, and B-work. A-work is actually hitting the sheet metal or the typewriter keys, cutting into cloth or patients; everyone understands that bakers must knead bread, cops grab robbers or farmers reach their sensitive experienced hands towards the overflowing udders of cows to adjust the milking machinery.

But no one understands anyone else's B-work. It includes lawyers leaning against one another's desks recalling the case of Rex v. Blackett; gardeners walking to the other end of the row to see if that was where they left the dibber. It is saying, 'I'll have a word with him', it's filling in the form, it's the site foreman saying to the contractor, 'It says here two by four, do you really mean three and seven-eighths, or what?' B-work is just as necessary, and needs to be better understood.

These were mostly serious pieces – well, fairly serious. But when they were collected in *Sunday Best* in 1976, we allowed ourselves some games, such as 'The Seven Ages of Scepticism':

If you eat up your carrots you'll be able to see in the dark.
Oh go on, tell me, I won't breathe a word.
We can't have a mature relationship if you won't.

Rinso banishes washday blues.

Poor Henry, his first wife was so unspeakably neurotic.

It's lovely, big grounds, only forty inmates, you'll love it.

Goodness, you'll be as right as rain in a day or two.

MONEY

The last of the mini-books was *How to Survive Your Money Problems*. ('Whatever you do, keep an eye on it, and if you don't understand it, don't do it'). The one and only typescript of this one was taken by mistake from the pub where my secretary was having a drink on the way home. The person who took it then disappeared untraceably into hospital – we got it back eventually, though, and our nerves did recover. There was a certain irony in my telling the world all about money; but then journalists are always supposed to be able to find out about things they don't know – another case of starting where the reader is, rather than being the great expert.

Our long and confused relationship with money began even before we were married, when we more or less pooled our money on our European journey. It was even suggested we only got married because we couldn't sort out the cash. We fairly soon wound up with a joint account, because when we had three – his, mine and the joint, into which we both were supposed to pay – one or other of us, usually Gavin, would forget and then say, 'Oh well, I'll pay the rent then', and the muddle got to be too much trouble. During the sixties we seemed to have a lot of it: Gavin often sold the film rights to his books, and prices of everything were lower in relation to journalists' salaries. But it didn't stop us having rows about it: Gavin thought I was extravagant. (My brother once said: 'Kath behaves as if money doesn't exist' – I sank to my knees and begged him not to say that in front of Gavin.) I worried that we had no life insurance, which Gavin resented because he thought it meant after-his-death money, though I meant an old age pension; and he worried that we didn't save.

But in the early seventies we made a move which had unintended consequences. I wanted us to have educational insurance to pay for the boys' school fees; we were advised instead to go in for a ten-year plan, where we invested the money and were to borrow against it. But then came the oil crisis, and things changed; ultimately the sky-high rise in interest rates ensured that we couldn't afford to borrow at all, and we were distinctly hard up for some years. At the original interview with the insurance broker who arranged all this, I said I supposed I'd better start paying my full national insurance stamp (not just the married woman's plus the 'accident' bit, presumably to be paid out if my fingers got stuck in the typewriter). 'Well, if you're so pessimistic,' he sneered. And damn right, I was: I did pay my stamp, and a bit of extra voluntary contribution as well, and now it means something like a hundred a week extra. So there.

More interesting than the ups and downs of our fortunes, though, are people's attitudes to money. Gavin and I came from totally different backgrounds in this respect. My parents were good about keeping accounts and so on – they had to be, they were far too hard up to be anything else. But we were educated on overdrafts. Gavin's father, who at sixteen joined the firm – Chalmers Impey – that he retired from at sixty-seven, prided himself on never having been in debt, never having had an overdraft – but he never went abroad, either. Both couples ended up with a freehold house, a car, such holidays as they wanted to take: identical outcomes from entirely different standpoints. My father was one of the few people I've come across who was absolutely not interested in money. He had a friend who was a Lloyd's underwriter who enjoyed seeing what money he could make; this my father found incomprehensible. He was like Captain Aubrey in Patrick O'Brian's *HMS Surprise* who, when he had had a deeply boring morning with a supplier in Malta, commented: 'But what can you expect of a man who sits and thinks about nothing but money all day?'

But it is the Gray attitude to money that I really value. To my mother's family, money was money: it never meant anything else. It didn't mean power, or that having it proved you were better than the next man, or being poor made you any worse – a useful attitude for hard-up teachers and ministers of the Church of Scotland, of course – and money could pass around the family with a minimum of hang-ups. My aunt Margaret helped her niece Elspeth start her gift shop with a lump sum; I could finance a break for Margaret when I happened to be flush. The pounds carried absolutely no overtones of obligation or improvidence or superiority.

The time came when the ten-year plan was due to mature; suddenly we had some money again and it was no longer a disaster if Bernard had broken his tooth-correcting plate or the income tax was worse than we feared. Of course a freelance's attitude to money is always going to be a bit more nervous than that of the salary earner. I used to tease Gavin that when the book he was writing was going well, we were rich, and when his plot was stuck we would perish in the workhouse, irrespective of what the bank statement actually said. But that was unfair. Money in the bank, if he saw no more coming in, was, understandably, no reassurance; in the end we kept far too much in the current account simply because it made him feel better.

But when I came to take my pension from the *Observer* – long before I stopped working for it – I received a rude eye-opener to my own supposedly admirable attitude to money. I was offered the usual choice between a bigger lump sum and a smaller pension, or a larger annuity and a smaller lump sum. My accountant said: 'Take the bigger lump sum, we can do interesting things with it.' So I said that was what I wanted. But I woke the next morning with a cold stone in my stomach: it was the wrong decision. I had to write and say no, sorry, not the lump sum, but the steady pension that would come in no matter what; I could not buy a boat with it which would then sink, or put it into a son's venture which would fail. And I realised that my carefree attitude to money had not, after all, been based on having a soul and mind above such things, but on having a safe and steady salary.

I suppose I've made some silly or improvident financial decisions in my time; but the only ones I remember and regret concern the boys. One was when Jake was quite a small boy, and had very carefully managed to buy a present for each of his people with his pocket money – all except for something like 70p. I was terribly impressed, thought he'd done marvellously, and offered to make up the difference. It was clear from his reaction that such an absolutely crass offer spoiled everything; that time, I was able to retrieve the situation and simply offer to advance him his next pocket money – a very different matter.

A DISQUIETING JOURNEY

Gavin and I often travelled separately for work, but one trip we made together in the seventies was to Israel, laid on by Lajos Lederer, an Anglo-Hungarian who worked for the *Observer*.

Gavin, quite untypically, finished *Blame the Dead* one hour before the car came to take us to the airport, and he was in a state of collapse when we got on the plane – only to find that we'd struck the middle of Passover and the flight was dry (this was before I had sworn never, ever, to travel, attend a conference, turn up to speak at a girls' school or go on a demo without carrying supplies of Scotch and chocolate – and in the case of a demo, aspirin and sandwiches too).

We had an interesting time in Israel; we stayed in the writer Lynne Reid Banks' dwelling on a kibbutz. I had Bruno Bettelheim's book *Children of the Dream* with me, which, to my mind, giant though he was supposed to be, got much of it spectacularly wrong, convinced as he was that only unadulterated parental care was any good. He would make an accurate and valid observation, but then follow it with an explanation entirely unsupported by what he'd actually seen. The one I remember concerned the children that he described going cheerfully back to the children's house after their two hours' uninterrupted time with their parents: they must be cheerful, he said, because they'd sadly given up hope long ago of ever staying at home. In fact the kibbutz was the most child-orientated place I've ever been – and the only place where I have ever been reproached for being so selfish as to have only two children. It is far from clear to me that the little Portnoys who get the full blast of maternal attention are actually better off than the cheerful kibbutzniks – and how many kids in Britain and America get two hours *uninterrupted* time every day with their folks?

In Israel we saw the shattering Yad Mordechai museum; we tootled briefly – too briefly – around Jerusalem; and at one point I was to interview a female politician. While I was talking to her, Gavin was talking to her husband, an academic scientist. He came away white-faced: 'My God,' he said, 'they've got the atom bomb; and these are the people who at Masada committed mass suicide rather than submit to the enemy.' It seems incredible that they put the hapless Mordechai Vanunu in prison for years and years for saying something which even Gavin, who was not a scientist, could deduce from a casual conversation years earlier.

Gavin contrived somehow to get to Beirut, via Cyprus, on a ticket that was actually an Israeli freebie, and wrote in *Judas Country* about the peacefulness of the place a few months before it all blew up. He said that wherever he went, there always seemed to be trouble afterwards – Beirut, the Dominican Republic – 'The Foreign Office ought to pay me to stay away.' When he started to write the books set in 1913, at the start of the Secret Service, he said at least it couldn't happen there . . . but then Sarajevo was in the news again.

LUCK

I yawn, that I may not sneer, when someone, usually a bit smug and fairly successful, says: 'I don't believe in luck' or 'I make my own luck', meaning 'I can claim credit for everything – clever me.' I don't say that what happens to people doesn't have a cause – but who is at the receiving end of any particular cause is, surely, a matter of luck and little else. Maybe it sounds better to call it good fortune.

Brian Inglis didn't even believe in *bad* luck, which I find even less believable: if you were ill, according to him, it was always because there was some inner problem or imbalance, something in your head that was being bodily manifested. You could say, 'What about epidemics?' or 'What about a workman dropping his hammer off a ladder and on to your head?'

He would then discuss what mental problem caused the work-man to fumble his hammer, which hardly seemed to me the point. But I have to admit that knowing that if you called in sick he would not say: 'What's wrong?' but 'What are you wor-ried about?' did ensure that his little workforce stayed remarkably healthy.

I have, on the whole, very good luck: starting with having low blood pressure, a good memory and an ability to sleep for ten minutes and rise refreshed; while those with worse luck have high blood pressure, poor memories and, if they snooze, snooze the whole afternoon. Gavin thought he had good luck in doing his National Service just when the Korean war was on, so he was trained to fly aeroplanes instead of simply greas-ing their inner parts; but in his writing life, though he had huge successes, he also had some very bad luck indeed. Listen to this.

Steve McQueen wanted to play Harvey in *Midnight Plus One* and MGM were buying it so that he could – but Steve McQueen dropped dead before he could do it.

A book of Gavin's was on the *Sunday Times* bestseller list – the one and only week when they printed the previous week's list by mistake.

In 1984 the BBC made a three-part television dramatisation of *The Secret Servant*; it was to go out in February; then some crisis at the BBC caused them to pull it back to December; nine million people watched it, but there wasn't a copy of the book in the shops.

A second series was eagerly planned by Charles Dance, who played Maxim, and the brilliant producer Alastair Reid, and the Beeb seemed keen. But then the man who was mas-terminding it fell foul of his bosses and was fired; and as Gavin bitterly put it, 'They burned down his huts, his goats, his wives and his scripts', and it never happened. I rest my case.

He and I both, though, belonged to what I can see, looking back, was a lucky generation. The war was over, and as we grew up things were gradually getting better all round. Our university fees were hugely helped by the state; we enjoyed the NHS during the days when it seemed marvellous; when we came to the stage of wanting a job, there were plenty around, and if you were fired there was always another one; ultimately we had excellent pensions. Compared to today, or what people had to go through before the war, I suppose we were lucky indeed.

JOHN, MY BROTHER

I had spent my childhood being envious of my brother John, and much of my twenties too; we were probably never as close as some brothers and sisters are, simply because he was away at boarding-school to begin with and in the RAF during my teens. But once I was no longer trying to catch up with his life, as it were, we got along fine. He spent most of his working life with the Confederation of British Industry – which started out as the Federation of British Industries (until, in the words of a scornful Frenchman, they just added the *con*). In the fifties he had married Josephine Plummer, who was at that time deputy head of *Children's Hour* at the BBC. She was somewhat stand-offish with us to start with, but we softened her eventually and grew to be very fond of her. When I had my second and worst miscarriage, in fact, she was the only visitor I wanted (she turned up not just with smoked salmon, but brown bread, butter, pepper and a lemon).

But gradually, over the years, Jo became more and more of a manic depressive, and wouldn't consider any treatment for it; this was because she was convinced that her sister had been driven over the edge mentally by the drugs she'd been given for, I think, cancer. John for a long time suffered and covered up – until at a conference in Cambridge he met Marion; and after a year he left Jo to marry her.

This was a shattering blow to our monogamous family, and it took us a long time to come to terms with it. Edith, who enraged me by writing immediately to John saying: 'If she makes you happy I love her already', also said later, to me: 'I don't think that young man has the slightest idea what this has done to his father.' But it has to be said that Marion became a very good wife indeed for John. She was of German origin, her family having come to England before the war; she had gone from her banker father's household in Potsdam, where there were footmen in white gloves, to almost a refugee status, and had made the best of it. She was highly artistic, later became an excellent sculptor and saw John through some very tricky times.

By the end of the seventies he was coming unstuck from the CBI, though he had other jobs later – notably with Eli Lilly, the drug company. This was run from Indiana by an uncomprehending set of Americans, who seemed to think that if John, as Corporate Affairs Director, had done his job properly, no one would have noticed that the drug Opren was killing old ladies. John had a couple of breakdowns caused by drink, and Marion ultimately got him off the hard stuff. Apparently she took him to one or two Alcoholics Anonymous meetings, and he loathed them so much he said: 'If I promise never to touch another drop as long as I live, will you let me off going to these ghastly meetings?' And so it was. They ultimately moved to Sussex where they had an idyllic dozen years – they were married for nearly thirty – before John died in 2003.

AN UNEASY TIME

But at the start of the decade, all that was to come; we were preoccupied with our own tangles. Gavin increasingly felt that I was neglecting things; maybe I was, but there was bags of help, with Trude, Mrs Ross, mother's helps and so on. Gavin began to think someone had to be in the house, even when the children were elsewhere; when *Blame the Dead* came out in 1972, Peter Preston interviewed him for the *Guardian*, describing him 'pacing his Chalk Farm cage', and charmingly headed the article 'Blame the Living'.

We had a stupendous row when I lost the lovely ring Gavin had given me for our tenth wedding anniversary; losing things, being scatty, rushing out and leaving other people to pick up the pieces or wait in for the delivery or take the messages – all these were the things that most irritated Gavin about me. Once I was given a flight back from Cumberland in – what a treat! – someone's private plane; but I left my glasses in it, and Gavin was the one who had to stay in till they arrived by messenger; he was understandably furious. He said I was always back twenty minutes later than I said, and he got fed up with fielding my phone calls. And even more fed up if he'd said I'd be back at 5.30 and they rang at 5.35 and I wasn't; he said he felt a fool.

When I and George and Linda were editing the women's page together, I *was* in the office too much; but I fairly soon gave up doing even half time there and came back to mend my fences at home. Arguably, I was still doing far too much – but the things that came up were so often irresistible. I would be asked to go on a TV programme, or a committee – I was on the Cambridge women's appointments board for a bit. I went to New Zealand to make a speech on their eightieth anniversary of women getting the vote and came back via the Philippines to see Lali, my friend from Cornell days. And I was part of a twelve-person delegation to a conference in Helsinki on cultural policies in Europe. It was a pretty footling affair. Interminable chat was conducted through simultaneous translation; much was made of how technology was the future and would change everything, though at no time were there not at least three delegates having trouble with their headphones.

But I was glad to visit Finland again, and that was where I met Willy Wright, then the top civil servant in the Ministry of Arts, which he regarded as a degrading demotion from being Number Two at the Ministry of Defence. Gavin once asked him what were the salt mines, as it were, for civil servants out of favour: 'Oh, the LSE ministries,' he said, – 'Health, Education, that sort of thing.' But, pressed, he could recall even worse – an occasion when some hapless chap, who had got Attlee and his wife in white tie and medals to the river entrance of the Savoy on the wrong evening, was rewarded with three consecutive postings to unhealthy African embassies.

Willy was not just a civil servant but a scientist and a scholar; long after his retirement he was given an honorary degree by Uppsala University for his work on ammonites. Once when Gavin and I and the boys were staying with him and his wife in Dorset, he picked up a bit of stone and charted its history first through Jurassic geology, then to the Beaker folk, the Romans, ending up in the seventeenth-century Civil War. I didn't – don't – know anybody else who knew *all* of that. I found him fascinating. To begin with he would take me to lunch at the Athenaeum in the dismal little basement room where ladies were grudgingly permitted to feed. After a few months I said: 'Willy, we can't go on meeting like this.'

He blanched: 'What do you mean?'

'We've got to go somewhere where the food's better.'

As this was an uneasy time for me, and Willy felt that he was coming to the end of his career without having got to the very top, we cheered each other up a lot. I suppose if we'd been that sort of people it would have been an affair, but we weren't so it wasn't; it was a highly enriching *amitié amoureuse*.

BRITISH AIRPORTS

I had been on various do-gooding committees, but it was not till 1972 that I was offered a serious public job; I was asked to go on the board of the British Airports Authority. Airports in the seventies seem as remote now as Biggin Hill and the Wright brothers; when I joined the board, the BAA was still a nationalised industry with all the attitudes of that: caution before flair, indifference to marketing. I was classed as the statutory consumer, not token woman, but it came to much the same thing. My name had apparently come up through the normal channels from the Department of Trade and Industry, which pleased me very much – not just a women's thing, then. Only years later did I discover that the 'normal channels' had in fact been Janet Cohen, then a DTI civil servant, who later became a banker and a novelist and a founder member of the London arm of the International Women's Forum, and a friend.

Being on a board was exciting and fun; there were visits to airports; you were treated with deference – I'd never been treated so politely. The chairman was Nigel Foulkes, a man of Cromwellian bent; he decided, for example, that we shouldn't be offered a full bar before our lunches, but just sherry. I loathe sherry and thought this was stupid and brought my own gin and tonic – which once misfired, literally, all over the sofa.

That wasn't the only mistake I made at the BAA; one of the worst was totally failing to appreciate the difference in culture between Fleet Street and the ordinary business world. Foulkes had a highly intelligent secretary who knew me from the *Observer* and had been delighted when I was appointed. On a magazine or a newspaper, secretaries are often shared – they cheerily help everyone – it's all pretty informal except at the very top. So when I realised that the minister was coming to visit us, and my tights had a ladder right up the leg, it didn't seem odd to me to ask her to send someone out for some fresh ones; but she was outraged and the story went right round the office. I realised that a great chill had set in; I asked Nigel if he knew why, and he took me out to lunch to explain the clash of cultures and exactly how office hierarchies worked.

There were other somewhat tricky social dilemmas: at a formal dinner of the board, did I go out with the women, or sit tight as a board member? I decided that as it was a social occasion I'd go with the women, who had just been buttered up with the usual speech about how wonderful they were and how the chaps, who had also been told they were marvellous, couldn't have done it without them. As the women rose to go, Gavin half rose out of his seat: 'What about me?' he said with a grin. 'Aren't I wonderful?'

Only years later did I learn of a much uglier instance of the same dilemma, in a far more important context. Geoffrey Johnson-Smith, at that time in charge of coordinating government information, went to a meeting in Brussels with

Barbara Hosking, who was then his private secretary – that's to say, she was the one who actually had the briefing on everything he was going to negotiate. But she was expected to leave a high-level dinner with the ambassadors' wives, and she reluctantly did – only to hear, as she left: 'Do move up gentlemen – now we can get down to business.' So she made her way back through the service door, shoving the waiters aside. The diplomats looked outraged – 'This will be *talked about*' – but Geoffrey said no, she must stay. Which was, of course, to his credit. But he shouldn't have let her be excluded in the first place, and nowadays she certainly wouldn't be.

Foulkes later went to the Civil Aviation Authority, where Gavin had many dealings with him when he was on the Air Transport Users Council. If he is remembered for nothing else, he should be admired for the formulation of Foulkes Law of Random Results: 'In parenthood (as in business, politics and war) the correlation between the efforts of the people in charge and the results – dazzling or disastrous – appears negligible.'

Was I any use on the BAA board? The woman who doesn't mind putting the question that none of the men wish to demean themselves by asking is always some use (you can see the male brows clearing as the answer is explained). I suppose I did a certain amount to remind the board of the needs of women with pushchairs and so forth; I must have done, because Norman Payne, the managing director, said angrily once: 'Why do you think all travellers are women with babies and people in wheelchairs?' To which I retorted: 'Why do *you* think the only passengers who matter are the ones with nothing but a briefcase?'

I did, however, contribute one thing. When they were building the new Edinburgh airport, Robin McLellan fussed a great deal to make sure that escalators were put in; they were still reeling from this when I asked about lifts. Yes, they said, there was one. In, I think, Departures. 'And what about the other way?' Kindly, as to a backward child, they explained that when a lift went *up*, it also came *down*, so that was all right.

'It comes down in *Arrivals?*'

They put in another.

DRINK

'It was no secret that Gavin liked a drink, and the one after that,' said Bernard in his memorial address. He did. And so did I. I can't write honestly about us without bringing it in, for it coloured a great deal of our lives. Gavin had drunk fairly heavily in the sixties, but he had a very hard head and it didn't particularly matter. When things turned more doubtful in the seventies – when he was less clear about what book he should be writing and the scripts weren't really coming off – he began to drink more. He stopped dead on at least one occasion, though, when he was ill with a ghastly pain in the leg – due not only to drinking but to smoking pipe and cigar tobacco, which he did for what he thought were health reasons. The neurologist knocked him off all drink and all tobacco for a time; he went back to drinking fairly soon, but not to cigarettes till the end of the decade. Then he compromised by smoking long, thin, mild Mores, and woe betide if we ran out of them. I'm still finding them even now in shoes and kitchen jars where I squirrelled them away.

Gavin got understandably fed up, when he wasn't drinking, with those who made a great fuss about his smoking while they knocked back their second Scotch: 'There can't be anything in passive smoking,' he would say, 'or you lot would be as relaxed and well adjusted as we are.'

The drinking reached a pitch at the end of the seventies, when he was switching to his Maxim books. When they were published they were a great success, but they were different from his earlier books and he was desperately on edge until he knew how the first one would be received. He turned in the manuscript of *The Secret Servant* and we went up to Scotland as usual for three weeks. When we came back, there was nothing from Michael Sissons, his agent; Gavin waited three days and then rang him up: 'Oh, he's just gone on holiday taking your MS with him,' said his secretary blithely – heralding one of the worst fortnights of my life, and the only time Gavin ever hit me. I hit him back. On the shins. With the dustpan brush with which I was sweeping up sugar *he'd* spilt. I hit Gavin twice – the other time he was driving down Queensway and accused me of being a bad mother.

KEEPING THE SHOW ON THE ROAD

In the second half of the decade we had great holidays in Scotland and there were always bright patches; but life was somewhat fraught. We were fairly hard up, there was Gavin's drinking and I was leading an unbelievably rushed life, with the *Observer* and the children and all. I even did the garden, up to a point, Gavin's view of gardening being that he thought it very selfish of a man to have a garden larger than his wife could handle. My parents once asked if he wanted something for the garden for his birthday. 'Yes,' he said. 'Six bags of concrete.'

In 1977, for example, I was sitting on final selection boards for the Civil Service and on the BBC's committee on the social effects of television, and doing an extra, shorter column for the *Observer*'s overseas service, 'Servob'; I went to China as part of Mrs Thatcher's press pack – a very different China from now – and only Ann Leslie had that newfangled wonder, a credit card. I also lectured my way round America for the Foreign Office for three weeks – 'Yesterday's men, tomorrow's women: helping the blokes to cope' – making what became four of my closest friends ever in St Louis. The letters I wrote to my mother that year make me feel tired even to read them. Here's a typical extract:

Came back from Corfu on Jubilee Day . . . next day in the office putting the pages together, writing my own column in the evening, more of the same the next day. On Friday I had eleven people to dinner, which was all the old *Spectator* gang, and arranged about last January because that's as long as it takes to get the more booked-up and far-flung ones together; as well as doing their dinner I lunched with Thea Porter to interview her . . . next day we went over to June and George [Grun] for their local celebrations because Jake had expressed sadness that we weren't doing anything for the Jubilee, though they'd been very anti-Jubilee the week before.

Next day we had two of our favourite Americans, Anthony and Linda Lewis, to lunch so that had to be cooked and so forth. Next day I was in the office again and lunching at the National Enterprise Board, finishing a Servob column in the evening . . . Thursday I got the pages away, went to Bush House to do a broadcast, finished my letters, met the others at the cinema . . . Then boarded the night sleeper to Darlington where I wanted to interview the girl at the centre of the closed shop row – turned out she used to be one of my babysitters, we had breakfast together, then I took train to Leeds where I was interviewing someone . . . then on to the Metropole where I was chairing a thing on Electoral Reform which was really why I was up there in the first place, then on to another night sleeper home – oh, I forgot to say I also did a TV short in Leeds in between. Then we packed Jake off to his history weekend in the country – he had to be at school by 8.15 – and we went up the hill to the Medawars who were taking us to Lords . . .

GROWING PAINS: BERNARD AND JAKE

At least during this time the boys were increasingly leading, as teenagers do, their own lives, Bernard at University College School and Jake at Westminster. Bernard has never been one to fit in easily, and his jealousy of Jake remained, but at least when they weren't in the same school the situation improved. Bernard started to write, did well in several subjects, got decent O-levels. At one point he got into a rather questionable group – Gavin, perhaps naively, thought this was like the jazz band of his own schooldays, but it was noisier and more suspect than that. I suppose they probably experimented with drugs, since one of the boys he admired got himself into a drug-induced psychosis which wasn't cured. After O-levels, though, deep discontents set in. Bernard simply couldn't see the point of what was required of him; it didn't seem to relate to the real world, or any issues in it. He decided he wanted to be a carpenter – and maybe a writer – and the school, which didn't have facilities for that, arranged for him to go for a day or two a week to the London College of Furniture.

We thought the problem was solved, but Bernard was desolate that he couldn't leave school there and then. He remained increasingly alienated from the whole thing, and in 1981, in what would have been the January before his A-levels, he refused point blank to go back. He got a job, initially in a Job Centre, which must have been a fairly unrewarding experience, but he did there meet his first serious girlfriend. At one point he worked for Jean Denton (later Baroness Denton of Wakefield) at Herondrive, the car leasing business, until he scraped one of her cars on the slip road leading to the M40 – the black mark was there for years.

But by the time he was twenty, he'd had enough, and wanted to get into the media; through Jeremy Isaacs he got a job editing TV films, which, interspersed with writing, has been his work ever since. Interrupted, though, by such things as motorcycling round Romania and America, scuba-diving in Belize and driving around Turkey with Donald Carroll, helping him with a travel book.

Which makes him sound a bit flaky, yet Bernard is pure gold, solid as rock. If you were in a jam you wouldn't wonder if he'd come and help, you'd *know* he would. He is a devoted father, an interesting writer and has married a really remarkable girl, Nancy Borrett – a violinist, now a music therapist, and fun with it. Bernard just has a tricky temperament, combined with his father's stubbornness. Jake once compared them both to limpets: you try and shift them, they become totally immovable. In Gavin's case it took the form, for example, of never ever letting his agent or publisher hurry him in any way – his books took the time they took, and that was that.

Nancy, who had been married before, had a charming

one-year-old, Megan, when they got together, and later they had Ruby – who was far more difficult than Megan as a toddler. One day I said: 'Oh Bernard she's *just* like you – so contrary.'

'Why, was I difficult?' he asked with surprise.

'You *always* did the opposite of what you were told!'

'Oh, I must tell Nancy – she thinks Ruby's like that because she's bringing her up all wrong' (Ruby being so different, I suppose, from the douce Megan).

But when I told this to my aunt Margaret, she said: 'But what about you?'

'Why, was I tiresome?' I said, astonished.

'You were *impossible*!'

Jake did well at the highly competitive Hall and easily got into Westminster. He didn't always see eye to eye with it, though: he disliked the team spirit, and indeed the cricket master, so much that he gave up cricket and instigated base-ball – well, softball – which they still play. Though, being Jake, when called back once to fill a gap in a house cricket team, he made fifty anyway.

Jake was extremely bright, notably at maths and physics; but he miscalculated the amount of work he had to do, and failed to get good enough A-levels to take up his place at Sussex – I only learned from him several months ago that he had been taught the wrong syllabus in maths for one whole year. He persuaded himself and us that he should go to a polytechnic to study electronics; but it was a very thin experience, with none of the surrounding culture or fun of a university, and he gave up after a year and got a job – a change which he only told us about six weeks after he'd been leaving every morning for the job, not his classes.

So much for the golden springboard of a classy education.

ALAN WHITEHORN

When my father Alan Whitehorn died in 1980, the letters poured in from pupils he hadn't seen for half a century, and there was an obituary in *The Times* (which I gather, to my satisfaction, annoyed one of his more pompous friends who didn't think schoolmasters should get them). One was from a man who had left the Foreign Office, where he was doing well: my father was the only person who didn't assume he must have blotted his copybook, but understood that he wanted a different life. Another was from a man brought up in a family of Plymouth Brethren, who hardly dared to think what his life would have been like if Alan hadn't 'prised his closed mind open' – which was one of the things my father thought was most important. One illustration of this I only learned about from a speech given at his memorial service, and it concerned his response to the Oxford Union voting in the 1930s that 'This House would not fight for King and Country'. As I mentioned earlier, Alan had been a conscientious objector in the First World War, but Mill Hill was fairly military. What he did was to go round his class and ask each one what he thought – and then make him write an essay putting the *opposite* point of view.

He used to make his sixth-form boys – he was always at his best with the older, brighter ones – learn a piece of poetry every night: Greek one term, Latin the next and English the last. They all protested and wailed, of course, but blessed him for it later. One, indeed, who was aide-de-camp to whoever was running the Mediterranean basin at the end of the war, fetched up in Eleuthera, and was made to stand in the middle of that marvellously acoustic theatre reciting Sophocles' *Antigone* while his boss in the back row heard every word perfectly.

People aren't supposed to learn things by heart these days, which I think is absurd, considering how easily small children, especially, do it; and if you don't give them poetry, they learn advertising jingles. I've always been pretty good at it; in fact, I came across a list of some 160 poems I once knew by heart (it's down to about eighty now). I don't see how anyone gets through traffic jams, committees and air travel without having some such thing in their heads.

My father thought he was teaching two languages, two literatures, two civilisations. I was surprised how insistent he was on the importance of the language side, but he said that, before you translate anything, you have to work out what you're really trying to say – 'You can't *waffle* in Latin,' said he. ('No? What about the Catholic Church?' said I. – 'Oh, well . . .') And he made the dead language a bit more fun than usual by, for instance, expressing the gerundive attraction in terms of 'Archie' and 'Priscilla', who got it together at the bottom of the page; and instead of sentences to translate such as 'It is pleasant in summer to swim in the sea' and 'Old men are wiser than young men', setting the boys: 'It is pleasant in summer to chase old men into the sea.' What I didn't realise, until I took him to Greece in the early seventies and got a taste of his teaching myself, was how extremely good he was at putting what he had to teach them in language schoolboys would understand. I remember him describing a battle where the Greek general Epaminondas had gone against the traditional move of putting his strong right wing against the enemy's strong right wing by putting his strong right wing against their weak left wing, and wiped it out – 'So Epaminondas's rabbits never had to bat at all.'

He had once, amazingly, thought of becoming a missionary, but became a total sceptic instead. In the event, he didn't have a funeral, because his wish to leave his body to medicine was fulfilled. After a year, though, a hospital chaplain wrote and invited John to contribute £100 to the cost of a service for all those whose bodies had gone for science; John wrote back that such would be in direct contravention of his father's will, but they could have the state funeral benefit – about £37, I think.

He had an eye for the ladies, Alan, though how far it ever went I don't know – I daresay I've deliberately avoided know-ing. My mother thought jealousy a demeaning and unlikable emotion, rather wished he'd sown some wild oats before they married; and on one occasion, when he was plainly smitten with Molly our nanny – in effect, more than a nanny – my mother asked if he wanted to leave; but he had no intention of doing that, and they remained a devotedly attached couple for fifty-seven years. My mother told me after he died that, during the confused and difficult days at the beginning of the war, Alan started a flirtation with one of the young matrons. Edie said: 'Alan, with all this, and the war, and John going to be sent to fight, I *can't stand* you having another flutter.' 'And he stopped,' she told me, 'just like that.'

When he retired from Marlborough, he and Edie went to live in Lilley in Hertfordshire and he was persuaded by his friend and old pupil Francis Cammaerts to teach Latin to young boys at Stevenage School, of which Cammaerts was the head. And about that time he started to have appalling endogenous depressions. Of course we cute little psychologists said it was because he didn't like the job – and he didn't; teach-ing reluctant twelve-year-olds a language they saw no use for was a totally different business from teaching a few clever boys civilisation. But the cause lay elsewhere. 'It runs in the family,' said my cousin Jean Sawers. 'They have these depressions in old age.' She, poor creature, had had them as a girl, in the days when you were likely to be told just to shut up and pray harder – which may well have been why she became a mental nurse. In the end his depressions were controlled, as they can so often be nowadays, by the right drug. He left Stevenage and went to teach a tiny but bright class at Berkhamsted School, where his predecessor at Marlborough, Garnons Williams, was head. He also drove over to Cambridge to do tutoring at Trinity Hall. He loved that – as a schoolmaster, not a don, he had retained a rosy view of Cambridge, and it was a golden time. My boys loved going to them; Edith and Bernard particularly had an incredibly strong bond, and when we told Bernard they were going to move, he was shattered: 'I always felt I had a wall at my back,' he said, 'and now I'm fighting 180 degrees.'

It had to come to an end. Alan had his first stroke in the spring of 1980; Jack Gallagher died about the same time. I had to dig out John, suffering badly from bronchitis, to hold the fort with our parents while I went to Jack's funeral in Cambridge. Alan was ill, Jack was dead; John and Gavin were up to their waists in whisky; I have never felt lonelier in my life. But my mother was, as ever, stalwart.

We finally moved them to Hampstead in 1980, when their doctor advised against their staying on in Lilley; but my father scarcely survived it. Edie hung on valiantly for another two years, but died in her sleep in 1982, while on a visit to Marlborough. And once we'd got over the first sorrow we were glad that she had: for the two things lip-reading depends on are good eyesight and fast reactions – neither of which could have been counted on for very much longer, and without the lip-reading she'd have been wretched. It's over twenty years now since she died, but somehow she doesn't seem any further from me now than she did, say, a couple of years after her death. If you've had a wonderful mother the memories are good ones and her comfort doesn't go away. After a few years we organised a memorial to her and my father: the Woodland Trust let us dedicate some Scotch pine woodlands near Carrbridge in Speyside; the plaque says: 'These trees stand in memory of Alan and Edith Whitehorn who loved the Highlands.'

For several years I would dream that my mother wasn't dead really, and we were giving her back her things; I never dreamed like that about my father. But they are odd things, dreams.

'You're dreaming you're flying?' said Gavin's friend Martin once, who was into psychology. 'Hmmm – that means you're thinking of sex.'

'Look, mate,' said Gavin, 'I am trying to learn to fly *aeroplanes*. When I'm thinking of sex I *know* I'm thinking of sex, for heaven's sake.'

Gavin's dreams got duller, he said, as life went on; he would dream that he had searched every known shop for a modelling part or a widget; next day he would think, I've tried everywhere – where can I look next? And then, Hold on – no I didn't, that was a *dream*. He complained loudly about this: 'I ought to be dreaming about naked houris, and I'm dreaming about DIY parts!'

He had pretty alarming nightmares, though: he would sometimes be thrashing wildly around, trying to speak or scream; the dream would have been about a man with a gun, a ferocious animal – real danger. My nightmares are quite different. Except for one vertiginous one that occasionally recurs, they are entirely social: people are coming to dinner, it is eight o'clock and I haven't even bought the food – in spite of the fact that, in reality, dinner parties are probably the most organised thing

I do. It reminds me of Bernard Levin, who never missed a deadline in his life, dreaming that he had missed one – and then woke and realised he should have been giving breakfast to his goddaughter. Dreams tell you something, no doubt, or try to, but they are absolutely lousy messengers.

JURY SERVICE

By the end of the seventies there seemed to be too many tricky cross-winds: Gavin was changing the sort of books he wrote and had taken an age about it; my father had given up most of his teaching and it was making him morose; Jack Gallagher was, we realised later, heading into his last illness; Bernard was growing out of being happy at school. I was in the middle of an ill-fated attempt to write about women and trade unions, and my mother was ill at the exact moment that I was put on jury service.

I got myself into an absurd moral tangle even before we started to try the case. When we were being sworn in, the clerk said: 'You're all Church of England, I suppose.' To anyone brought up in a nonconformist atmosphere this is a red rag to a bull – at least, it was to this cow. 'No,' I said, 'I wish to affirm.' Panic: I didn't know how you did it, and any true Quaker would, of course. However, they had a card for that, so it was OK – until the judge asked: 'Are they all sworn in?' and was told 'No, one affirmed', and I was asked why. 'Society of Friends,' I mumbled. He nodded.

But here's the thing. Why do Quakers affirm? Because their word is as good as their bond, they don't *ever* tell lies. And I had just told one, in saying I was a Quaker. There seemed nothing for it but to become one, and I did get hold of some literature; but I can't say I've ever exactly joined, though I do go to Meeting from time to time.

The case concerned a receiver of stolen goods, who had already admitted to most of it, and his wife – and the degree to which she did or did not know what was going on. The defence was exercising its rights in the matter of jury selection by admitting any young woman, who would presumably sympathise with the wife, or older man, who might be charmed by the defendant, while excluding all the presumably less sympathetic, beady-eyed, middle-aged women. So I didn't expect to get through – but I did. Why? One of the other jurors overheard the defence say, 'It's all right, she's reading *New Society*.'

We were an odd band because there was another journalist, there was a teacher, a social worker and a cousin of the convicted murderer Hanratty – so altogether not really the random sample of a cross-section of society that a jury is supposed to be. The case took a long time, and we got to know each other pretty well; I don't think I'm breaking the law when I say that though we finally returned a guilty verdict on the wife, there was a great reluctance among some to convict anybody of anything, only to be overcome by realising that it wouldn't benefit the wife at all to have to go through another trial.

What we all loathed was the way the lawyers smiled at each other and licked their fat lips whenever either made a 'good point'. I wasn't wild about the judge's perception of modern life, either. A stash of the loot was found under a bed; the defence was that the man was about to leave his wife and he'd packed it all up to go – including her wedding ring. 'But surely a wife wears her wedding ring all the time?' Well, I do, my mother did; but this was 1979 – plenty of women didn't follow such a rigid pattern. There was a certain black humour in the fact that though the entire defence had rested on the husband saying he was leaving his wife, which was why there was a stack of jewellery under the bed ready to go, the social worker's plea for a light sentence rested on the fact that they were such a loving couple. We all felt that maybe the husband did deserve punishment, maybe the wife did, but we were quite sure all the lawyers should be sent down for ten years.

We took our leave of each other, we took our per diem, but we all felt as if it was in some sense blood money. It wasn't a cheerful experience, but it made me feel more strongly than ever that juries are essential. Chesterton said in his essay 'The Twelve Men' that it was not that the legal people 'were wicked (some of them are good) or stupid (some of them are quite intelligent), it is simply that they have got used to it; they see only their own workplace, they see the usual man in the usual place'; so you must have people from outside who see it as 'a terrible business to mark a man out for the vengeance of men'.

PART 8

CRUISING ALONG

SIMPKIN *AND THE RIVER*

By 1981 we had agreed we would get a boat, we'd worked out what it would cost; then we did the sums and realised, sickeningly, that we couldn't after all afford it. We'd been expecting to have our summer holiday on it, but instead we blundered about the house feeling awful; Gavin was reproaching himself for not being a millionaire, I was reproaching myself for not having put us into austerity mode so that we could have afforded it. 'Do you think we're too old to be happy again?' said Gavin morosely – on the brink of the single thing, I think, that made us the happiest ever.

But eventually we were ready: we ordered in October 1981 a Norman 20, a bright little boat twenty feet long, with a cockpit and a saloon that turned into one almighty double bed when you slotted its table into the sides. We called it *Simpkin*. It was to be delivered in February to the yard where we were to moor it, near Reading. I spent the whole winter planning it down to the last knife and saucepan; everything had to do two jobs. Gavin wrote to his father:

'Kath is like a kitten learning to swim in cream, making Lists of Things To Take Aboard The Boat, and Lists Of Things For Gavin And Bernard To Make For The Boat, and Meals I Shall Cook On My Boat, and People I Wouldn't Let Near My Boat Not Even If They Crawled 100 Miles Across Hot Cinders To Plead With Me. For her, it's a childhood dream come true. I haven't seen her so bobbish for ages.'

And in February we took delivery of it. I had yearned so long that I thought of course it must be spring by now; it wasn't; but we went out anyway, and it snowed.

'You have a boat!' people would say, impressed. 'Where do you moor it?' – expecting the Bahamas or Cowes at least. Their faces rather fell when you said 'Reading'. But it was a river boat first and last. Theoretically it slept four people, but in practice they had to be small and tough and we rarely had the boys overnight once they'd learned the ropes. They both became extremely good at steering and ropes and everything else from the very first, and preferred to take the boat out with their own friends; I imagine they slept in heaps like puppies.

Your whole view of life changed once you were on the river. I would spend the morning scrubbing the deck and be beaming with pride by lunchtime; if I'd been cleaning the floor at home I'd be in a pig of a temper. Gavin was endlessly happy putting up a new shelf for a camera or an ashtray, figuring out some-where extra to store things.

'What happens when you've finished all you can do on the boat?' I asked.

'That day will never come.'

I can't say we never had rows, or the sour little spats you get when one or both of you are worried about something else; but they didn't last. We also had a row at least once a season because I felt that Gavin was doing all the interesting boat things while I, apart from scrubbing the deck, was mostly doing the washing-up and emptying – eternally – the Portapotti. But about the third year I suddenly thought halfway through: We're having our boat row! and laughed – which of course stops a good row in its tracks.

I did do the knots on the fenders and such – Gavin admitted that when he had to do one, he would check that no one was looking and go down into the cabin to consult the tea-towel on which knots were displayed. It didn't always help when I did get Gavin to do a chore or two, either. At the end of one long annual trek, I won the argument about who should take the trash to the huge containers kept at the boatyard; fine. But I had put all the clothes of mine that needed washing – which was most of them – in a black plastic bag, and he unwittingly took that too. Fortunately the dustman hadn't been and I could drive down from London the next day and collect them.

Whatever we were worried about in London seemed to evaporate on the boat; in the days before mobiles and laptops, you were in another world, you were completely cut off – especially above Oxford. Downstream of Oxford the road and the railway criss-cross with the river, and you're never very far from them, or from towns and villages. Above Oxford the rail and road are at the edges of the valley, you're back in the Middle Ages and alone in the world (we used to take an evil pleasure in hearing confident youths in the hire boats ask the lock-keeper where they could get a pint and some bread, and being told 'Over those fields a mile away').

Jeering at the hire boats was only a minor pleasure of the river, but it had its marvellous moments. Gavin's favourite was an occasion when an ineptly handled hire boat lost a child overboard just outside a lock: the man at the wheel immediately dived in after it, leaving the boat totally adrift and not turning off the engine – which is the one thing you *must* do – it's the propellers that are the real danger. His wife, distraught, ran along the boat, crying – for help? – for the lock-keeper? – for a rope? No – 'Someone put on a kettle to make a cup of tea!' We gathered the child was fished out of the water OK.

The boat shared one characteristic with a country cottage: whatever you thought you'd brought was actually in London, and when you wanted something in London it had probably been left behind on the boat. But things are easier to lose on a boat, just because there are so many places to tuck things away. Once we were going to have Parma ham and melon for supper; we ended up having just ham, because I'd left the melon in London, I thought. The next morning, I found it under my mattress: no longer the soccer-ball shape of a cantaloupe but more a rugger ball. 'Do you think,' said Gavin, remembering the princess who couldn't sleep for a pea under seven mattresses, 'that you are *not* of the blood royal?'

Simpkin was canal width, and we had a canal licence, because we had dreams – at least I did – of exploring the whole canal network. So eventually we ventured up the Duke's Cut into the Oxford Canal.

It was dreadful. Not only did we have to work the locks by hand, but there were little bridges that you had to hold up while the boat went under; there was only about half an inch clearance for the boat at each side, so Gavin had to steer while I hung on grimly to this huge piece of wood, knowing it could crack down on the boat and break the cabin top. When we moored, just for a bit, because it was pouring with rain, we were knocked off our moorings by an iron-sided barge fifty feet long: we were canal width, yes, but not canal strength.

Finally we reached the place we could moor for the night –
in a row with six or seven other boats. You were surrounded by
people, so you had to shut the boat up if you went on shore.
On the river, you moor between two alder bushes and a willow
on a wide, curving bank and you think you are alone in the
world. In the morning when sixteen exhausted pricks stumble
on to the bank to relieve themselves, they realise they have
been surrounded by other boats all night, but these haven't
impinged at all. Here, though, on the canal, we might as well
have been in a shopping mall for all the real privacy. Of course
I know there are desolate stretches on canals, too, but how
many days away were they?

Gavin was exhausted. I told him to go up to the pub while
I buttoned up the boat, and when I joined him he was sitting
like something out of Zola's *L'Assommoir*, head in hands, gazing
sightlessly into his pint.

'It's . . . not quite what we thought,' I ventured after a while.

'No, it's not.' He went back to staring gloomily into his
beer.

Long pause. 'Maybe . . . I wonder . . . I mean, do you think
we should go back to the river?'

Gavin clutched my arm. 'Oh Kath I'm so glad, I was afraid
you'd say we had to keep trying longer.'

So the next morning we made our way back to Duke's Cut;
and it stopped raining, and a shaft of sunlight fell on the bank,
where there were some goats; goats of a nutty brown colour
with long silky hair . . . 'Nature at its tamest,' sighed Gavin
happily. And when we finally got a bigger boat, it was too wide
for the canals anyway.

We kept a log on the boat, and I seem to have recorded in
enormous detail things that are of no interest: what we ate, for
example, or, for practical reasons, crucially, exact amounts of

petrol relative to distance travelled (our second, bigger boat was diesel, much easier to come by on the river). These entries provide yet another proof of the shaky nature of memory. I suppose where the boat's concerned I have a sundial memory, I 'record only the sunny hours'; but leafing through the boat book I'm amazed how often it seems to have rained. Every now and then, too, it says: 'Kath fell in' – and I know I did every now and then, though usually only up to my knees or waist while mooring. But there's only one incident I can actually remember. It was below the Rose Revived inn, at a favourite mooring that got to be called Eel Mooring because a fisherman caught an *immense* eel there once, and we were the only people around to be shown it.

But before the eel, it was a good bathing place, and one day when we had Geoffrey and Elspeth Howe on board, Elspeth and I swam happily for a long time. (Geoffrey still has a framed copy of the photograph he took of us which he calls 'The Water Babies'; I have thought of hiring a burglar to get in and smash it, but he's still officially protected against the IRA.) We dropped them back at the Rose Revived, and as we went downstream again I was moving along the deck to jump with a mooring rope – and fell in so deeply that there was green weed on the top of my sunhat.

Apparently one of the struts that held up the hood had got twisted out of shape, and it was sticking out where I didn't expect it and knocked me into the water. I hit my leg on a cleat on the way down; then, stupidly, decided to be a Brave Girl about the resultant wound, and simply put sticking plaster on it. So by the time I took it into Eynsham to a doctor it was too late for the stitches it should have had. It was a crater that had to heal from beneath, which takes forever, especially as it was on the shin, where there is very little blood supply.

In London I took it to my GP, John Barlow, who said the key to its healing was to keep it up: 'I am sure the meetings you go to won't mind,' he said.

'The only meeting I have this month is the British Medical Association,' I replied, and sat the whole meeting with my bandaged leg on a chair, feeling for once I had the moral edge on everyone.

The boys often took the boat out, and were enjoined to keep the log too. So we have an account of Jake and Kym on their honeymoon being asked to rescue a fishing-rod which a distraught woman said a swan had stolen off her husband – which they did; or a wry comment: 'Paula was not the best of crew but probably not *quite* the worst' – that was Jake; or Bernard describing an invasion by cows as if he was a nineteenth-century explorer beset by savage African wildlife; or writing: 'B. in indulgent contemplative mood out of bed 11-ish, considered Life and The World. Concluded that Life is short and The World round. And this from a man without A-levels. Not bad, eh?'

I longed to spend a whole summer on the boat, and in 1983 I had a sabbatical from the *Observer* and it seemed possible. It wasn't such a good idea for Gavin, though, who had brought his typewriter with him and was trying hard to finish a book. We managed to manoeuvre the car up and down alongside the river and I would sometimes vamoose for the day rather than stick around being disliked; by the end, though, we were old shipmates again and entirely accustomed to the restrictions of our tiny craft.

I was so in love with *Simpkin* that I could hardly bear the idea of a different boat; only when I realised that for six years poor Gavin had had to kneel down to pee did I finally give in and we got *Theodora*, named after Gavin's best aunt, twenty-six and a half feet long (the boat, not the aunt). With a fridge! Hot water! A real stove with an oven! It really was more comfortable. I was aware that at some illogical level I had not realised that the *river* would stay the same.

I loved bathing in the Thames when the weather was right. Gavin never bathed, and he never went for walks – 'I'll stay and see that no one steals the boat,' he would say (which meant that when I and friends would roll out to Hampstead Heath to walk off a heavy Sunday lunch he would say, 'I'll stay and see that no one steals the house'). I walked, a lot; mostly along the flat, because that's where rivers go; but below Eynsham Lock you can climb a steep bank, and I'd look down and see the boat and Gavin in it, and think: 'There is all my happiness.'

The river was ours. We totally owned it, we knew the moorings, the locks – which one had a slimy set of steps, which one had a lay-by too far away to see the lock-keeper, which one had the sign 'DO NOT TRUST CAT' – the cat would apparently wait till the boaters were preoccupied with mooring and nip on board to steal their steak. We were – at least we felt we were – totally alone; we could read in the cockpit on a summer evening till nearly ten. For me the distant cooling towers at Didcot, industrial to some, hold treasured erotic memories; the light fading on the quiet water, a bird settling in a distant tree; watching the moon come up and knowing there were days and days of peace to come . . . we had never been happier.

By 1982 there had been another health scare, and Gavin was scarcely drinking at all – the inscription he wrote to me in the second Maxim novel, *The Conduct of Major Maxim*, promised 'improved conduct from me'.

But gradually it built up again. When we went to France on

holiday in 1985 I was slightly worried, but during that month he was only drinking wine – of which we had a small barrel in the top-floor terrace room in La Colle-sur-Loup where we were staying. (We had stayed with a friend, Cecilia Gillie, in Mirabeau on our drive down, and she'd had this barrel filled from something which looked like a petrol pump; she also set us up with enough garlic to suffocate a platoon of vampires and we never got the car to smell right again.) And it was in 1985 that I sat in a café in Antibes and reflected that Bernard had at last got a media job; Jake (we thought) was headed for Sussex; they'd just moved my column to an immensely prestigious place, Gavin's books were doing well and he didn't seem to be drinking at all heavily. Everything I wanted when I first came here has come true, I thought. I didn't have the wit to say, like Napoleon's mother at his coronation, '*tant qu'il dure*' – 'while it lasts'. But I should have done. There was much to follow.

RECTOR OF ST ANDREWS

Soon after my mother died, in 1983, I found myself, to my and everyone else's surprise, Rector of St Andrews University. The rector of a Scottish university is an odd hybrid: you're elected by the students and supposed to be their champion – but you actually chair the 'Court', the governing body of the university. I became Rector more or less by default, with none of the traditionally noisy campaigning, as the only nominee whose supporters managed to get a name in on time: 'Whitehorn elected unopposed!!' was the horrified headline in the student newspaper. So I had to work pretty hard to justify my existence.

Being Rector is a bit like getting married: glossy ceremony to start with, the hard slog later. For the inauguration I came in by boat (my predecessor, Tim Brooke-Taylor, had come in by helicopter). The quay was lined with cheering students in their red gowns – it was one of the most moving moments of my life. Then I was dragged round the town in Kate Kennedy's Coach, pulled by muscular students.

What had won the students round was a simple thing: the first grievance they brought me was the fact that the student travel office was not empowered to sell British Rail tickets, and when the bus got to Leuchars, the nearest rail link, there was no time to buy them there. Fortunately I knew Peter Parker, who was running British Rail at the time; he thought the whole thing a great jape and arranged for the tickets to be sold as wanted. So I was, by then, really welcome. Next day I was installed and made my inaugural speech; fortunately I didn't know till afterwards that the students, in traditional Scottish style, had brought all sorts of bangers and whizzers to let off if they didn't like it. Then there was a ball. It was after that that the real job began.

To sail into a Court of distinguished lay members, academics and university officers and sit down and start chairing it, when I had only ever – and only once – chaired a roomful of ten, was a terrifying business. Mercifully I was excellently steered by the university's secretary, Martin Lowe, who briefed me on what was on the agenda and, even more importantly, on what wasn't – the plotting, the gossip – so that I knew what was what. Always before I'd been the down-table pest who cracks inappropriate jokes and makes the Chairman's a life a misery; now it was me who actually had to get things decided – and in a reasonable time

There was always a certain amount of 'creative tension'

(you don't have rows at that level) between the lay members wanting the university to be run more like a business, and the academics, always more interested in getting something exactly right than in getting anything done in the least soon. Just as you thought you'd reached agreement, some Good Committee Man would say: 'I don't want to take your time, Rector, but there's just one small point in Annexure Sixteen . . .' The Court didn't deal with the academic side: we discussed land, buildings, the latest dire missives from the University Grants Committee; student grievances. There was a running problem about a lavatory to be put up near the cliffs, and another one about coast erosion; I rather think the failure to solve the second issue ultimately took care of the first.

But apart from the Court, there was a great deal to do, and as I hadn't stopped working for the *Observer*, it all had to be fitted into four or five weekend-length visits a year. I had to make speeches at clubs, societies, meetings; listen to student complaints – I held a surgery, like an MP – anything from the food in the halls of residence to possible injustices in their courses. This is a big part of the Rector's job – at least if she's around: when Winnie Mandela was elected Rector of Edinburgh University (after me – I was the first woman Rector) she wasn't able to set foot in the place. I managed pretty well on the whole. though in one direction I failed completely. St Andrews's dominant body is the all-male Kate Kennedy Club, which is the swank home of, among others, all the English students who have failed to get into Oxbridge. They run things, they greet the spring in Kate Kennedy's Coach; until recently 'Kate' was always a man in drag. Traditionally, they have always made rather a pet of the Rector, but they left me severely alone. They had me classed –

rightly – as a feminist and they certainly weren't in favour of that.

I made some real friends, but the trouble as far as the students were concerned was that I was not studying with them or teaching them, so the exciting, expanding part of their minds was not accessible (with one exception: I found the medical students weren't getting anything on medical ethics, so I did a few seminars on the subject myself, which was far more rewarding). I could only share the students' leisure, where the age difference was, of course, most hampering.

But there was one exception: Scottish dancing. I loved it, and eventually became Vice-President of the Caledonian Club; it was mainly full not of Scots, so much as Americans and Egyptians and such, who seriously wished to learn about Scottish dancing. At the end of my last year I went to their ball, in a new dress with six inches chopped off the bottom – the Rector must *not* trip up; our party led the dance and acquitted ourselves well. After a couple of hours we moved on to a ball in a hall of residence, and came in just at the point where they'd stopped the strictly ballroom dancing and were moving on to more popular reels scorned by the Caledonian Club. We danced an eightsome, the Dashing White Sergeant and so on; then they started Strip the Willow, which is known to be the most boring dance in the entire world. But one of our party suddenly said: 'It's the same beat as Mistress Montgomery's Rant!' – one of the esoteric dances we'd learned for the Caledonian Club – so after that there was no stopping the Rector's party; we danced that instead. It was terrific. I couldn't have agreed less with Gavin's definition of it all: 'the re-enactment of the Massacre of Glenlivet to the sound of massed tomcats'.

WOMEN AT THE TOP

It was in 1983, too, that something I thought I probably shouldn't have done had some wholly excellent consequences. As part of the 'Britain Salutes New York' week, the Women's Forum of New York invited half a dozen achieving British women over as their guests. As I had got back from India only a few days before, and as my oldest American friends Sol and Elinor Glushak were staying with us in London at the time, I should really have turned down the invitation, but I couldn't resist. So I left them to Gavin; and I hate to think what I would have missed if that had been the road not taken. For this was the start of my involvement with the International Women's Forum, and from that has sprung a fair proportion of the most agreeable occasions I have ever enjoyed – dinners, conferences, jaunts – and some of my best friends ever. There were various forums, simply collections of successful women who meet to enjoy the company of other women like them-selves; to provide female connections to match the ubiquitous old boys' networks. There is no American forum, but a Boston one, a Colorado one and so on, and now the International Women's Forum has forums in twenty countries and a leader-ship foundation and so on. But this one was strictly New York's, run by Elinor Guggenheimer, the remarkable woman who had started the first one.

It was an amazing week. We were flown over free, put up at the Regency Hotel, taken to all the openings of exhibitions and such, and actually had breakfast at Tiffany's – champagne and strawberries. We also went to an AGM of the forums. When we came back, a few of us resolved to start a London Forum. Mary Baker – who is the wife of the politician Kenneth Baker, though that is not the most interesting thing about

her – had chosen the original group for the New York trip. She
was then head of the English Tourist Board, President of the
organisation Women in Management and on the board of
Thames Television, in whose boardroom the first dinner was
held. The founding four were, besides Mary and me, Heather
Brigstocke, the brilliant High Mistress of St Paul's Girls'
School in London, and Barbara Hosking, then head of information at the Independent Broadcasting Authority. Barbara,
whose father ran a milk factory in Cornwall, had risen to be
private secretary to a Cabinet minister without ever having
gained a degree; she had, however, run the office of a mine in
Kenya, among other things.

To these four was very soon added Rosalind Gilmore, who
was at that time Marketing Director for Girobank the GPO's
banking arm, though she had been in the Civil Service and
returned to it in the eighties as a highly successful building
societies commissioner.

This Gang of Five ran the forum for years. We met about
five times a year for a dinner in somebody's boardroom; no
money changed hands, there were no committees, no elec-
tions, no rules. We kept the numbers down to about thirty
(not all of whom could turn up at every dinner) so that we
could more easily have a general discussion. The people we
invited to join were all eminent in their fields: Janet Cohen,
ex-DTI, then a director of a bank (and later a thriller writer);
Anna Mann, founder of headhunters Whitbread Mann; Liz
Nelson, co-founder of advertising firm Taylor Nelson; Anne
Mueller, one of the few really senior civil servants; Prue Leith
of the cooking school, the books and the restaurant; Eileen
Cole, Director and Chairman of Unilever's research firm;
Patricia Mann of J. Walter Thompson; Elizabeth Butler Sloss,
the judge, and so on.

We deliberately left out the politicians, because Mary thought the confidentiality aspect, not to mention the seating, would make it too difficult; and we didn't invite authors and artists and other such creative people, because they would have swamped it. The idea was to have people who ran things; I think I got in mainly because of being Rector of St Andrews, where Mary had been an undergraduate. It's interesting that in 1983, given that we excluded those categories of people, plus a couple of dozen others known to be a pain in the neck, it was quite possible to point to the top hundred or so women in British life. By the end of the decade that would have been impossible – there really was a substantial upward movement of women going on.

At our early dinners, all our talk around the table was of female advancement – how we could get more women into top jobs, what the barriers were, how we'd arrived there ourselves and so on. After a while we grew bored with that, and discussed general things like education and China. It was only after two or three years, I suppose, that we trusted each other enough to talk about personal things. Eileen Cole told us about her mother, whom she supported. Steve Shirley, who founded F International to use the computer skills of women whose young children kept them away from the workplace, told us about her disabled son.

'How could you do what you've done if you had all that to cope with?' I marvelled.

'How could I have stood coping with Giles if I hadn't had something else as well?' was her answer.

I don't suppose any of us bared both breasts, so to speak; this wasn't group therapy, for heaven's sake. But we got to know a lot more about our non-work side as well as networking on jobs and plots and inside knowledge. It was only at our tenth anniversary, though, when we went round the table saying what Links – as the organisation was by then called – had meant to each of us, that one of the most startling revelations was made. There were several there – I remember particularly Sara Morrison, an executive director of GEC during its great pre-Marconi days – who had never been in the least attracted to women's groups because they saw them as preoccupied with the 'feminine' side of life (cooking, babies, clothes and so on). But this was the first time they had met a group of women *like themselves*.

BOARDS AND COMMITTEES

When the Nationwide Building Society decided it was time to admit a female element to their board, they wisely thought it was better to have two than one; then no one could accuse them of having just a token queen bee. So in 1983 they co-opted both me and Rosemary Day, who came from London Transport, and we were duly elected by a compliant member-ship. The Society had originally been the Co-op Society, and still had some charmingly folksy ways about it, such as giving company cars to non-executive directors. It was, and I'm delighted to say still is, a mutual society, so that, in theory, the margin between the savings we took in and the mortgages we paid out should have been as narrow as possible. In practice, of course, its managers, many of whom had come up through such outfits as local government and similar, tried as hard as they could to think like real businessmen and were intent on making that margin as wide as possible. In the long run it didn't make that much difference.

One of the things I got involved with was their Charities

Committee, in which most board members weren't interested; I and another board member, Michael Haines, ran it together, and it was delicious to be able to lob a few thousands at some good cause – particularly something like a minibus for sick children that could put the Nationwide name on its side. Michael was an accountant, and left when his firm was taken over by a larger one that didn't want its people sitting on other boards. But he had a great retirement lunch many years later, at which he recalled his Nationwide years. He said in his speech that he had never known a nicer set of people make more really bad decisions.

I guess he was right. The biggest bad decision was to try to take over estate agents, which we did at colossal expense. I was in favour because I naively thought we were going to be Good and never do all the horrible things that estate agents did; in practice, all we did was buy up existing ones for vast sums, which we later had to sell again. Another barmy one was amalgamating with the Anglia Building Society. The board was offered masses of convincing information about how economies of scale were to be made. A few years after the merger, when it became for a time quite hard to balance the books, it was sadly admitted that the cause of the trouble was, in fact, the merger. Let's hope they're doing better with their proposed merger with the Portman.

On that board I could display a certain useful bewilderment, as at BAA, about things I didn't understand. But one thing I came to understand very well indeed: any management worth its salt can usually bamboozle the board quite well, simply by proceeding without drawing breath from 'It's too early to decide now' to 'It's too late to change it.'

When Mary Baker was on the board of Barclays, she got all their literature rewritten so that it was unisex; I suppose I hoped I would be able somehow to promote the rise of women in Nationwide, but I can't say I did. We used to go the rounds of branches from time to time, and when I raised the matter of women as managers I was always given the standard excuses: women weren't so dedicated and anyway they couldn't move about the way rising managers had to do. It was never quite explained to my satisfaction *why* they had to move, or why it couldn't be accommodated if they preferred not to. I remember having the argument with one chap, keen to explain why one very smart woman in the branch we were about to visit hadn't been offered another possible branch, which had gone to a man. It turned out that this branch was as much as *twenty-five minutes* away from where she lived. I laughed ruefully as I told him how long it took most commuting Londoners to get to work. And I noticed that when they had a promising *male* manager whose wife had a very good job in the Patent Office, they found no difficulty in moving *him* around so that he was always within commuting range of London.

Nationwide nowadays has extremely enlightened policies – at least, according to their house magazine – about such matters as job-sharing and home working, not to mention gay marriage and career breaks. It's a very good and efficient society and still mutual, to its credit, having fought off over the years the carpetbaggers who'd be happy to destroy its special qualities for a quick buck. But the entire middle management is still male, and there's only one woman, now, on the board.

While I was learning from St Andrews and Nationwide about committees, Gavin was heavily involved with the Air Transport Users Council. I had once written that though you never meet, outside the fortunate ranks of the zoo or the nursery school, anyone who doesn't sit on a committee of some sort, from the Cabinet to the West Wittering Oyster-catchers'

Water Pollution Subcommittee, you never meet anyone who approves of them either – let alone admits to liking them; but Gavin did. He got involved with things like the design of airports and the grievances of passengers, and drew cartoons for their newsletter. But what fascinated him was the committee itself: its movements and procedures, all of which he put into the Maxim books – especially *The Conduct of Major Maxim*; I had to urge him to shorten such scenes quite as often as I had to get him to cut down on the details of guns. All this tied in excellently with his continuing fascination with aviation; long after he'd stopped putting flying scenes in his books he used for years to review books for *Pilot* magazine, and *Flight* landed regularly on the doormat. It remained his hobby, a closed book to me; as was, to him, what he regarded as mine – things medical.

MEDICAL CONNECTIONS

One way and another, I have had a lot to do with medical matters; and people have wondered why on earth, given that I've no medical training at all and was never a medical correspondent either. It all started with my being asked to join a working party in the early seventies to decide whether the world was ready to have doctors take out organs for transplanting without asking.

It was a preposterous gathering of some forty people, representing religions, viewpoints and vested interests, medics, and others who were vaguely supposed to represent the public, such as me. It was chaired by an august Scottish doctor, Sir Hector MacLennan; he wore a dark coat – maybe it wasn't actually a frock-coat, but his monocle was certainly attached to it by an impressively heavy black ribbon. Possibly a gathering of different breeds of dog, or perhaps a get-together of Trotskyists, Republicans and the Pope might have been slightly less harmonious, but I doubt it. The actual shape of the rows we had escapes me after all these years, though I remember the agonised baying of the Chief Rabbi and the ritual sneers of some of the medics. Anyway, after a few sessions the Ministry of Health had the wit to disband that group and convene another, consisting of only a dozen or so halfway sensible people, none of whom were greatly given to frothing at the mouth, and I was one of them.

We studied the matter for about two years, and finally concluded that the public simply weren't ready for anything so draconian, to the annoyance of MacLennan, who thought we had failed to do our job.

But in the course of it, I had to put up with a good deal of the obligatory denunciation of the press with which every profession warms itself up before discussing anything else; piqued by this, I wrote a column asking why on earth the medical profession didn't *use* the press instead of just raging at it. And one of its members, an extremely agreeable brain surgeon from Southampton called John Garfield, rang me up at about ten one evening to say: 'OK. I'm taking you at your word: you've got to write about the scandalously low pay that nurses get.'

Even then I knew enough to be stunned that a surgeon should be worrying about nurses, and set to work to do as he asked. It was what we called a 'Review front', the long piece at the beginning of the Review section of the *Observer*. I was just, as it were, emerging from the nursery, I put far more work into it than it really needed, and got hooked. There followed the mini-book *How to Survive in Hospital*, and somehow I became classified as a statutory patient.

This led to my being invited in 1976 to take part in a conference on 'Patient Counselling' in Holland. The patients at this impressive event seemed to consist of one man in a wheelchair, Queen Juliana and me; the rest were some four hundred doctors, mainly American, trying to figure out how to get their patients on anti-inflammatory drugs at age twenty and keep them on them for the rest of their lives. My speech was about the second one on the timetable and it made Queen Juliana laugh, so after that I had a great time enjoying myself – including going around the canals on a tourist barge with, of all people, the baby-doctor Benjamin Spock, and being taken to lunch, at 3.30 one afternoon in a Japanese hotel in Amsterdam, by Michael O'Donnell, the brilliant editor of *World Medicine*.

World Medicine was a free magazine for doctors, and it was outstandingly readable: the principle on which it was edited was that anyone who could write could write about medicine, and anyone who was a doctor could write about anything. Michael himself wrote a column at the back, and, getting bored with doing it every issue, he suggested I should write it alternately, which I did under the heading of 'Outpatient'.

It was huge fun to do, particularly as no one I knew was going to read it (especially not Gavin). And it didn't clash with the *Observer*, who would only have minded my writing for a rival newspaper. I suggested a 'Doctor Most Like His Patient' contest along the lines of 'Dog Most Like Its Owner' (for example the dermatologist – 'You scratch my back, I'll scratch yours'); I sympathised with the sewer rat who presumably consumes all the myriad pills NHS patients flush away; and suggested ethics for patients, such as keeping the doctor's confidence (not telling the neighbours his breath smells, for instance) or wasting the doctor's time by wearisome

comparisons between your condition and your mother's and
that of your Aunt Emmy who suffered something terrible; and
actually saying what is really bothering you and not discussing
the weather, your children and your slight cough, or only mentioning at the door that you feel after meals as if you've
swallowed a tomcat.

While I was writing that column, I was searching about for
subjects, and started going to the odd lecture at the Open
Section of the Royal Society of Medicine – the only part of it
you could belong to if you weren't a doctor. Somehow I got on
to the section's Council, and for three years was its President.
I stayed on the Council right into the next century, when I
finally resigned.

'Why are you resigning?' they asked.

I said: 'Well, it says here you aren't supposed to stay on for
more than ten years, however many different jobs you've been
doing.'

'How long *have* you been on then?' asked these newcomers.

'Twenty-two years,' I replied. 'I'd better go.'

But I am still a Fellow, and as the RSM is wonderfully handy
for John Lewis, Marks & Spencer and my hairdresser, I'm there
quite a lot.

Far more involving, even unto the edge of sanity, was the
Patients' Association. Dame Elizabeth Ackroyd – Betty – who
ran it, asked me and Claire Rayner to be Vice-Presidents, and
in those days I didn't know enough to run a mile from anything
offered as 'Just your name on the notepaper'. (Either that's
really what it is, in which case they do something frightful
and you're blamed for it, or you get sucked into working half
the week.) A temporary secretary who didn't know that vice-
presidents weren't asked to meetings asked me to one, and I
went – to this meeting where Betty, who was in fact dying, was

proposing to close the Association down. I got caught up in the rescue party, and spent the next ten years trying to keep it afloat. Which, more or less, we did.

I talked Rabbi Julia Neuberger into being Chairman; she promised us a year and gave us three, and was marvellous. My hope was that as she was vaguely involved with the College of Health (the patient pressure group founded by Michael Young) and also with the Medical Advisory Service (a phone helpline run by two amazing nurses more or less on their own), she might somehow weld us all together into something as strong for health as, say, Shelter is for housing. This, alas, has never happened; but through its various upheavals the Patients' Association has kept going, helped in large part by Claire Rayner as Chairman and then President.

While all this was going on I wrote several articles for the *Observer* on health subjects, and went to various cheerful conferences, again as statutory patient. I also fetched up at a conference on primary care in London, Ontario, which was interesting enough; but the most arresting part was a conversation in the bus going to the airport with a GP, who was also a professor, from Belgium. He had become worried, he said, that a large number of refugees from the Congo came to him complaining of heart trouble; but there didn't seem to be any. He had the wit to consult the university anthropologist, who said that a great deal of their worry really concerned a fear of bad magic deriving from the stormy scene from which they had fled.

The anthropologist suggested that the GP, having checked that there actually was nothing wrong, should give the next patient (1) an injection, preferably painful; (2) a serious-looking bottle of medicine; and (3) a certificate saying he was now well. This he did; and the man folded the paper carefully, and placed it over his heart – as a talisman. Ah well, to one who worked under Brian Inglis, none of this should have come as a surprise.

A TIME FOR MY FATHER'S VALUES

It was the eighties that made me appreciate my father's values; come full circle back to them, if you like.

I had been brought up to despise commercialism; I suspect that a good left-wing distaste for filthy capitalists meshed seamlessly with a slightly snobbish disdain for people in trade. Certainly during the seventies there was a good deal of complaint that whereas, in Germany, engineers and manu-facturers were honoured and well paid, in Britain you scored far higher if you weren't actually making anything. At that time I thought that my father's values had to be wrong: that professionals were, far more than they realised, drones who relied on the worker bees they despised, unfairly immune from the pressures of making ends meet. In Ogden Nash's words:

> Professional men have no cares.
> Whatever happens, they get theirs.

But then came the eighties, and Mrs Thatcher. Fair's fair: we really, badly, did need the woman. It's easy to forget how absolutely despairing we were towards the end of the seventies. The all-powerful unions constantly mucked things up with strikes and called far too many shots. Management was flaccid and feeble and seemed almost content not to be able to do much about them. And we took for granted, I suppose, the fact that we still had the best broadcasting in the world, an educational system that wasn't bad and a health service which had so far been wracked by only one or two ruinous 'reforms'. I often think that history will find it odd, given that situation, that Britain decided suddenly to model all its institutions on the thing it did *worst*.

Her reforms – or at any rate some reforms – were needed; but their legacy was sometimes dire. Everything became budget-oriented; the internal market caused as much trouble as an internal ulcer; putting the cleaning of hospitals out to the lowest-tendering companies meant that the lowly paid were not only even worse paid, but had lost the one thing that had sustained them: the feeling of belonging to a warm, useful, known environment where they were appreciated. Now they were just casual workers with no interest in the hospital or the patients. Even Hereford Cathedral was invited to draw up a business plan and asked what was their 'unit of resource', to which one cleric ventured: 'One saved soul?'

Competition was supposed to solve everything, and didn't, of course. I felt, glumly, that for the first half of my life I'd kept being told, with no evidence at all, that everything would run better if it was run publicly – that is, by the state – and that now I was spending most of the second half being told, also with no evidence at all, that everything would be run better if it was run for private profit. It was as if the whole country had stopped wanting to make money in order to do things, and began only to do things in order to make money.

I wasn't alone. Early in the nineties I wrote an article bewailing the fact that though you could disparage someone who was caring and concerned by calling them a do-gooder, mock anyone who did up their house with the word 'yuppie' and sweep any liberal or humane objections to one side by denouncing the chattering classes, we had no word for the increasing numbers of dung beetles who could think of nothing but money. I invited the readers to come up with one.

I knew I was angry myself about such people, but I didn't quite grasp the extent of the readers' fury, irritation and occasional despair until the letters started pouring in like molten lava. Teachers complained that all meetings of governors and staff centred on cash and balancing the books; education was hardly mentioned. One nurse sighed that 'some nurses believe the bean-counting nonsense and question whether particular patients are worth their bed space'. A publisher wrote: 'It is horrifying to think what accountants have done to that once noble profession.' Some of the most damning stories came from the business world itself: there was the man who wrote that he had always believed in making a profit, but had never thought that was the *only* thing that ever mattered.

We never did come up with a name that got into general currency, though there were 'ledger-louts' and 'profiterolles', 'bottom-liners' – and hence 'nappies'. I quoted John Garnett, inspiring former head of the Industrial Society (and Virginia Bottomley's father): 'It's the creation of worth, not wealth, that's important. One will follow the other.'

Perhaps we had thought the money would last for ever; perhaps we were naive about what could be done by public fiat; perhaps times move on and some such shift was inevitable. Some of the readers said we didn't need a new word – just say 'Tory'. But that wasn't it: rural Tories raged when the pensions people cut costs by paying money into bank accounts, thus pulling the rug from under a main source of income – and survival – for vital village post offices. Indeed, Old Labour and One-nation Tories have more in common with each other than either of them have with Thatcher herself or her blasted clone, Tony Blair. Both groups believe in public service, in doing things for their own sake – in my father's values, in fact.

WOMEN'S PROGRESS

By the end of the eighties it was obvious that there ought to be a much larger women's forum on the lines of the various American ones, and Jean Denton (not then a Baroness) said she would start it up. I had known Jean since she wrote to me, long before she became well known, to query something disobliging I'd said in an *Observer* article about women and machines, and she sounded so interesting I went down to interview her. She had been a round-the-world rally star, in spite of never having put hands to wheel till her twenties, and at that time was running five garages in the hinterland of Southampton. She sold Fiats, and bettered Fiat's national figures by a factor of five, simply because she realised that lots of these small cars were sold to women as the family's second car, and that it might therefore be a good idea to stop treating them as morons when they came into the garage, to listen to what they had to say about the noises under the bonnet, to send them Valentines and even put a bit of carpet down in the showroom.

However, after various other jobs Jean found herself in politics, and did an enormous amount for the advancement of women, getting them appointed to positions where others (such as Mrs Thatcher) might not have bothered. And when she was made Under-Secretary for Northern Ireland she had an amazing rapport with the women she encountered; they would sometimes demonstrate outside her office for hours, then come in for a cup of tea and a chat. She became extremely disillusioned with the Northern Ireland Office, which she saw as being just as obstructive as any of the political factions. And when the wind of power changed, she spent serious time turning over to her successor, Mo Mowlam. 'If I'd had Mo,' Jean sighed when she came back, 'we could have changed the world.'

PART 9

THE BEGINNING OF AUTUMN

BACK TO THE BOTTLE

By the summer of 1986 it was clear Gavin's drinking was back in force and I was getting increasingly desperate. But that autumn I went to Greece to take part in a conference on human ecology at Delphi, and afterwards I was sitting on the Acropolis in Athens when a young couple, happily in love, came by arm in arm and laughing. That was us, I thought; nearly thirty years ago that was us. I am *not* giving up on us.

I went and saw Dr Jack Dominian who ran the organisation One Plus One, and discussed the problem; I went to him because I admired him, and also because he was a Catholic, so I knew he wouldn't suggest splitting up. What he did suggest was that I give up drink too – which horrified me, and delayed my bringing Gavin to a consultation. Finally we came, and turned up for it a bit early; the conversation we had in the car before we went in may have been the most valuable part of the whole process. Gavin did give up for a bit, though I didn't; the idea was he should hold off until he'd finished writing *Uncle Target*, the last of the Maxim series. Which he didn't, quite; but when I found he was drinking again we had a series of rather useful rows. 'Life was very cosy at the bottom of that bottle,' he said. And maybe I was too bossy – we batted it back and forth, hashed out an agreement that he would hold it down, and we would go on a holiday on which *he* would make all the decisions, which seemed OK – and make all the bookings, too, which surprised him.

This was the summer of 1987, which was an exceptionally wet one; there were only about thirteen fine days that July in the whole summer – but those were exactly the halcyon days that we were away. We started on the boat; then drove away after the weekend – and found Gavin had left his jacket over the boat's steering-wheel with his wallet and everything else in it. We had to go back for it: oh joy, it was *so often* me who forgot things! We visited Ironbridge, we went to Lincoln – and saw a remarkable service, this being July: the cathedral was full of holly and ivy and carols – they were filming for Christmas TV. And so home, with all problems ironed out and a golden future before us.

But 1987 has stayed in my memory as the year of the false dawn. We had six weeks in America, a prolonged holiday, in the autumn, and by the end of that I realised that nothing had really changed. I had shot my one bolt: from now on it was just a case of putting up with it, surviving as best I could. We got our new boat in 1988; somehow nothing was ever really bad on the river and we spent a lot of time on it. *Uncle Target*, about which the agent had said 'It's a knock-out!', attracted little publicity, mainly because his publishers weren't doing much; Gavin didn't exactly fall into the whisky but it was a disappointing time. And as the winter wore on he was becoming ill; his figure became – his own word – 'grotesque'. The Cold War was beginning to peter out and so he had to

abandon the next Maxim halfway through. By June I had persuaded him he must have a check-up. They told him his lungs
were OK – good for such a heavy smoker – but that he had cir-
rhosis of the liver.

For a week he thought he was dying. Then our GP, John
Barlow, convinced him that it wasn't a death sentence if he
gave up utterly; and for the next thirteen years, until he died,
he never touched it – he would even spit out a liqueur chocolate if he got one by mistake.

Sometimes he said, 'I don't know how you stood it when I
was drinking', and I would say, with perfect truth, 'You were
always more Gavin than anything else.' And I was spared most
of the things which women whose husbands drink have to put
up with. He wasn't violent, never went missing, never fell into
the wrong bed, never suffered from boozer's droop, and it never
affected his work. In fact he thought his work needed it: one of
the times when I most wished I could see the entire staff of
Hodder & Stoughton revolving on a spit in the fires of Hell
was when Gavin said sadly: 'I haven't had a successful book
since I stopped drinking.' As if *that* was the trouble.

If Gavin wasn't touching a single drop, though, he was
going to notice every single drop I took – and they weren't
single, they were double, mostly. Our patterns of drinking were
quite different: when Gavin was drinking he'd start early and
keep himself gently topped up all day – which is apparently a
lot worse for the liver than binge drinking, because the liver, a
long-suffering organ with great powers of revival, never gets a
chance to recover. I was – am – much more likely to drink too
much when happy, at a party, out to dinner with friends,
though at worst I can get into fierce rows on points of ideology,
rows which would make Gavin cringe. Everyone else too, I
daresay; but mostly they'd be drinking too, so they wouldn't be

too bothered. It didn't happen all that often, but Gavin hated it; occasionally he'd berate me for it. And I realised, when it was me, just how you feel the next day when people are being sniffy about whatever you drank the night before. Miserable, shamed, that's how. Enough to drive anyone to drink.

I was into another pattern, too, in the early nineties. It was a vicious circle: I would be terribly tired, pour myself an immense gin and feel better – but worse the next day, occasioning another enormous gin come six o'clock.

At one point I said, almost weeping, 'I'm supposed to be half retired and I'm supposed to be at the top of my profession but I still work *all* the time and I'm still tired *all* the time and I still buy my shoes at Marks & Spencer!'

Gavin decided to take the last point first: 'You only buy your shoes at Marks & Spencer because you've got bunions.'

'Yes! I've got bunions too!' Boo-hoo!

Eventually I went for a check-up and they said I had mild macrocytosis, something to do with the red blood cells; the kind doctor struggled quite hard to find some explanation other than drink, failed, and I did try a bit harder to watch it – or at least to recognise the onset of the vicious circle.

The question remains: why did Gavin drink so much? We discussed it, of course, over the years; and I'm quite sure that plenty of people – possibly his parents – thought it must be the strain of being married to me. But he didn't think that; I have a card that says: 'Darling – thank you for the happiest years of my life – and particularly for the years when I didn't deserve your support, but which made all the difference.' Gavin himself never vouchsafed a firm opinion, though he did say, which is certainly the case, that once you've started for whatever reason, the drink itself becomes the reason you go on. If that's so, the fact that his hard head enabled him to go too far, once he no longer had to worry about what it cost, would have started it off. He himself thought he must have an addictive personality – once he stopped drinking he smoked even more. I sometimes wondered whether the gulf that had to be bridged between the highly moral, lovingly domestic, faithful man he was in real life, and the violent killers in whose minds he lived in his books, was somehow bridged by the drink; it's possible.

What I blame myself for, which didn't occur to me for a long time, was not realising what effect Gavin's drinking had on the boys. When Jake – who I much later learned had even gone to an Al-Anon meeting – was in Bali trying to find himself, he faxed us a long and dreadful letter reproaching us for the way we dealt with him, and life, and the drink – particularly the drink. He said we'd never tackled it 'as a family'. I imagined he meant in some sort of Californian let-it-all-hang-out group session, and responded, robustly enough, that I'd kept the show on the road and I thought that was what mattered. Besides, how did he imagine such a session would go? *With* Gavin, how would he have felt? Without him, making him feel even more left out?

But I think I missed the point: that I thought the drink had only to do with Gavin and me, that the boys were leading their own lives and weren't too affected. I did remember one occasion when Bernard was trying to discuss his A-level options and Gavin was past it, and kept saying why didn't we all just go to bed? – but that was about it. Indeed, I once innocently asked Jake why he didn't bring friends home; there was a terrible pause before he cooked up some other explanation. Thank heaven none of it stopped them loving and admiring him.

I remember talking about all this once with a married friend: she said she wouldn't have been too upset by the odd girlfriend, but couldn't have stood the drink. I said I couldn't have put up with the possibility of other women for a moment – but the drink, yes, I could. I suppose if you stay married, even joyfully married, you must have been dealt a hand that you can play. And if I was asked whether we'd have had a better life if we'd been teetotallers, I'd have to say: absolutely not. If some of the worst bits were due to drink, so were many of the best times: the highs were part of what we had, too.

GOING THE DISTANCE

How do you write about forty-five years of married life – Philip Larkin's 'joyous shot at how things ought to be'? It isn't chronological – some things crop up here, and then, ten years later, there; some things are trends or long evolutions; it's a characteristic of the state that sometimes you wake up to something only after it's been going on for years and neither of you could tell where it started. The same with children: you can document the year they went to nursery school, the year they went to camp, the year they gave up playing the violin or kicking their brother or dying their hair green. But it doesn't tell you a lot about who and how the child actually was (which is one reason those ghastly Christmas letters that tell you every success of their faceless offspring are so tedious). I know, too, that the young Gavin who started out as a journalist, doing up our first flat and dashing about on assignments, was a different man from the thoughtful writer sitting behind his desk, cooking, drinking, living in his own mind; endlessly curious about the things that interested him, poring for days over book catalogues, over the memoirs of generals, over histories of European politics. But it isn't a simple narrative, not a road with milestones – more a rugged heath with occasional sign-posts.

One factor in what happened to us was our up-and-down relationship with – I hesitate to call it fame, it wasn't that – being *known*, being recognised. Gavin once said, in our very early days: 'One day they're going to say: "That's Gavin Lyall's wife over there."' It wasn't easy for Gavin when they just said: 'That's Katharine Whitehorn.' But, being Gavin, he didn't think he ought to complain about it, and just how deeply it bothered him I don't know to this day. In the sixties, after he started to write successful books, there wasn't a problem: Gavin was selling film rights, getting awards and accolades, while I had ceased to be quite the flavour of the month once other columnists, notably Jilly Cooper, were coming to the fore.

We had rows, of course – rows about money. These only stopped in the seventies when we didn't seem to have enough financial information to have rows *with*. Rows, which never really ceased, about my doing too much outside the home. Gavin didn't mind what I did for the *Observer*, indeed insisted on it. There was never any problem about an assignment, about the column. But he resented all the extra things I was inclined to take on – a committee, a series, an involvement with a cause. After such a row, about once every half-dozen years, I would offload this committee or that, shake the thing down to an essential few, and life would be calm again – until it gradually built up once more. Gavin would complain that he was coming last in the queue, whereas all my friends thought I was absurdly concerned about his reaction to absolutely any-thing, to giving him his due. Probably, as usual, the truth was somewhere in between.

Our son Bernard, in his speech at Gavin's memorial service, said: 'Gavin married Kath over forty years ago. Any honest couple have their ups and downs and maybe there were some I wasn't aware of; but in all that time no one would have doubted the depth of his devotion to Kath, or hers to him.' The downs never included unfaithfulness, beyond the odd kiss, for either of us: the ancient Cornish motto of Margaret's school, Godolphin and Latymer, seems to me to sum it up (though I don't imagine it was talking about marriage): *Francha leale toge*, 'Free and loyal thou art.' He gave me incredible freedom; the loyalty wasn't difficult.

But can I actually claim virtue? Frankly, I doubt it. Did I ever, *really*, want to be naked in bed with anyone but Gavin? No. I knew which side my bed was buttered. But something more. Jack once said I could never expect to find someone who was both kind and intelligent – which was plainly rot because *he* was both. But there's a subtler assumption, that anyone who is rock-solid dependable must be, in some sense, a bit *too* rock-like: that you won't find anyone who inspires the most passion you can feel who is also someone who makes you feel totally secure. 'Too hot not to cool down,' says the song; 'All true love must die/Change at best into some lesser thing,' says the Yeats poem – 'Prove that I lie.'

I can't, of course; but I can say this. After Gavin died – quite a while after, I couldn't have done it sooner – I wrote an article for the *Guardian* about losing him. And I got letters from other wives, husbands too, who had lost the person they loved, who had found someone who had been absolutely the right one, whatever their difficulties, for thirty, forty, fifty years. And I wished that all the people who say it's unrealistic to think you can love someone all your life – the people who've been unlucky themselves, or lightweights wanting an excuse to move on, or the young who can't really imagine such a long future – could read those letters. In the play *Shadowlands*, about

C. S. Lewis and the love he married late in life who then died, the author William Nicholson has Lewis say: 'I find that I can live with the pain after all; the pain, now, is part of the happiness then. That's the deal.' I doubt if many of us would have wanted any other.

FINISHING THE CENTURY

The 1990s were to be our last decade together. Gavin didn't hold with dividing time into decades, rightly pointing out that it's entirely artificial, that trends flow over the edges – and certainly half of what they ascribe to the Swinging Sixties actually started halfway through the fifties. But the nineties did have a distinctive flavour for us.

At the beginning, Gavin was coming to terms with not drinking, and with the collapse of the Cold War and therefore the end of Major Maxim; he wasn't too well for a while. There was a period of confusion and misunderstandings when Ann, Gavin's mother, died, and his father went to live with Barbara and Dennis. It turned out to be a difficult arrangement, the Drinkwaters didn't think we were pulling our weight; finally Joe was installed in an Abbeyfield home and good relations were gradually restored.

The boys were living elsewhere, Jake's exit only engendered by my writing a disobliging article on 'Whatever Happened to Young Men Leaving Home?'. Bernard was working as a film editor and coping with a bad back (he'd inherited his father's height and his mother's negative attitude to exercise, a very bad combination), and frequently taking his motorbike or his scuba-diving suit to foreign parts. Jake spent his twenties alternately working in London as a software expert and, when he'd got together some money, buying the next stage of his flying training in America, finally achieving both a commercial and an instructor's licence. He adored that, but couldn't do it for long as the pay was cripplingly low – they don't have to pay instructors much because would-be airline pilots build up their hours by doing the job for peanuts. He finally got his instrument rating after working for weeks in San Antonio, living on $4 a day of which $1.40 was cigarettes. Later I realised I knew rich and friendly women in that town, but I was glad I hadn't put him on to them; for seeing just how dedicated Jake could be when it really mattered helped Gavin realise how serious he was about flying.

I had talked the *Observer* into letting me do the column only every other week; Gavin started a series of books set in 1913, the first being *Spy's Honour*; we both revelled in the larger boat; we began to go every summer to the Languedoc. And though we still had spats, even occasional real rows, there was mainly a new serenity between us.

Could we always have been like this? I wondered once; we thought about it, and decided no. The peaceful harbour is welcome after a life on the high seas; but if we'd never been out there, facing the storms and the jagged rocks, we'd just have rotted on the beach.

It wasn't until the early nineties that Gavin started taking me along on his work trips. The first one was researching *Flight from Honour*, in northern Italy; he said it was the first time that on such a trip he hadn't, at some point, fallen into a total depression in which he was convinced the whole idea of the book was a wash-out. We had a great time on that one: I loved Turin, tourist-free and attractive. Gavin, however, got far more out of Trieste, which was creepy and sinister with all sorts of dank alleys and dark corners. We were lashed by the Bora wind – 'Beware any town where the wind has a name,' said Gavin. But what suits a thriller writer is a bit different from what suits the simple holidaymaker. When we went to Turkey to research *All Honourable Men*, we hired a car in Adana to ride up into the craggy mountains where, in the book, they were building a railway and having sundry gunfights. The day we went, it rained; the mist was practically at sea level; the alleged mountains were nowhere to be seen; and when we finally came to a sodden village there was mud everywhere, Turks scuttling across between the dismal houses with sacks over their heads. 'Perfect!' exulted Gavin. 'This is just what a railwaymen's camp in 1913 would have been like!'

He had great fun writing the 1913 series – *Spy's Honour, Flight from Honour* and so on; and he also put an enormous amount of time into a fantasy – he rewrote it twice as a book and also made a TV script of it, but it was never published. It supposed that Lord Hamilton had shot Nelson ('cleaning his gun – without his *trousers?*' – 'Old naval custom'), so we'd lost the Napoleonic wars and the French had taken over London, compelling the city to take to the sewers and build up a civilisation there, with hellscrapers instead of skyscrapers. Eventually they'd dug so far down they'd got to Hell, and had to wrestle with the dilemma of whether it was ethical to use anything acquired from the devil as an energy resource; this they badly needed as the methane gas hitherto derived from French-generated sewage was running low because the French had taken to *la nouvelle cuisine*. The devil, traditionally unable to create matter, was interested in the city's consumer goods in exchange.

Once, Gavin opened the door to a couple of evangelists who asked him if he believed in the devil; Gavin eagerly tried to engage them in conversation about this, citing Thomas

Aquinas . . . the horrified girls thrust pamphlets into his hands and fled.

He also started to draw and paint more – he had, after all, seriously considered being an artist and not a writer. He began to draw our Christmas cards, always a black and white drawing involving both Christmas and cats. He'd done it before, in the sixties – there was one where all the ornaments on the tree were cats, one trying to get at the tree-top fairy, but the next one he drew had been the Three Wise Men done as Victorian savants, with side whiskers and sextants; the printer had said it was blasphemous and refused to print it, and Gavin, busy and affronted, had stopped drawing them. Now it was just a matter of going round to the local printing shop.

When he finally realised that Hodder had given up even *trying* to sell his books – though mercifully the Japanese kept on doing fine with them – and began to tire of friends and fans asking him if he was still writing, he switched to writing TV scripts. At first this seemed splendid: he sold the option on the first one right away. I remember him coming home from a celebratory lunch with the company that bought it saying, 'Oh Kath, it's so good to be admired by someone outside the family!' The script was an extremely witty comedy thriller, but it was turned down by ITV as being a bit too like *Midsomer Murders*. So the company that had bought it, Red Rooster, made him rewrite it and rewrite it. When I was given it to read six months later, they'd made him make it far *more* like *Midsomer Murders*; they'd managed to remove all the wit and subtlety, and it had completely lost its flavour.

There was no help for it but to spit in the eye of Red Rooster and start again. But nothing came of other scripts, and Gavin gradually came to regard himself as retired. I don't remember after which reverse it was that he said: 'So long as I've got you nothing can really hurt me.' He was wrong: there were illness and death to follow. But before that, there were good times still.

And bad ones. In 1996 I nearly got sued for slander, broke my ankle jumping from the boat with my glasses on, and was told the *Observer* was stopping my column. Will Hutton, the editor, assured me that I still had a great future writing bigger pieces. I believed him, but no one else did, especially not Gavin. In my view, the trouble was, in two words, Jocelyn Targett, deputy editor, who effectively ran the show. For example, I wrote a piece on a clutch of Bangladeshis in Bradford who were not even beginning to integrate. Being a racial subject, I naturally watched every word, but it ended up with the headline 'Blame the Asians', so no one I was trying to reach would have read it without fury. And when, long after I'd finally decided I couldn't stand it any longer and ended my contract, I wrote a history of women's writing in newspapers, I included one sentence about the prissiness of early women's magazines, saying that in those days we didn't have orgasms on the front page. Of course, that was the headline he chose: 'We Never Had Orgasms on the Front Page'. 'You should have known if you had orgasm or penis or vagina anywhere in the article, that would be the headline,' said Edie Reilly, my longterm assistant and friend at the *Observer*. And when, later, Targett was disappointed that he wasn't made editor (Roger Alton was, thank heaven) and a colleague reported that he was desperately upset, all I could say was '*Splendid!*'.

The last straw came in the spring of 1997, when the Features editor asked me to do a piece on nursing, which I duly set up with the aid of Christine Hancock, a friend and head of the Royal College of Nursing. The Features editor had asked for it for one Sunday, but still hadn't printed it by the next two. I said she'd better print it soon because the clinic I'd written about was moving: 'Really, Katharine, I have twenty-four freelances telling me why their piece has to go in next Sunday,' she replied. And I suddenly thought, What the *hell* am I doing waiting for this chit to deign to print my nursing piece? And that was it.

1998: A GOOD YEAR

If 1996 had been horrible, 1998 was the opposite. It was, for a start, our fortieth wedding anniversary. We had a party where Bernard, ever good at speeches, quoted Donne's 'Anniversary': 'This, no tomorrow hath, nor yesterday . . . But truly keeps his first, last, everlasting day.' It was also the year of my seventieth birthday: Gavin took me off for a romantic weekend to a hotel on Monkey Island, in the Thames, where he'd booked a suite. The next day we met Bernard, Nancy and their girls at the Beetle and Wedge, a familiar and lovely hotel, where they don't mind a bit of mess – just as well, as they were ages late, and the baby had been sick over Nancy, twice; she'd brought a cake and they put a firework in it instead of a candle. And a day or so later I had an all-women lunch: it was magic.

Then the boys both announced they were getting married that summer, and I was impelled to lose ten pounds without giving up alcohol. And we hosted an International Women's Forum conference in London; which was highly successful, in spite of the diligent and indeed infuriating efforts of the Americans, who had no concept whatever of local conditions. They had no idea, for example, that the privilege of booking the Durbar Court at the Foreign Office for a reception was no ordinary achievement, let alone getting a member who worked for Smirnoff to come up with serious vodka. And when I discovered at the last minute that our Chairman, another American resident here, had been conned by a florist into ordering cute little straw pigs and chickens with bandanas round their heads for the formal dinner – totally unsuitable for the Whitehall Banqueting Hall – I got hold of the firm Molly Blooms and asked if they could do flowers for thirty-seven tables for £20 each the day after tomorrow. They simply said: 'Yes. What colour are the tablecloths?' It was *beautiful*.

Gavin's sister Barbara and her husband Dennis had their fortieth anniversary too, which they celebrated with the entire clan on an open boat tootling round Chichester Harbour. By that time two of their three sons, Tony and Neil, were married and there was an assortment of small boys as well. The invitation said: 'Time and tide wait for no man, woman *or child*' – a wholly happy occasion.

A NEWNHAM ANNIVERSARY

That year we also had the fiftieth anniversary of women getting proper degrees in Cambridge, rather than just a certificate through the post. I actually did get my degree – I remember it vividly because when I got up from kneeling I trod into my gown like a priest in a bad pantomime. But as there were no such degrees when I came up in 1947, I was included, and keen to come to help my aunt Margaret, who was in her turn helping a frail contemporary.

That day of celebration in 1998 was a wonder. All the women were in gowns; most walked, though some were very elderly indeed and came in a bus; we processed down King's Parade, with the bells tolling and the populace cheering us on, to ceremonies in the Senate House. The services were divided into three, to accommodate the different age groups. The person who spoke for our tranche was Margaret Anstee, whose mother had been a lady's maid, who got to Newnham on scholarships in 1940 and became the first woman to head a UN delegation. I spent a lot of time with her and she showed me the tiny ground-floor room in which she had lived. On one occasion a young man had come to tea to ask her to marry him; she'd said no; he said then he wouldn't see her again, and stalked with great dignity through the door – into her clothes cupboard; it took her ten minutes to disentangle him. She and I did a BBC item together; the crass young interviewers kept trying to suggest we'd been terribly repressed In Those Days. We tried, I'm not sure successfully, to express on the contrary the marvellous sense of freedom we had experienced on getting there. It was an open gateway to the rest of our lives.

I had been delighted to get into Newnham, but I had no particular feeling for the college as such. The day of women wanting to do things as women was over – or not yet begun; the college was shabby and uninspiring because it was 1947 and it was still in wartime mode. We were told not to take more than one bath a week; I found my friend Felicity took one every day on the reasonable assumption that plenty of girls never took one at all. And while Newnham showed the shabbiness of wartime neglect, the men's colleges were grey and immemorial and in any case full of men; we related mainly to them.

But when I went back for that fiftieth anniversary I saw it differently. They had built fresher, interesting buildings, done good things to the rose garden; the undergraduates who looked after us were helpful and well turned out and intelligent; they all wore T-shirts on which were the names of distinguished ex-Newnhamites *including me*. I suddenly thought of so many new universities' premises, with their streaked concrete and the crisp packets and Coke cans rolling around the echoing vestibules and everybody slouching about in grubby jeans, and it seemed to me that, the academic aspect completely aside, Newnham these days offers an enviable experience of civilisation, one which, when I was up, we had only found in the older colleges.

There's a big debate going on – has gone on for years – as to whether Newnham should stay single-sex or whether doing so condemns it, in the public eye at least, to contain nothing but Muslims, lesbians and those with a convent mentality. I hope they do stay single-sex – and for mainly one reason. At the moment all the colleges are vying for such female academics as are around. But if you've any sense of history, you know that climate can change all too easily. Men admit women when there's a reason for doing so; but there's a powerful magnetic pull, always, that tends to make the chaps go back to preferring other chaps around them. At the moment it doesn't matter whether there's an all-women college or not. But in fifty years? It wouldn't surprise me if it turned out that by then the men's colleges, now so eager to recruit promising females, had just one or two tokens, in not very high positions.

It's no accident that the Oxford colleges had girl undergraduates long before they had an even passable number of women academics; for the male desire to have pretty girls around can often overcome their general reluctance to grant prerogatives to women. Girls saying 'Very true, Socrates' with shining eyes are a lot more acceptable than middle-aged women saying 'Just what do you mean by that?' I think it would be imprudent not to keep just one citadel that the men can't take over, and I admire Lucy Cavendish College, which is prevented by its statutes from having men until there is a fifty-fifty split between men and women in the university as a whole. Which is not about to happen any time soon.

TWO WEDDINGS

The year 1998 saw both Bernard and Jake married; and Bernard still is. Jake had a marvellously romantic wedding under the redwood trees in California. The altar consisted of tree-stumps draped with a white cloth, the groom and the father of the bride wore kilts, the bride wore ankle-length white velvet with bare feet; all stunningly romantic. But Jake and Kym hadn't as much in common as they first thought, though they were fiercely in love. And when Jake finally achieved his goal of becoming a flying instructor, and it didn't work out because the airfield was too far away and the pay too bad, and other differences arose between them, they finally split up.

Bernard's wedding was almost as unconventional, though in a Unitarian church in Hampstead. The procession up the aisle consisted of Bernard in the first suit he'd worn for ten years, Nancy in a knee-length sea-green dress and high heels, and Megan, her daughter by her earlier marriage, in ivory satin. They were followed, after a certain amount of scuffling, by the preacher, female, in a maroon dress, holding the hand of Ruby aged fourteen months, who had to be picked up during the actual taking of the vows. Of the sixty or seventy people present, at least twenty were very small children, who roamed freely around the church. It was all hilarious, but incredibly moving.

MILLENNIUM

So we came to the end of the century, sharing the millennium in Washington with Chuck and Anne Korr from St Louis and their and our good friends Tom Whitford and Charlotte Grimes. Charlotte was a journalist, now a very prestigious professor of journalism; Tom is a painter. When we first knew them they lived on a boat in Washington with a white German Shepherd dog. It was getting on a bit, this dog, and had to wear a blue nappy – very striking on a white dog. It was to their favourite riverside restaurant that we went. By that time they were living in a Winnebago, but we spent the two millennium nights in a hotel, leery of driving back perhaps through a chaos of non-working traffic lights; we were issued with a bottle of water and a torch just in case civilisation came to an abrupt end, as predicted.

The general impression afterwards has been that the idea of all computers crashing and life being totally disrupted had been a pointless scare; but I have it from Gwyneth Flower, who masterminded the British preparations, that if nothing too bad did happen it was to a large extent because firms took amazing precautions (BT had spent £600 million and Unilever £500 million on disaster prevention). Even so, there were actually some thirty-six thousand failures – Japanese ATMs, for example, were out for more than twenty-four hours – but no country wanted to admit to them.

GAVIN'S LAST MONTHS

We were creatures of the twentieth century; one way or another we welcomed the twenty-first, but changes were afoot.

We were getting too old for the boat, but had rented a marvellous little furnished cottage in Oxfordshire; and that was where we were in September 2002 when Gavin said he thought there was something wrong. He thought it might be the tiny gallstones he'd had for years (they'd decided they were too small to operate on). So off to Murray Lyon, his gastroenterologist, who set up a lot of tests and then passed him on to Professor Roger Williams, brilliant but chilly, who said there were three bumps on his liver, to be removed at six-week intervals by chemo-embolisation. Naively, we were actually relieved: they knew what was wrong, and now they were going to fix it.

Before that, though, there was the fiftieth anniversary of his passing out of the RAF at Pershore which Gavin was very keen to attend. At the fortieth, there had been a marvellous and totally spontaneous happening when they'd visited the old runway and lined up in their cars – and without any pre-arrangement at all they'd all roared off down the runway, and I'm quite sure most of them expected their cars to achieve take-off. This time it was all set up and organised: the men were to stand by their cars, flares would be lit, a plane would fly over and take a photograph from above . . . except that the mist was so thick we couldn't even see the plane; I've no idea whether it could see us.

In the afternoon of the fiftieth, some of us went into Stratford to see a play, but Gavin slept. When we got back we found the hotel plunged into darkness: there had been a power cut. The grand dinner was safe, cooked by gas, but there was no heating, and this was the end of October. OK for the chaps in their thick dinner jackets, but what about us in our flimsy dresses? I chopped my woolly tights off at the knee so I could wear them as knickers under my frock. So far so good. But then it turned out the laundry had sent back the wrong dress shirt for Gavin, one designed to have studs not buttons down the front, so I spent the last quarter of an hour crouched with my needle by the skirting-board emergency light in the corridor, desperately re-attaching the top and bottom buttons.

Still, the dinner took place as planned and Gavin enjoyed it. The next day, after more inspection, in the rain, of yet another deserted airfield (which makes a damp point-to-point seem like Disneyland, I have to say), we went back to the cottage. Gavin had had the reunion he wanted.

I was supposed to be going as a lecturer on a Saga cruise in November, but a day or two after the chemo-embolisation it was clear Gavin was feeling worse, not better. I thought, I don't care what Saga does to me, I simply can't go – and what Saga did was send me flowers of sympathy; they are like that. And I still didn't know how bad things were.

Did Gavin know that he was dying? With long hindsight, I realise he must have known in the end he wasn't going to get better. And of course when we were young and fit, we'd said certainly we'd tell each other . . . but by the time we were into his final illness, we were past having that kind of conversation at all. Now it was only about could I get more watermelon? should I bring his clothes down? maybe I could get something to help him sit up in bed . . . Gavin had told his first specialist, Murray Lyon, that he didn't want any medical information at all, so he had been passed on to Professor Williams with that instruction. It was only when I, largely at the insistence of the insurance company, saw the doctor alone that I finally realised what it was.

'What *are* these bumps?' I finally asked Williams.

'Tumours,' he said.

'How long?'

He shrugged. 'Six months perhaps.'

It was actually to be about six weeks, and no one could have wanted it to go on longer. 'Was he in awful pain?' people have asked; and the answer isn't easy: I don't think there was much actual pain as such, but discomfort to the point of real pain – a bedsore, constipation, aches, sleeplessness and weakness. (I didn't know then, and no one told me, that the temazepam he was prescribed can, if taken over a period of time, be a depressive.) Through December he was still getting up and getting dressed, and we had wall-to-wall visitors – in particular our friends the Gregos from Rome, which actually helped: helped *me*, anyway. For the first three days after I knew the score I couldn't eat or stop thinking about it, but then I had to get on with things. I could kid myself – sometimes – that he might get a bit better, that we still might have a little time together.

We had already sent out the invitations for our usual neighbours' Christmas party and went through with it, with Jonathan Grego doing the drinks and Gavin sitting with a cushion in his lap; maybe that was a mistake, but it did mean that everyone around knew what was happening. He made a marvellous job of Christmas Day, but after that, went down fast. He needed to go back into hospital; Jake came over from California. They tried a new treatment which, with hindsight, I realise was futile: Jake saw it was making things worse and we stopped it. Jake was also the one who said it was absurd to try and take Gavin across London for a last consultation, when the palliative care team had gently made it clear there wasn't long to go.

I had not been going out for a month except to buy necessary things, but on the Thursday before Gavin died I did go to a Links dinner. I went to say goodnight to Gavin; he put his hands on my pink silk jacket and said: 'You're going out.'

'Not for long.'

By then there was a night nurse from the Marie Curie, so that I could get a bit of sleep. She woke me at five: Gavin was sitting on the edge of the bed: '*Kath! Kath!* Give me a sleeping pill, *two months* I haven't slept . . .' I gave him another temazepam; he seemed to sleep. Melodie Francis, marvellous head of the palliative care team, came in the morning and gave him an injection which I suppose had morphine in it. That was the Friday. I spent it lying on the other bed (I'd moved us downstairs by then), reading one of his books; it was as if in a way he was talking to me still. Jake and I were not leaving him alone at all by then, but on Saturday afternoon Melodie was doing something to relieve his throat, so we were upstairs. That was when he went. I believe this happens quite often: it is only when the watchers at the bedside are absent for a few minutes that the dying person finally lets go.

Our doctor, John Barlow, came; and the undertakers. Bernard was there, though he had to rush home for a bit to continue desperately getting his unfinished home ready for an imminent move; but he came back to sleep the night in Gavin's study. He said it seemed to help. The undertakers asked if we wanted to come and view the body. No, absolutely not. I realise that I had increasingly felt that when Gavin did die, I would in some way get back the real Gavin. I wanted to forget this gaunt, silent, skull-like figure on the bed. And in a way that was true. There are stages of grief, and I don't believe it's the same for everyone; but part of the process of healing, for me and for one or two others I know, is the gradual fading of the memory of the awful last days, compared to the solid happiness of forty-five years.

PART 10

LEFTOVER LIFE TO LIVE

A TIME OF TRANSITION

So you soldier on. Quaker funeral, mostly silence, a few words from Bernard, a reading from Barbara, another from Jake. I broke ranks with Quaker tradition to the extent of having 'Brother James's Air' as the coffin slid away, which is an unbearable moment. Then outside, and thank heaven we live in a culture where men can sob too.

Two months later we had the memorial service in St James's, Piccadilly. Simon Brett spoke movingly about Gavin's books – their moral complexity, their expert technology, especially about aeroplanes, and how funny they were. Jake talked about his flying, and Bernard recalled him as a man – with the sort of wry humour Gavin would have appreciated. The choir sang the spiritual 'My Lord, What a Morning' to a well-filled church. Then we had a reception at the RAF Club. The boys had said they didn't want it to seem just another party, and they'd unearthed some green baize screens at the club and put up all sorts of pictures of Gavin – and one or two by Gavin, as well. It was right.

*

Gavin was only seventy when he died. 'It is an amputation,' said one of the letters I received – a good analogy. Nothing can put back what's gone, but sooner or later the person who has lost a leg learns to walk with a crutch, the woman with only one hand left somehow manages to cope, even if she feels phantom pains in the limb that's no longer there.

To begin with I went from raging misery to total numbness, which was just as well as there was so much to be done. At that stage everyone's being solicitous and kind. It was when the drama was over, and Jake had gone back to America and the grey mudflats of the future stretched endlessly ahead that the real widowhood began. The death takes longer than you might think to sink in – sink in at all levels, that is. Joan Didion wrote in *The Year of Magical Thinking* that she found it very hard to give away her husband's shoes – wouldn't he need them when . . .? I remember, too, that years ago I once commented to my old friend June Grun that a widow we knew seemed unduly bowed down still, although it was a year since her husband had died. 'Oh no,' she said sadly, 'that's when you realise it's for ever.' For a long time I thought, subconsciously, that I only had to get through all this somehow and things would return to normal. I found myself – still do, occasionally – thinking that Gavin will approve or disapprove of something I've done, and I imagine that for those who really do live in 'the sure and certain hope of the life to come' the feeling may not ever go away.

Do I so live? Not really. And I doubt it would be much comfort if I did. If there is an afterlife, which seems improbable, I can't think that Gavin would be there waiting for me: whatever his soul's journey he would have travelled on without me, and I find that thought even more lacerating than simple extinction.

But is it likely? It has always been the most tiresome thing about philosophy that it has to take its clues from the physical world – such as Socrates thinking you couldn't rely on your senses because of the way a stick looks bent if half of it is in water – and I don't think the universe really goes in for the continuation of individuals. Nothing is wasted, but it is not the same bird, the same cell, the same cloud that goes on and on. The nearest suggestion that I've come across of what might happen to everything that is not physical is in Arthur C. Clarke's *Childhood's End*, where they are all swept up at the end to be part of 'the great dance'. Or in Rupert Brooke's poem 'The Soldier', so hackneyed that no one realises any more that it's brilliant, where he writes of 'this heart, all evil shed away/A pulse in the eternal mind'. Perhaps. But all we can do, as Prof Broad said at the end of a book that my father was fond of quoting, is 'to wait and see – or, as the case may be, not see'.

So life goes on. In some ways, it stays the same: I haven't moved, I'm still working and we never did breakfast together except on holiday; breakfast, we felt, being no time for human relations. The cats have reluctantly realised that I am now all they've got and are as demanding as ever – and they are a help: they prevent the bleakness of a dark empty house. Even when there were two of us, Gavin used to talk with approval of a house being 'centrally catted'. I'm inclined, too, to say yes to any event that offers, even boring talks (some of them given by me), whereas Gavin would never go out three evenings in a row and made a serious fuss if it was even two running.

I see a fair amount of Bernard and his family: his wife Nancy, the girls, Megan and Ruby – they are great. Bernard, the awkward, wayward one, is now the one with an attractive house, a friendly and amusing family; he is writing novels and has plenty of work as a film editor for TV documentaries. Jake writes software for a living in California, where the voltage is low, which is just as well since when he can't pay the rent he works as an electrician. He has also reinvented the wheel – the RIOT wheel (Restoration of the Wheel) – a sand vehicle which has been featured on the US Discovery Channel. But as Bernard says, you never know what Jake's doing till he's done it. At least he's no longer spending the summer juggling around the fairs of Europe on stilts. We talk endlessly on the telephone, proper conversations, not just how-are-you and the weather – more, maybe, than if he lived across London.

Real friends are a godsend, and not just by being a shoulder to cry on. Even from the earliest days they can distract you or do things with you or at least pour the alcohol without which I don't see how anyone gets through this. And they don't mouth the false comforts, the usual platitudes that excoriate one so. I particularly disliked people saying, 'You'll get over it', as if it was an illness or a busted love affair. I groaned, too, when someone said: 'I know how you feel – when my brother died . . . when my aunt died . . .' I wanted to snarl: 'It isn't the same *at all*.' When my brother died, the spring after Gavin, I felt very little: maybe because John's mind had already gone, maybe because we weren't that close; but I think much more because, as it were, the grief slot was already full.

Being a widow is not helped by also being old. It's a relief, in a way, that my sagging curves no longer have an audience, but being on my own makes the prospect of being really ill and frail alarming. When I broke my wrist, there was Gavin to drive me to hospital and fasten my bra. An exceptionally well-endowed woman on his Air Transport Users Council committee sympathised with me about this: she told Gavin that when she broke a wrist, she'd had to get the janitor's wife to fasten hers. 'The janitor's wife,' mused Gavin, 'must have been a *very strong* woman.'

Losing your husband has two separate aspects: there's missing the actual man, your lover; his quirks, his kindness, his thinking. But marriage is also the water in which you swim, the land you live in: the habits, the assumptions you share about the future, about what's funny or deplorable, about the way the house is run – or should be; what Anthony Burgess called a whole civilisation, a culture, 'a shared language of grunt and touch'. You don't 'get over' the man, though you do after a year or two get over the death; but you have to learn to live in another country in which you're an unwilling refugee.

Some widows play bridge – I can't, I wept my way through a whole summer when they tried to teach me and finally gave up. Some are absorbed by their grandchildren, but I don't know which of us would dislike that more, the girls or me, agreeable though they are. I am luckier than most, I know: I don't live at the end of a muddy lane two miles from anywhere, I'm not broke and I've friends to do things with. But as Felicity Green, doyenne of journalism, put it: 'I have plenty of people to do things with – I just have no one to do nothing with.' Exactly.

Soon after the memorial service for Prue Leith's husband Rayne Kruger, she and her sons found themselves having lunch in the garden at three p.m. 'Father would never have allowed this!' said Prue lugubriously, and one of them said: 'Look, Ma, there's not much of an upside, but you might as well enjoy what there is.' There are widows who can find nothing to cheer them at all, but for most of us, after a time, there *are* a few upsides –lifelines to be grabbed at (and I don't just mean wardrobe space).

To have been in some way answerable to someone else for half a lifetime was not wretched; but to be released from that does have something to be said for it. Not having to own up when you're an hour late home because you've been inept enough to drive from Kennington to Hampstead via a road labelled A23 Brighton is, there's no denying, a relief. And I make my own decisions about money, when to get up or what colour I should paint the house – a sort of brownish grey with a turquoise door, in the end – which were apparently Lillie Langtry's racing colours.

So much depends on whether you do enjoy doing things on your own. Two and a half years after Gavin died I found myself kicking around Nice for a long afternoon and early evening, sitting for the odd coffee or drink, and suddenly thought, When I was young this was one of my favourite things – and I haven't done it for decades. It was some sort of a milestone.

I had hoped that after a while the good memories would drive out the ghastly last weeks of Gavin's life, and to an extent they did; but never completely. What does happen is that the good memories become a source of pleasure and comfort, tinged with the same autumnal ache, the same regret one feels about having once been young, of the unreturning years. A phrase can bring them back, a smell. Proust may have talked of his *madeleines*, but in my case, sorry about this, it's the smell of gin on a cold day. It brings back the boat and the river where we were always happiest and where we scattered Gavin's ashes.

We did that two years after he died, because we wanted Jake to be there as well as Bernard and Nancy and the family. It was a bitterly cold day, but bright: most of us had colds and were held up by Nurofen and whisky; we walked to his favourite mooring on the river, which we called Goose Bay, across frozen fields and an ocean of mud. We passed round chocolate and Scotch, recalled good moments on the river, happy memories of Gavin. Each of us flung handfuls of the ashes – they're not like fire ashes, they're like fine sand – into the gentle wind and they became nothing, they were gone. Totally. It was right.

Then we had a meal at the George in Dorchester, and drove home – but something happened on the way back which I remember with pride. Bernard, driving his brood in one car, suddenly stopped, got out and ran back, and Jake, driving me, did the same: there was a man lying by the side of the road. The man turned out to be just an agreeably woolly drunk who hadn't quite made it home; they helped him on his way and all was well. But I thought, Neither of them would hesitate for a moment to do that; plenty of people would just think: 'Let's not get involved' and drive on. Well, we must have done something right.

AGONY AUNT

I am lucky – there it is again – to be still working, particularly being agony aunt for *Saga*. It was originally, I suppose, my parachute out of the *Observer*; but it has become very rewarding in its own right. Journalist friends would react with derision: 'Do *Saga*-age people *have* problems?', *Saga* being for the over-fifties – well, that's what it says, since no one minds admitting they're over fifty rather than the age they actually are, which averages about seventy. Indeed they have problems. People ask, too, if I make them up, and occasionally, when you need exactly eleven lines in a hurry, you concoct one from a known problem, or one that someone has sobbed on your shoulder rather than actually written in a letter. But quite often you simply couldn't.

Could I have made up the man whose lover liked him to wear her nightdress when he visited, which he didn't mind because it was comfortable; but she wanted him to wear it when her sister came for Christmas . . .? (Answer: Get a dressing gown.) Or the couple who worried that when they died, their two daughters-in-law would spend their money instead of investing it wisely, and then divorce their sons – surely they couldn't both be married to Ivana Trump? Or the man who wanted to bequeath his 'collectibles' – bought by him, not family heirlooms – unto the third generation. I gently wondered how much his descendants, perhaps living in small flats with little money, unable either to insure or sell Great-grandpa's hideous objects, would bless his name? Or the son who won't leave home, and after four years of counselling has turned from a sweetly dysfunctional child into an aggressive and frightening personality; not to mention the fifty-eight-year-old son still living with Mother, who wants to get her into an old folks home now he's realised he's gay and wants the house to himself for wild parties?

The commonest problems are dilemmas about moving house; about sons, daughters and daughters-in-law who have broken off contact or who make their parents' life miserable; access to grandchildren after a divorce, and couples of which one is still keen on sex and the other isn't. But I never know what's going to come up; and after all those years of having to think up a subject every single week, it's miraculous to have all these flooding in non-stop.

People often ask, in various roundabout ways, why on earth I should think I know how to answer the letters. The answer is that a good two-thirds of them could be answered by anyone with a bit of common sense. It's just that the unhappy person is like a fly buzzing endlessly at the glass when there's an open window a foot away. A few are pretty well unanswerable – the occasional sad man who has never, in a long life, found any reason to be happy – no friends, no mate, no work that means anything to him. I only get about one of those a year, thank goodness. The remainder, on the whole, can be referred to people who know everything there is to know about a specific problem, whether it's alcoholism or shoplifting or wigs or schizophrenia or disabled holidays. I sometimes feel that if an Indonesian lesbian grandmother with in-growing toenails wrote in I would be able to find, in one of the directories, an organisation that dealt with just that.

One thing I have learned over the years: it's fatal to say anything remotely disobliging about a dog or a cat. I had one man write in who began with a quotation from 'The Miller of Dee': 'I care for nobody, no not I, and nobody cares for me.' He lived in a big house with a wife he scarcely spoke to, had hardly any friends and no serious interests. After much thought I advised him to get a dog, on two counts: even if his wife hated it, they'd have at least to talk – about its walks, its food, its tendency to chew the carpet; and, as I knew from a friend's recent divorce, a dog can be a source of real emotional comfort. The readers were outraged: how *dare* I consign an honest dog to this dysfunctional family? Ruefully I remembered that Marge Proops, the greatest of all agony aunts, had once had a woman ring up in tears because her husband was having it off with their Alsatian in the corridor; if that had been in *Saga*, the readers' concern would have been entirely for the dog.

Saga is a great place to work. It has a big circulation – Paul Bach, its original editor, had built it up to over a million before

Emma Soames, the current and very successful one, took over. They pay well and they operate from Folkestone, so there's no nonsense about having to go into the office. Our only complaint is that so far they have resisted the pleas of contributors to have a big party every now and then where we could all meet each other. Most of us, too, have lectured on Saga cruises. Gavin and I lectured our way across the Pacific on the *Saga Rose* (where his books sold in no time to people who said: 'I didn't know he was still writing!'). Which sounds fun, but wasn't: we couldn't land on either Easter Island or Pitcairn, and there's an awful lot of the Pacific – 'And that's just the top,' said one mean sea-dog. They hadn't got everything organised then as they have now.

I did another stint on the *Saga Pearl*, which was fine, except that when I turned up at Casablanca I found the ship had already sailed, so I had to fly back to Madrid the next day, take the midnight plane to Tenerife and pick up the ship there. But in the hotel in Casablanca I had a book and some whisky, and I'm pretty cool in most crises for which I can't be *blamed*. Best of all are the shake-down cruises – small test voyages to see which bits fall off or need fixing. They last only a day or two, when Saga gets a new ship, and the seagoing guinea-pigs are Saga personnel and media folk and are great fun. So it goes on.

Saga is now my main job, but I write for the *Guardian* sometimes; the odd TV and radio project crops up; I seem to go abroad a lot – for a conference or a speech, for occasional jaunts; people come to stay. I swim, ponderously but determinedly, in a local health club. '*You?* A health club?' say incredulous friends, till I explain that I have a 'social' membership which allows me to use the pool and the bar but expressly bans me from the gym and those ghastly machines.

AS FAR AS IT GOES

How do you end an autobiography? The most decorous way would be to drop dead in the middle of a sentence and have someone else finish it with a tearful appreciation. But I am not keen to do that – nor to stop living at my present pace. I have a vivid memory of Gavin, in a lurid pair of swimming trunks, changing the propeller on *Simpkin* before we tried the canals, where they have a very low speed limit. He was putting on a smaller propeller, so that the engine would not have to idle: 'This engine doesn't work well at low revs,' he said. Nor do I. So for the time being, I'll just keep going.

There are ways, after all, in which age can be usefully linked with the present. I had inherited my grandmother's sewing-machine, made in 1917. Bernard, wishing to hang blinds across the windows of the attic where he writes, came round to borrow it and sew them up. I had had the thing serviced ten years ago; it was working all right and we managed the complicated threading of the needle in the top part, and I went out and left him to it.

When I came back he was, to my surprise, only just finishing. It turned out that our threading of the shuttle part had been wrong. So Bernard had looked it up on the Internet, found six colour pictures showing how to thread this part of a 1917 machine, printed them out and finished his sewing. 'It's a wonderful old machine,' he said approvingly – and I've put the pictures in its box.

So it goes or, at any rate, can go.